1

PARAPSYCHOLOGY: GHOSTS AND HAUNTINGS

I would like to dedicate this book to my wife Sharon and my two children, Callum and Spencer.

Secondly, I would also like to dedicate this book to parapsychologists Dr Andrew Nichols, Dr Barry Taff, Loyd Auerbach and Steve Mera, and also to the late great psychical researcher, Peter Underwood.

PARAPSYCHOLOGY
GHOSTS AND HAUNTINGS

*When one experiences something strange and inexplicable in their life,
it stems from the mind of the beholder* — Robert Young, Ph.D., 2013

Robert Young, Ph.D.

with a Foreword by

Prof. Andrew Nichols

THE OFFICE OF PARAPSYCHOLOGICAL STUDIES

ISBN 978-0-9926404-3-9

Published by
The Office of Parapsychological Studies
Nottingham, UK

parapsy.co.uk

A catalogue record for this book is available from the British Library.

CONTENTS

FOREWORD

The concept of ghosts, apparitions, and haunted houses is as old as recorded history. Pre-biblical accounts from Babylon, ancient China, Egypt, and many other cultures furnish evidence of encounters with spirits of the dead and a host of other spectral entities. These eye-witness accounts are remarkably consistent, whether originating from cuneiform tablets and scrolls, or from modern sources, and create a world-wide and cross-cultural pattern which requires the attention of serious researchers. Dr Robert Young is such a man.

I first became aware of Rob's talents when he was a student in my courses on parapsychology and psychic research. He soon demonstrated his exceptional scholarship, psychological insight, and a willingness to challenge the *status quo*, sometimes questioning the conclusions of both establishment scientists and those of seasoned parapsychologists. Since his student days, I have had the privilege of knowing Rob as a colleague and friend, and I was delighted when he accepted a position as the UK representative and consultant for the American Institute of Parapsychology. I was equally pleased when Rob asked me to write a foreword for his book. Having known him for years, I can attest to his extensive knowledge, experience and integrity.

Rob Young is no 'armchair savant'. The special contribution that he makes in the following pages is based upon his own extensive experience as an investigator of paranormal phenomena, and Director of the Office of Parapsychological Studies. This book is particularly appealing for the author's own experiences – his personal encounters with haunting-type phenomena. Rob shares with me a conviction that many academic parapsychologists lack the personal experience with the paranormal that guided his path to current insights. In my view, academic parapsychologists often minimize or even deny the validity of their own subject matter, in an attempt to conform to acceptable scientific standards.

Robert Young, by contrast, clearly describes his motivations for extensive studies in a subject matter which is both esoteric and often fear-inducing as well. His approach is far from dogmatic however. By combining historical case studies with his own findings, Dr Young's book provides variety, but also strikingly illustrates an overall pattern. He enables the reader to approach this challenging field of inquiry with equal amounts of skepticism and open-mindedness. An important element of his approach is to point out the links between haunting and other types of reported paranormal phenomena.

Readers should not look in this book for total confirmation of their own views. Dr Young makes it clear that these extraordinary human experiences, occupying the borderland between the psychic and the psychological – between the paranormal and the normal – defy easy explanation. He does not replace one dogmatism with another, but rather stimulates the reader toward independent thinking.

This book should interest anyone who has wondered about reports of 'haunted houses' and whether there is good evidence to support the concept that spirits of the dead or non-human 'demonic forces' can invade or interfere with our lives. There may never be agreement about the extent to which such events have been exaggerated, or even fabricated, but there remains a residue of cases which cannot be explained away as fraud or delusion. For those of us who increasingly suspect that the totality of human experience is not explained by modern science, this book may offer an important contribution to parapsychology, and it has the additional advantage of being an entertaining read!

Prof. Andrew Nichols, Ph.D.

American Institute of Parapsychology
Gainesville, Florida, USA

INTRODUCTION

Parapsychology is the scientific study of anomalous phenomena associated with the human mind (MHs.M16 Paranormal Science). Today, it is also referred to by some as Anomalistic Psychology (Chris French 2000). Parapsychology is the study of phenomena suggesting that the strict subjective (here in the head) and purely objective (out there in the world) may instead be part of a spectrum, with some unusual anomalous phenomena falling between the subjective and objective (Dean Radin 1995).

We call such phenomena *anomalous*, as they are difficult to explain with current scientific models. Mainstream scientists and scholars still refer to the field as a pseudoscience, but thanks to media coverage and 'unreality' television paranormal investigation programs, it has become rather more popular and known to the general populace. Those involved in Parapsychology study and research many kinds of anomalous phenomena. The main sub-fields of study are Extrasensory Perception (ESP), telepathy, psychokinesis (PK), clairvoyance, and precognition. Other sub-categories of study are haunting phenomena, poltergeist disturbances otherwise known as Recurrent Spontaneous Psychokinesis (RSPK), apparitional experiences, reincarnation, Out of Body Experiences (OBEs), Near Death Experiences (NDEs), metaphysical science, unconscious awareness, cold reading, psychic fraud, and others.

To some people, however, all supernatural, preternatural, and paranormal phenomena are regarded as parapsychological in nature, but this is not the case; studies in UFOs, cryptids, Fortean Phenomena, etc. are not usually placed in this category of study in Parapsychology. I beg to differ regarding ufological phenomena as there are many parallels between them and parapsychological events. Sometimes people who are allegedly psychic may call themselves parapsychologists, but most parapsychologists are highly skeptical and scientifically minded, and debunking phenomena, so to speak, is the aim of Parapsychology as well as discovering whether some phenomena are truly anomalous in nature. It is true that there may be parapsychologists out there who may have genuine psychic ability, but they are individuals who also possess scientific credentials and are highly regarded in their chosen scientific field. They are also open-minded and are highly regarded in the parapsychological community.

This book is mainly focused on my own personal research into ghosts, apparitional experiences, haunting and poltergeist (RSPK) phenomena. The book will not only contain personal accounts and investigations from my own organization in apparitional experiences and hauntings, but will also contain many classic cases already known in parapsychology and ghost lore. The first five parts investigate what parapsychology is and how it is trying to develop into a genuine scientific discipline. In 2005, I established and founded what is now the Office of Parapsychological Studies in Nottinghamshire, England. The organization's main aim is to study and research apparitional experiences, haunting phenomena, poltergeist disturbances otherwise known as RSPK (Recurrent Spontaneous Psychokinesis), and other psychic phenomena.

My research into the poltergeist phenomenon also suggests RSPK as an explanation for this fascinating phenomenon. Several years ago, I had a friend who was an investigator for my Office of Parapsychological Studies. We went on many investigations with him in attendance and much paranormal activity followed. At one particular location, I concluded that RSPK was involved. The Ancient Ram Inn in Gloucestershire, England was reputedly a very haunted location, and over several investigations, we had witnessed and recorded much paranormal activity. We experienced rappings and banging noises which would shake the floor, stools moving across the floor, beds being lifted up then dropped to the floor, coins being thrown, whistling noises and breath sounds being heard, footfalls which would respond to human investigators, and much more.

Some members of the group began to call my investigator a possible cheat and hoaxer (but not to him personally), as the activity always seemed to centre on him. To me, it did not seem possible for him to have achieved this *consciously* without being caught, as he was always with us at the time the different types of phenomena were experienced. But *unconsciously*? That is a different matter entirely. In his personal life, he used to have his own business as a car mechanic which ended up down the pan, so to speak. He had just split up with his wife as she was seeing someone else behind his back and would not allow him to see his own daughter. It also turned out that he got into trouble with the police over some matter, which we did not know about until later.

All-in-all, his situation turned out to be the perfect catalyst for him as an RSPK *agent*. An RSPK agent is someone who is going through a traumatic period in his or her life. All the emotional anxiety, turmoil, anger, etc. is unconsciously built up and then unleashed in an explosive amount of psychic energy, which manipulates the physical environment around the person, causing objects to move about by themselves and other seemingly paranormal phenomena.

Physics, as a science, may explain much paranormal phenomena in the future, especially Quantum Theory. Quantum Entanglement (MHs.M2 Advanced Metaphysical Concepts) is a concept that states that when two particles are entangled, they remain connected regardless of how far apart they become, even across space-time. When an action is performed on one particle, the other entangled particle responds instantaneously, not at the speed of light, but as though as if it the same particle. It is also known that all physical objects—animate or inanimate—are essentially made of the same types of atoms and molecules (although sequenced differently). So it may be theorized that if an RSPK agent becomes entangled with any physical object (animate or inanimate) at the quantum level by touch or even thought, then by some unknown psychic factor, it is probable that we can manipulate the physical environment around us by just thought alone, whether consciously or unconsciously.

Currently, another research project I am engaged in focusses on the rarer phenomenon of Spontaneous Dream Visitation (SDV). This is a phenomenon whereby a person, whilst in their sleep/dream state, experiences apparitional type phenomena. I had a personal experience in this phenomenon many years back which led me down the path of studying scientific Parapsychology. Parapsychologists theorize that in our sleep state, when all external stimuli are eliminated (sight, sound, touch, taste and smell), ESP and other psychic phenomena can come into play.

PART ONE

INTRODUCING PARAPSYCHOLOGY, GHOSTS AND HAUNTINGS

ONE

A SHORT HISTORY OF PARAPSYCHOLOGY

The term 'parapsychology' was coined by philosopher Max Dessoir around 1889, the word *para* meaning 'alongside', 'something going beyond', or 'besides the ordinary'. The word 'Psi', which is a neutral term for parapsychological studies, was coined by biologist Berthold P. Wiesner and was first used by psychologist Robert Thouless. In 1942, Psi was argued for by Thouless and Weisner as a non-theoretical manner of referring to extrasensory perception and psychokinesis (Arthur Berger & Joyce Berger, 1991).

Originally, parapsychology was known as Psychical Research and some researchers still refer to it as such. On 20 February 1882 the Society of Psychical Research (SPR) was founded in England. The SPR was founded principally on the initiative of some academics and scholars at Cambridge University, all of whom believed that various claims for the existence of paranormal phenomena warranted scientific scrutiny. In those early days, a number of SPR members were skeptics; others were philosophers concerned fundamentally with the metaphysical implications of parapsychological experiences, if those should prove to be genuinely paranormal in nature.

Nevertheless, the founders of the SPR were united in their conviction that the investigation of parapsychological phenomena was called for, despite the prevailing lack of interest in such research among the established divisions of science. That lack of interest that still applies today, with mainstream science saying that paranormal phenomena are unworthy of scientific study and a waste of valuable time and resources. Parapsychology began when spiritualism was at its most humble beginnings and in its most prominent era. Mediums such as Daniel Dunglas Home (1833–1886), Leonora Piper (1859–1950), Helene Smith (1861–1929), and Charles Bailey (1870– 1947) were some of the individuals tested under early scientifically controlled conditions by early psychical researchers. Cases of crisis apparitions and haunting phenomena were also some of the main studies carried out during the early days of psychic research.

This research led to the establishment of the SPR's American counterpart, the American Society of Psychical Research. Unfortunately, many so-called mediums were, in the early years, exposed as frauds (including Helen Duncan) by such prominent figures as magician Harry Houdini and psychical researcher Harry Price. Furthermore, many spirit photographs during this era were exposed as hoaxes, such as the photographs taken by William Hope. In 1917, J. E. Coover, a psychologist at Stanford University, was one of the first researchers to apply experimental techniques to the study of Psi abilities in the laboratory. Parapsychology became an academic science in 1927 when plant botanist, Joseph Banks Rhine (1895–1980), became the father of modern-day experimental parapsychology.

Rhine studied botany and plant physiology at the University of Chicago where both he and his wife, Louisa Rhine (also a noted parapsychologist), obtained their PhDs. This may seem an odd background for a person who taught psychology and engaged in parapsychological research, but two factors conspired to help Rhine along his chosen path. First, in the 1920s, botanists were at the forefront of work in statistical theory, and Rhine's knowledge in this area served him well in his later efforts to design laboratory experiments involving ESP. Secondly, Rhine's interest in parapsychological research endeared him to William McDougall, the newly appointed head of the Psychology Department at Duke University. Rhine thus became an instructor in psychology in 1928 and an assistant professor in 1929. Rhine and his colleagues developed original experimental techniques to study Psi abilities in an academic laboratory setting and helped popularize the term ESP (Extra Sensory Perception) and Parapsychology.

In 1935, Rhine created the first academic Parapsychology laboratory at Duke University, Durham in North Carolina, USA. Rhine's laboratory was initially part of the Psychology Department and developed a worldwide reputation for pioneering scientifically sound Psi research. In the early 1960s, Rhine retired from Duke University and moved his lab off-campus. Today, the *Rhine Research Centre Institute for Parapsychology* (of which I am a member) conducts state of the art research into Psi abilities and consciousness (Harvey Irwin & Caroline Watt, 2007). Although parapsychology was and is a university-based study, there are now more members of the general public becoming interested in parapsychological phenomena. There are now separate colleges and institutes available to study Parapsychology, either through online courses (such as the Institute of Metaphysical Humanistic Science's PhD program, the American Institute for Parapsychology's certificate program, and the Scientific Establishment of Parapsychology's BITC and AITC certificate programs in anomalous phenomena and Parapsychology), where the subject of Parapsychology is taught without the need to study psychology as a major, as at many universities. At these universities, the learner must undertake several years of psychological study before asking to learn Parapsychology as a separate module, which unfortunately is not considered very significant. But the need to study basic psychology is critical for a greater understanding of parapsychological phenomena.

In 1985, the Koestler Parapsychology Unit in Edinburgh, Scotland was established as a research group based within the Psychology Department at Edinburgh University. It consists of academic staff who teach and research various aspects of Parapsychology. Parapsychology has been part the University of Edinburgh since the appointment in 1962 of the late Dr John Beloff as a lecturer in the Department of Psychology. Beloff researched and taught Parapsychology at Edinburgh until his retirement in 1985, although he maintained his connections with Parapsychology and the department for another two decades. Many of Beloff's students are still active today. Beloff played an important role of bringing the Koestler Bequest to Edinburgh. The Bequest was intended to further scientific research into the capacity attributed to some individuals to interact with their environment by means other than the recognized sensory and motor channels.

Robert Morris was Koestler Professor of Parapsychology at Edinburgh University. He recruited additional staff and research students to form the Koestler Parapsychology Unit. Over nearly two decades as Professor of Parapsychology, Morris supervised over 100 undergraduate students' projects, and over 30 postgraduate students, many of whom went on to establish research units and teach Parapsychology at higher education institutions. During that time, he also served as President of the British Association for the Advancement of Science, showing that Morris succeeded in his aim to integrate parapsychology with the wider academic community (Harvey Irwin & Caroline Watt, 2007).

Some noted parapsychologists and psychical researchers (deceased and still living) and their research are: Frederic Myers, William James, Harry Price, Peter Underwood, Maurice Grosse, J.E. Coover, Joseph and Louisa Rhine, William Roll, John Beloff, Michael Thalbourne, Robert Morris, Loyd Auerbach, Dean Radin, Andrew Nichols, Barry Taff, Christopher French, Richard Broughton, Robert Schoch, Susan Blackmore, Harvey J Irwin, Caroline Watt, Carlos Alvarado, Hans Holzer, Richard Wiseman, Hans Bender, Michael Persinger, John Palmer, John Kruth, Russell Targ, Hal Puthoff, Rob Young, Steve Mera, and many more who are currently engaged in Psi and psychical research.

Noted universities, colleges, and institutes engaged in Psi research are: the American Institute for Parapsychology, Florida; the Koestler Parapsychology Unit, Edinburgh; the Society for Psychical Research, London; the American Society for Psychical Research, USA; the Institute of Forensic Parapsychology, London; the Scientific Establishment of Parapsychology, Manchester; the Office of Parapsychological Studies, Nottinghamshire; the Rhine Research Centre, North Carolina; the Parapsychology Foundation, USA; the Parapsychological Association, USA; Goldsmiths College, London; Hope University, Liverpool; Northampton University; the Institute of Metaphysical Humanistic Science, Florida; the Institute of Noetic Sciences, USA; the Windbridge Institute, USA, and many other privately funded organizations and institutes.

Those interested in becoming full-time parapsychologists may be greatly disappointed in the job prospects as most researchers in the field study and teach it on a part-time basis; most come from other scientific backgrounds and have an interest in parapsychological research on the side. University placements in this field are rare, as competition is fierce. There are only a small handful of full-time parapsychologists, and about a dozen or so in the world.

TWO

EXPERIMENTATION IN PARAPSYCHOLOGY

In 1947, experimentation in laboratory-based Parapsychology began when Dr Joseph Rhine introduced a pack of cards called *Zener Cards*. These cards are used for testing the ESP ability of clairvoyance. The Zener Cards were developed in conjunction with Dr Karl Zener and consisted of a pack of twenty-five cards each with the symbol of a star, cross, square, wavy lines, and circle. The chance factor is considered five correct guesses out of twenty-five cards. More correct guesses than five in repeatable card sessions may indicate a possible paranormal Psi factor.

In the early days of the Rhine laboratory, several high-scoring subjects emerged, notably Hubert Pearce, Charles Stuart, and A. J. Linzmeyer, who were capable of averaging around seven or more hits (correct guesses) per run over a large number of card runs, thereby producing enormous odds against chance. There are a number of other tests conducted using the Zener cards. Another experimental test that was frequently used was the transmission and receiver test, an early testing method for telepathy. This test involved two individuals who were separated into two rooms. One of the participants would look at a random picture and then try to create a telepathic link with the receiver in the next room. Then, the sender would try to transmit the picture telepathically so that the receiver would psychically pick up the image that was sent.

Rhine also introduced the dice-throwing test, a method no longer used experimentally. This test involved testing for the Psi ability of PK (psychokinesis). In this test, the volunteer concentrates on a number on a dice roll, and then sees the result once the dice are shaken. By chance alone, the volunteer should guess at least one out of six guesses and repeats the process several times. Rolling three dice and guessing the total score over repeatable sessions is another experiment used in the dice method. Tests for PK now usually involve Random Number Generators and statistical analysis. Tests that were carried out several decades ago are sometimes now used as preliminary tests. If participants have successfully passed these preliminary tests, then large-scale tests using sophisticated scientific equipment and computer programs are carried out in Parapsychology departments in universities, colleges, and scientific institutes.

So what are the current experimental methods and procedures used in Parapsychology? The advent of electronic and computer technologies have allowed parapsychologists to develop highly automated experiments studying the interaction between mind and matter. In one experiment, a Random Number Generator (RNG), which is based on electronic and radioactive noise from decaying radioactive matter, produces a data stream that is recorded and analyzed by a sophisticated computer program. In the experiment, a subject attempts mentally to change the distribution of the random numbers, usually in an experimental design that is functionally equivalent to getting more heads than tails, such as in the flipping of a coin.

Meta-analysis of a database published in 1989 examined 800 experiments by more than sixty researchers over the next thirty years. The effect size was found to be very small, but remarkably consistent, resulting in an overall statistical deviation of approximately fifteen standard errors from a chance effect. The probability that the observed effect was actually zero (no Psi), was less than one part in a trillion, verifying that human consciousness can indeed affect the behaviour of a random physical system. True random numbers cannot be generated by a computer, but there are devices that can be connected to a computer that will generate near-random numbers. Since not every researcher has one of these devices, there are services that make these random numbers available over the worldwide web.

Another experiment in PK research has concentrated on the effect of psychokinesis on living systems and has been called Bio-PK. Some parapsychologists refer to it as *Direct Mental Interaction on Living Systems* (DMILS). This is the ability to monitor internal functions of the human body including nervous system activity using EEG and biofeedback technology. This has provided an opportunity to ask whether biological systems can be affected by intention in a manner similar to PK on random number generators. A particularly successful experiment using DMILS is one that looks at the commonly reported feeling of being stared at. In this experiment, the *starer* and the *staree* are isolated in different locations and the starer is periodically asked to simply gaze at the staree through closed circuit video links. Meanwhile, the staree's nervous activity system is automatically and continually monitored. The cumulative databases on this and similar DMILS experiments provide strong evidence that one person's attention directed towards an isolated person can significantly activate or calm that person's nervous system.

Experimentation in ESP and telepathy uses a method called the *Ganzfeld* (whole field) *State*. This is when an individual is isolated in a sound-proof chamber whilst lying relaxed on a couch or reclining chair. All other external outside noise is eliminated from the chamber. The eyes of the individual are covered with half ping pong balls or an equivalent, and headphones are placed on the ears while white noise or calming music is played through them. The light in the chamber is also subdued using red coloured light or an equivalent. During the Ganzfeld Experiment, the person's vital signs such as heart rate and EEG brainwaves are monitored. Whilst the subject is relaxed, the sender, which is in another room, is shown a video clip or asked to look at a picture, and is then asked mentally to try to send the picture to the receiver in the Ganzfeld Chamber. The receiver is asked to continually report aloud all mental processes including images, thoughts, and feelings. At the end of the session (which lasts approximately 20 to 40 minutes), the receiver is taken out of the Ganzfeld Chamber and is shown videos or still pictures, one of which is the true target image while the others are decoy images. The expectation of picking the correct target picture by chance alone is one in four times for a 25% ratio. After the collation of scores of such experiments (as of 2007) totaling about 700 individual sessions conducted by about 24 parapsychologists worldwide, the results show that the target image is selected on average 34% of the time, which is a highly significant result, and suggests that telepathy exists (Harvey Irwin & Caroline Watt, 2007).

Currently, another unusual experiment is ongoing throughout the world called the *Global Consciousness Project* (MHs. M2: Advanced Metaphysical Concepts). This is a psychokinesis experiment to try to effect positive change throughout the world and, according to the research, it appears that we can. Dr Roger Nelson at Princeton University in New Jersey, USA, has been researching consciousness since 1997 using random number generators located around the world.

These random number generators are electronic devices connected to computers and generate numbers in the form of binary numbers of 0s and 1s at a rate of 200 per second. This again is the same concept as tossing a coin repeatedly. The data is uploaded to a main computer at Princeton University and logged. Probability dictates that if you toss a coin 100 times, it will land on heads 50% of the time and tails 50% of the time. This is typically what the random number generators do, most of the time.

The fascinating aspect of this research is that these random number generators seem to become less random when global consciousness is focused on one single issue. The most stunning example of this was on September 11, 2001. Not only did the random number generators become less random when the planes were hitting the Twin Towers in New York City, but, according to Dr Nelson, 'the random number generators started changing 4 or 5 hours before the first plane hit'. Another example is when Hurricane Katrina hit New Orleans, Louisiana, and the gulf coast in August 2005 (Douglas Kelley).

As we have looked into some of the current experiments carried out by parapsychologists in the laboratory, what about research into apparitional experiences as well as haunting and poltergeist (RSPK) disturbances? Unfortunately, in the field of parapsychological research, observations, case collections, and environmental monitoring seem the only answers currently to this question. In addition to historical research, parapsychologists have to use observers as well as past and present personal experiences for research, as well as a host of environmental monitoring equipment. Equipment currently used in this type of research includes Electro-Magnetic Field (EMF) meters, Tri-Field meters, temperature and air monitors, ion counters, ultrasonic amplifiers, Closed Circuit Television cameras, video and digital cameras, night vision, thermal cameras, audio recording equipment, and beam breaking alarms.

Although there has been evidence captured on the above equipment, the evidence is scarce as well as elusive, and does not provide conclusive proof that ghosts or apparitions exist. Above all this, the equipment stated was not even designed for this kind of research. In poltergeist (RSPK) disturbances, most parapsychologists think that unconscious psychokinesis from an individual somehow manipulates the environment and is, therefore, not attributed to invisible discarnate entities causing havoc, so testing the individual in the laboratory using some of the above experimental methods may be a necessity. Unfortunately, testing people under laboratory conditions seems to dampen and negate alleged Psi abilities, as the individual unconsciously knows that they are being tested and does not want to fail the tests being performed.

There are many people who set up amateur paranormal investigation teams who want to investigate ghost and poltergeist phenomena, but unfortunately, there are few people who know how to properly use and read the equipment they are using. Because of reality TV shows and programs, people may buy the 'in fashion' equipment without realizing how to actually read the data shown and get many false readings which have a natural rather than paranormal cause. One thing for certain is that, due to ghost-hunting paranormal shows, Parapsychology and related matters are becoming increasingly well-known to the general lay person, and people want to know more about the science that lies behind paranormal phenomena. Just recently, I spoke to parapsychologist Dr Barry Taff and he stated that these 'unreality' TV shows have set the field back 75 years or more because of the hoaxing and falsifying methods used during the shows to boost ratings. It must be remembered that these shows are for entertainment value only and do not reflect what really happens during a proper scientific paranormal investigation.

THREE

REMOTE VIEWING: THE BEST EVIDENCE OF PSI ABILITY?

Remote viewing is a neutral term for general ESP introduced by parapsychologists Russell Targ and Harold Puthoff. Remote viewing is generally recognized within the scientific community as the psychic ability to access and provide accurate information regardless of distance, shielding, or time about people, locations, and objects or events inaccessible through any normal recognized means, sensory or otherwise. There is much laboratory evidence suggesting that this particular psychic ability is a scientifically proven phenomenon. Some parapsychologists believe that the Pineal Gland, which is a pea-sized mass of nerve tissue which is attached by a stalk to the posterior wall of the third ventricle of the brain, set deep between the cerebral hemispheres of the brain at the back of the skull, functions as a gland which secretes the hormone melatonin. Some evidence suggests that the pineal gland is a vestigial organ, the remnant of a third eye, and it is this third eye which some parapsychologists believe is the source of Psi phenomena. Since the 1960s there have been many CIA (Central Intelligence Agency) and military projects associated with remote viewing experiments such as Project Stargate and Project Scanate.

From 1972 until 1995, the United States military and intelligence organisations conducted experimental parapsychological research and operations involving remote viewing. Official confirmation of government research into remote viewing occurred in 1995 when a small portion of the voluminous classified research material was made publicly available via the FOIA (Freedom of Information Act). Paranormal research involving parapsychological research and psychic functioning has been perceived as a controversial field by American academia and the scientific community at large, who have responded to its reported results with outright skepticism and deemed them controversial.

The Stargate Project created a set of protocols designed to make research into clairvoyance and out-of-body experiences (OBEs) more scientific and to minimize, as much as possible, session noise and inaccuracy. The term *remote viewing* emerged as short-hand to describe this more structured approach to clairvoyance. Project Stargate only received a mission after all other intelligence attempts, methods, or approaches had already been exhausted. It was also reported that there were over twenty-two active military and domestic remote viewers providing data.

In 1969, whilst participating in a scientific conference at Big Sur, California, a leading Russian scientist presented a research paper that, when subsequently analyzed by the US intelligence community, indicated that the Soviets were involved in some form of distant influencing with mind control implications.

The Russians' organizational structure and funding for parapsychological research, combined with the lack of any research undertaken by the United States' scientific bodies, created a Psi gap. Furthermore, this lack of research and the corresponding potential for Soviet scientific breakthroughs were deemed enough to pose a national security threat to the United States, which could not afford to fall behind. The US intelligence community was concerned that the Russians could have developed the ability to replicate paranormal phenomena and harness their potential. This threat, in an area of research historically disregarded by the scientific community, prompted American intelligence services to begin accelerating efforts for a counterpart US program.

Given prevailing attitudes towards parapsychological phenomena, the CIA did not know where to begin, since most Western scientists generally regarded this whole area of research as nonsense and non-scientific. The CIA thus began to look for a discrete research laboratory, operating outside mainstream academia, which could manage a quiet, classified research project. At the time, the Stanford Research Institute (SRI) at Menlo Park, California was conducting annually funded government research, so it seemed suitable for the CIA's purpose. In 1972, several CIA officers approached Dr Harold Puthoff, an SRI LASER research physicist and parapsychologist. Dr Puthoff also worked as a former Naval Intelligence Officer who had worked for the National Security Agency (NSA). Owing to Dr Puthoff's military and scientific credentials, the agents confided in him their concerns regarding Soviet research efforts in Parapsychology that the CIA had been monitoring for over a decade.

The CIA's interest in SRI and Dr Puthoff had been triggered by a report Puthoff had drafted earlier that year regarding his observations of Ingo Swann, a New York artist and alleged psychic. Dr Puthoff arranged for Swann to visit SRI after they corresponded regarding experiments to investigate the boundary between the physics of the animate and inanimate. Prior to Ingo Swann's SRI visit and without Swann's knowledge, Dr Puthoff arranged for access to a shielded magnetometer used in quark detection experiments by Stanford University's Physics Department. Quark experimentation required that the magnetometer be as well shielded as technologically possible to preclude outside influences.

While visiting the laboratory as part of Swann's facilities tour, Dr Puthoff challenged Swann (who claimed he could perform psychokinetic effects) to see if he could affect the magnetometer, as it could not be affected from the outside by normal external means. Intrigued by the challenge, Swann observed the magnetometer in a manner that eventually became known as remote viewing, and with pencil and paper in hand, Swann sketched the interior of its unpublished construction. According to Dr Puthoff, the magnetometer 'went berserk' during Swann's sketching. Essentially the output signal for the magnetometer became visibly disturbed, demonstrating a disturbance in the internal magnetic field.

Astonished, Dr Puthoff asked what Swann had done; Swann replied that he had done nothing but look at it. When Puthoff asked Swann for a repeat demonstration, the magnetometer again reacted in the same manner. Later, Dr Puthoff reported that Ingo Swann's remote viewing demonstration had impressed him more than the magnetometer's reaction. Apparently, the CIA was impressed as well for several weeks later, its representatives approached Dr Puthoff. Ingo Swann was the driving force behind the development of coordinated remote viewing, which is the ability to remote view using geographic coordinates in lieu of an outbound target person at a designated location serving as a sort of beacon.

Ingo Swann felt that his abilities were not being tested or utilized to their fullest potential, especially during early remote viewing experiments. Swann made suggestions that helped the remote viewing program develop and mature. He even confided that he could remote view anywhere on the planet and beyond its limits, which Dr Puthoff initially thought of as preposterous. In response, Swann suggested that an experiment was needed to determine whether someone was required at the target location site during a remote viewing experiment, and recommended a remote viewing of the planet Jupiter, prior to the upcoming NASA Pioneer 10 flyby.

During this experiment, Swann described a ring around the planet Jupiter, and at first thought he might have remotely viewed Saturn by mistake; astronomers and others readily dismissed Swann's description until the subsequent NASA 10 flyby revealed that the ring did, in fact, exist. From this initial effort, the protocols were expanded and numerous experiments were conducted using geographic coordinates, latitude, and longitude in degrees, minutes, and seconds. Scanate, short for 'scanning by coordinates', was the name given to this method of remote viewing. When provided with the geographic coordinates for any given location on the planet, the remote viewer was asked to describe the location in as much detail as possible. One of the major challenges facing parapsychologists at SRI with this form of remote viewing was developing protocols the precluded the possibility of a remote viewer somehow memorizing all of the world's geographic coordinates.

Using Ingo Swann and Pat Price, another remote viewer, SRI conducted a long range test of Project Scanate's procedures for the CIA in 1973. The purpose of the experiment was to determine remote viewing effectiveness under conditions that approximated to an operational scenario. The experiment's results were profound, significantly impacting not only SRI's remote viewing program, but also the CIA support it received. The target site coordinates were for a West Virginia mountain home owned by a CIA employee; however Swann and Price, who were located at SRI in Menlo Park, described a nearby facility that, in their opinion, was more interesting. The site proved to be a highly sensitive National Security Agency (NSA) facility, and both Swann and Price were accurate in their physical descriptions of the facility as well as in their identification of its general purpose.

Additionally, Pat Price psychically penetrated a secured vault and thereby obtained the facility's codename along with those of various programs, one of which was extremely sensitive. He also accessed the names of individuals who worked at the facility, but this information proved to be inaccurate. Such was the result of the first ever long distance operational remote viewing test accomplished by SRI during the initial pilot program for the CIA. In the following year (1974) the CIA presented SRI with a long distance remote viewing experiment intended to test more fully the operational utility of this extraordinary method of intelligence gathering. Thus, Psi warfare was established. The CIA requested that SRI employ long distance Scanate procedures in a manner similar to the West Virginia site experiment.

The CIA provided information about a Soviet military site of ongoing operational significance. SRI employed Pat Price for the experiment. The CIA provided the map coordinates for an unidentified research facility in Semipalatinsk, USSR, a highly secret Soviet nuclear munitions site where work was thought to involve development of particle beam weapons. Price accurately described the facility and the highly sensitive work that was being accomplished there. In particular, he sketched a giant crane-like structure that literally rolled over the tops of the buildings it straddled. Additionally, Price described ongoing work inside the facility that involved problems the Russians were experiencing in welding together thick metal gores for the construction of a 60-foot sphere. According to Dr Russell Targ, the team did not get any feedback from this information for more than three years. The team discovered how accurate Price's viewings were when this sphere-fabricating activity at Semipalatinsk was eventually described in Aviation Week magazine on May 2, 1977. Unfortunately, by then, Pat Price had passed away.

Russell Targ observed Price during the aforementioned experiment; they were both in an electrically shielded room of SRI's Radio Physics building located approximately 10,000 miles from Semipalatinsk. Targ knew nothing of the Semipalatinsk site, in order to guard against the potential for cueing or telepathy. Regarding the experiment, Dr Targ stated, 'The accuracy of Price's drawing is the sort of thing that I, as a physicist, would never have believed if I had not seen it for myself'. During an early outbound experiment, Price proved extremely accurate in describing a San Francisco Bay area site. Two water tanks that he had reported as being at the site were not there, however, and this observation was dismissed as inaccurate. Years later, SRI researchers discovered via an old photograph of the same site that the two missing water tanks had stood in exactly the same locations described by Price, but many years prior to the actual remote viewing.

The SRI team realized that it was therefore crucial to specify exactly when in time the remote viewing experiment was to be focused. As a result of these experiments, Dr Kenneth Kress, a physicist, wrote a synopsis entitled *Parapsychology in Intelligence*. He concluded that the research and experiments demonstrated paranormal abilities. In July 1978, INSCOM (US Army Intelligence Support Command) initiated a three-year remote viewing program, code named Gondola Wish, in which the first year would be devoted to training, the second to testing, and the third year to evaluation and reporting. Five months into the first year's training program, however, the Iran Hostage Crisis developed. The training program was terminated and INSCOMS's cadre of six remote viewers immediately went operational. Since Gondola Wish had been the codename for the initial training program, it was named Grill Flame, concurrent with the program's operational status.

With five months training under their belts, the Grill Flame remote viewers began receiving a massive influx of taskings and associated intelligence support requests from the National Security Council (NSC). One of the original obstacles faced by the NSC was identifying exactly which of the 400 Americans known to be in Iran at the time were in fact being held hostage. The Grill Flame remote viewers were successful in identifying all 64 American hostages. Further, they identified three Americans who, due to the sensitive nature of their assignments, were being held at a separate location from the main body of hostages. Had the Grill Flame remote viewers not identified the three Americans thereby enabling their government to negotiate for their release along with the others in addition to letting the Iranians know that INSCOM knew they were holding them hostage, they would have likely been tortured to death.

Throughout the Iran Hostage Crisis, Grill Flame psychics accomplished over 600 remote viewings for the NSC. One of those remote viewings involved them identifying a potential underground rescue route, discernible only to those with old Persian or Roman maps of Tehran's sewer system. One of the Grill Flame remote viewing images involved diagonal-like grid work with blue and orange diagonal squares that covered an oval-shaped object. It proved to be a canopy which covered a manhole cover. It was located about a half a mile from the US Embassy compound in Tehran. United States personnel discovered that only Iran has these types of manhole covers; most countries use round ones to stop people and objects from falling through.

The manhole led to underground telephone lines that, disappointingly, ran perpendicular to the embassy. Archived area maps, however, revealed a long-forgotten sewer system dating back to pre-Persian or pre-Roman times and was unknown even to the Iranians. It was physically located beneath the telephone line system. The sewer system ran under the embassy compound, exiting into one of its garages. The remote viewing thereby providing the information requested for a potential rescue attempt. As with all intelligence information, intelligence gathered by remote viewing must be verified by independent sources; remote viewing information cannot stand on its own. Ray Hyman, Professor Emeritus of Psychology at the University of Oregon and a noted critic of Parapsychology, stated in an Air Force report that if Ed May's conclusions are correct, remote viewers were right 20% of the time and wrong 80% of the time (Ed May is an experimental nuclear physicist whose interests turned conclusively towards the research of parapsychological phenomena) (Robert M. Schoch & Logan Yonavjak).

In 1995, Project Stargate was transferred to the CIA, and a retrospective evaluation of the results undertaken. The CIA contacted the American Institute for Research for an evaluation. An analysis conducted by Professor Jessica Utts showed a statistically significant effect with gifted subjects scoring 5% to 15% above chance, although subject reports included a large amount of irrelevant information, and when reports did seem on target, they were vague and general in nature.

Ray Hyman argued that Professor Utt's conclusion that ESP had been proven to exist, especially precognition, was premature, and that present findings have yet to be independently replicated. Based on their collective findings, which recommended a higher level of critical research and tighter controls, the CIA terminated the 20 million dollar project, even after the successes with Pat Price and Ingo Swann, to name but a few, citing a lack of documented evidence that the program had any value to the intelligence community. Time magazine stated in 1995 that three full-time psychics were still working on a half-a-million-dollar-a-year budget out of Fort Meade, Maryland, which would soon close (Robert Schoch & Logan Yonavjak, 2008).

Recent studies into remote viewing suggest more positive results. Dr Michael Persinger, cognitive neuroscientist, parapsychologist, and professor at Laurentian University in Ontario, Canada, has published increases in the remote viewing accuracy of Ingo Swann, as measured by a group of ratings of congruence (between Swann's drawings and the locale being viewed) by 40 experimentally blind participants during stimulation with complex magnetic fields using a circumcerebral (around the head) eight channel system. In 2010, Persinger et al. published a report of their work with the alleged psychic Sean Harribance, reporting that blind rate accuracies in his apparent psychic insights correlated with specific quantitative Electroencephalography (EEG) profiles, specifically congruence between activity over the left temporal lobe of those being 'read' by Harribance and his right temporal lobe. Persinger stated that 'The results indicate even exceptional skills previously attributed to aberrant sources are variations of normal cerebral dynamics associated with intuition, and may involve small but discrete changes in proximal energy' (Michael Persinger & Steve Mera, 2012).

FOUR

PARAPSYCHOLOGY AND UFOS

Parapsychology is the scientific study of anomalous phenomena associated with the human mind. As this book has already covered, it incorporates studies in ESP, psychokinesis, precognition, apparitional experiences, haunting phenomena, and poltergeist disturbances as well as a host of other psychic experiences. Ufology, the scientific study of Unidentified Flying Objects (UFOs) (MHs.M16: Paranormal Science), incorporates studies in astronomical, meteorological, and aeronautical fields along with a belief in extraterrestrial/inter-dimensional craft.

In the field of Ufology, there is more hard and overwhelming evidence than for any other paranormal phenomenon, suggesting that extraterrestrial/inter-dimensional beings do, in fact, exist. Unfortunately, the field of Parapsychology does not study many aspects of ufological phenomena, but there are good reasons to believe it should. If parapsychologists look into cases regarding psychic phenomena and Ufology, then they may realize that certain phenomena studied by parapsychologists and UFO researchers may, in fact, be the one and the same, depending on the belief system of the witness or experiencer. It is conceivable that an unknown paranormal intelligence may manifest itself as a ghost or apparition to one witness and as an alien entity to another, depending on that person's religious or personal belief system.

This is by no means a new idea, and Carl Jung, the famous psychologist, theorized that UFOs might have a primarily spiritual and psychological basis. In his 1959 book, *Flying Saucers: A Modern Myth of Things Seen in the Sky,* he pointed out that the round shape of saucers corresponds to a mandala, a type of archetypical shape seen in religious images. Thus, flying saucers might reflect a projection of the internal desires of witnesses who see them. However, he did not label them as delusions or outright hallucinations; it was more in the nature of a shared spiritual experience. However, Jung seemed conflicted as to the phenomenon's possible origins. At times, he asserted that he was not concerned with possible psychological origins, but that at least some UFOs were physically real, based primarily on indirect physical evidence such as photographs and radar contacts in addition to visual sightings. He also considered the Extraterrestrial Hypothesis to be viable. In 1958, the Associated Press (AP) quoted him as saying, 'A purely psychological explanation is ruled out'.

There are cases documented by Ufologists which witnesses have had a close encounter with a UFO and have afterwards been subjected to a host of other psychic phenomena. There have been reported psychokinetic effects around the person who has had a UFO experience, manifesting poltergeist-type phenomena around the home as well as ESP and premonition warnings about future events. When a UFO experiencer has witnessed an alien entity, some of the beings have been reported as almost apparitional in nature. They have been seen to walk through bedroom walls and also vanish at will, almost like a ghost. The beings themselves also seem to produce a telepathic bond between the said entity and witness, and state that they can regularly contact the beings that are abducting or contacting them. In the 1950s and '60s, the alien contactee movement was rife with people who were allegedly in regular contact with alien creatures from another world. In parapsychology, this is known as channeling or clairvoyance, where the psychic is said to contact the spirits of the deceased.

Balls of light (orbs) are also studied by researchers in both fields, those seen with the naked eye in haunting phenomena and those reported as UFOs. When a person experiences an alleged alien abduction, they are said to become paralyzed and are then seen to levitate through a tunnel of light into a waiting UFO above. These experiences seem remarkably similar to Near Death Experiences (NDEs) or Out-of-Body Experiences (OBEs) where a witness claims to have travelled through a tunnel of light into the spiritual plane where they communicate with deceased loved ones or friends. In the case of UFO abductions, they meet alien beings rather than loved ones or friends.

If a witness never experienced psychic phenomena before having a UFO encounter but then did so after the experience, then parapsychologists can look for what instigated this new-found ability in the first place. Did the UFO somehow alter their chemical and biological makeup or physiology during the encounter? Some have speculated that the electromagnetic field of a person may have been somehow altered, allowing him or her to produce psychic phenomena (if indeed electromagnetic fields cause paranormal occurrences in the first place). There are also reported cases of people becoming artistic or musical after a UFO encounter, as well as of some who become psychic healers. Although they had never claimed or shown these abilities before having the UFO encounter, it is valuable for the parapsychologist to study what may have occurred during the UFO event, asking why these physiological changes occurred to that person or caused psychic disturbances to happen.

There are parapsychologists who study certain aspects of UFO phenomena, specifically alien abductions associated with sleep paralysis. Dr Susan Blackmore is one such person and Professor Chris French is another. In Canada, Dr Michael Persinger has conducted much research into the alien abduction phenomenon. The described experience usually begins at home in bed, asleep, or sometimes on a deserted road whilst driving a vehicle. In the bedroom, a blinding light is seen through the window. On the road, a glowing UFO is often witnessed. In the bedroom scenario, the witness becomes paralyzed and is usually only able to move his or her head or eyes. On the road, the witness is usually found to be driving along the road with a missing time episode. In the bedroom, the witness encounters small grey creatures about four feet tall which are seen to enter the room, sometimes through walls; at other times they are already there. The beings are usually described as having overly large heads, large black almond-shaped eyes, a small mouth, and just barely a nose.

The witness is then levitated out of bed to an awaiting UFO above, subsequently having medical procedures performed on them. Afterwards they wake up in bed with no recollection of the night's events. They sometimes find small scoop marks on their bodies, wondering where they got them from. Later, they may recall strange dreams about being on the craft and then they may want to undergo 'questionable' regressive hypnosis to try to unlock the strange night's encounter. These are the usual phenomenological characteristics of a typical alien abduction case. But are people really being abducted by extraterrestrial or inter-dimensional beings? Or are they experiencing a lucid dream associated with sleep paralysis? Some abductees recall their experiences spontaneously, whilst some only remember in therapy, support groups, or under hypnosis.

Psychologists know well that memories can be changed and even completely created using hypnosis, peer pressure, and/or repeated questioning. Confabulation can often take place. However, there are many reports of conscious recall of abduction experiences without hypnosis or multiple interviews, but the role of false memory is still not clear. Another theory is that the experiencers are mentally ill. This theory receives little support from the literature. The late abduction investigator Budd Hopkins found that his abductees had above average intelligence and displayed no signs of serious psychopathology, based on a study of nine of his subjects (*Phenomena Magazine*, Issue 39, July 2012).

In 1988 psychologist June O. Parnell (University of Wyoming) found no evidence of psychopathology among 225 individuals who reported seeing a UFO, although they did not report having been abducted. More recently, in 1993, another psychologist, Nicholas Spanos (Carleton University) compared 49 UFO witnesses with two control groups and found that they were no less intelligent, no more fantasy prone, and no more susceptible to hypnosis than the control group, nor did they show any signs of psychopathology. They did, however, believe more strongly in alien visitations, suggesting that such beliefs allow people to shape ambiguous information as well as diffuse physical sensations and vivid images into a realistic alien encounter (Steve Mera, *Advanced Investigators Training Course in Anomalous Phenomena*, 2010).

Temporal lobe lability is also another theory. People with relatively labile temporal lobes are more prone to fantasy and more likely to report mystical and out-of-body experiences, visions, and psychic phenomena. However, psychologist Spanos found no difference in a temporal lobe lability scale between UFO witnesses and control groups. In 1995 psychologist Marcus Cox (University of the West of England) compared a group of twelve British abductees with a matched control group and, again, found no difference in the temporal lobe lability scale. Like Spanos' subjects, the abductees were more often believers in alien visitation than those in the control group. The final theory, which I consider more plausible, is that abductions are elaborations of sleep paralysis, although sleep paralysis fails to explain all aspects of the alien abduction experience (Steve Mera, *Advanced Investigators Training Course in Anomalous Phenomena*, 2010).

In a typical sleep paralysis episode, a person wakes up paralyzed, senses a presence in the room, feels fear or even terror, and may hear a humming or buzzing sound or even see strange lights. An invisible entity has been known to sit on their chests, shaking, strangling, or prodding them. Again, this is also reported in diabolical hauntings where witnesses are said to have been attacked or even raped in their sleep by alleged demonic spirits referred to as an incubus (male demon) or succubus (female demon). Attempts to fight the paralysis are usually unsuccessful. It is reputedly more effective to relax or to try to move the eyes or a single finger or toe. Descriptions of sleep paralysis occur in many accounts of abduction and haunting (Steve Mera, *Advanced Investigators Training Course in Anomalous Phenomena*, 2010).

FIVE

FUTURE APPLICATIONS IN PARAPSYCHOLOGY

Future parapsychological research and experimental techniques may find a key to unlocking conscious, subconscious, and unconscious super-potential, which could change the way scientists think about many things. If the secret of Psi phenomena can be unlocked, it could change approaches to life, death, and physics. The potential practical applications of parapsychological research could be used to further scientific investigation, as well as for finding lost objects, archaeology and historical investigation. Parapsychological insights could also be brought to bear on improving human life, in medicine, psychotherapy and counseling, care for the disabled, environmental improvement, making education and training more efficient, and forecasting the future to avert or predict natural or manmade disasters. Parapsychology could even be deployed by governments in executive decision making and the gathering of military intelligence, and regrettably it seems likely that the weaponisation of psychic abilities might be attempted. Likewise, governments might deploy psychic abilities for criminal investigation, social control, weather prediction and even health and safety inspections. On a commercial level, psychic abilities could aid industrial espionage, entertainment, agriculture and pest control, exploration for natural resources and even gambling on games and sports. More speculatively, Psi abilities may make possible interspecies communication between humans and animals. The possibilities are endless.

There are also other areas where parapsychological research could benefit mankind in the future. For instance, there has been much research in the ability of Direct Mental Interaction on Living Systems (DMILS), also known as Bio PK (as explained earlier). This is the ability whereby a psychic can influence the human body's physical system. This could, in the future, help in the field of medicine as well as healing and alleged psychic surgery. With this in mind, would it be possible in the future to use these paranormal abilities without the use of controlled drugs? Or even for an individual to undergo surgery without the need for flesh to be cut or sewn and diseased parts removed?

With the ability of PK still in mind, might it be possible for paraplegic or other disabled people to be able to lift and move objects with just a thought? It may seem a far-fetched idea, but nonetheless, it presents quite an astonishing thought. Unfortunately, parapsychologists wish that these abilities were easy to unlock than they seem to be. Many parapsychologists believe these psychic abilities exist; the problem is that they do not know why, how, or what causes them to happen. Although there is evidence that suggests some of these paranormal processes do seem to exist, the best evidence is statistical analysis of repeated experiments by different researchers that provides statistically significant results above chance, but nonetheless intriguing. What about life after death? Can we imagine being able to resolve scientifically the one question that has plagued our minds since time immemorial; the question of whether our consciousness or soul does indeed survive bodily death?

There is a long history of criminal cases in the annals of psychical research in which an alleged psychically gifted person is said to have assisted in the apprehension of the perpetrator of the offence, for instance by using dowsing tools and psychometry (paranormally obtaining information about the crime from holding an object that had been in contact with the victim or the offender). There have also been successful cases where the predominant method of psychic detection involved waking clairvoyant visions in which the psychic gives hints, clues, and information relating to the crime. This information has then led to the offender being caught and the victim being found alive or dead.

Although there are many benefits that parapsychological research could give to the world, there are also concerns over those who might abuse it for nefarious purposes. Some national governments are interested in the prospect of utilizing parapsychological research findings for military purposes, as explained earlier in this book. It has been claimed that the world's superpowers have been investigating the use of ESP and Out-of-Body Experiences in espionage as well as PK for sabotage of radar equipment and missile guidance systems. (*Phenomena Magazine*, Issue 33, January, 2012). Some reports of government involvement in these applications may be instances of disinformation, the objective being to incite rival nations to waste some of their defence budgets on monitoring parapsychological research. Many parapsychologists are disturbed by the idea of their field being subverted towards military ends. Yet if parapsychologists provide evidence of Direct Mental Interaction of Living Systems or of psychic healing or psychokinesis, there is no logical reason why such abilities might not be directed towards harmful rather than beneficial ends.

Can we imagine a soldier or an individual being able to psychically kill or harm a person using PK? What about stopping the heart using Bio PK? Or being able to control the thoughts of others to do harm to others or themselves? It is quite a frightening prospect. On the other hand, the inability to control the phenomena and the minuteness of effects typical of Psi experiments give little reason to believe that military applications or, indeed, many other mooted practical applications could be successful in the near future. Only time and future experimentation in parapsychology as a science will tell.

SIX

GHOST HISTORIES: CHANGING EXPERIENCES OF GHOSTS

By Francis Young

Whether someone comes at the question of ghosts as a skeptic, a believer, or an agnostic, no one can fail to be fascinated by the existence of ghost stories themselves. Why do people feel the need to record, treasure and share their supernatural/parapsychological experiences? Ghost narratives, as I prefer to call them in preference to ghost stories (a term that implies fiction) have an intriguing life of their own, worthy of study, quite apart from the question of whether they are true. Ghost narratives do not stay the same over time, but evolve, change and adapt to the surrounding culture. It is not just the narratives that change over time, but also the way that people seem to experience ghosts. This phenomenon is not unique to ghosts, either: a similar phenomenon is found in our attitudes to dreams. In the ancient world, most recorded dreams featured encounters with a figure of power and authority who imparted a message to the dreamer. Such dreams are now rare, and most people in the West report narrative dreams, in which they did or experienced something. There are many theories about why this may be; one reason is that people in the ancient world expected to receive prophetic messages from the gods in their dreams, and so they did. Whereas modern people are accustomed to the idea, derived from Freud and Jung, that the messages in dreams are usually hidden in symbolism.

So how have our experiences of ghosts changed? There are comparatively few recorded ghost stories from medieval England, but many of them feature revenants, dead bodies that refuse to lie quietly in their graves and emerge to torment the living, similar to 'zombies' in contemporary culture. Stories of non-physical or semi-physical spectres are unusual in this period. This may be because medieval people took a literal view of the body. For instance, in a medieval court, a murderer could be convicted if the body of the alleged victim was brought into his presence and started bleeding. Likewise, if someone had unfinished business when they died, then not just their spectral soul, but also their physical body might manifest itself. Medieval ghosts served very prosaic purposes, often directly punishing those who had cursed their deaths or defrauded them in some way. These stories were told by priests and monks, probably with the intention of frightening people away from the sins of murder, fraud and theft. Having said that, however, there are some vivid stories in the chronicles that sound like they were based on eyewitness accounts.

In the sixteenth century, England experienced the upheaval of the Protestant Reformation. Henry VIII rejected the Catholic doctrine of Purgatory, which said that the souls of the dead were waiting to get into heaven through the help of their living friends and relatives.

Masses for the dead were abolished. Part of belief in Purgatory had always been the idea that the souls of the dead might return to ask their loved ones for prayers directly; ghosts were part of the religious culture of Catholic England. Ironically, however, the sixteenth century saw a huge increase in sightings of ghosts. Catholics declared that this was the result of abolishing prayers for the dead. If you stopped praying for the souls in Purgatory, a plague of ghosts were exactly what you should expect. To this day, there are those who argue that England has more recorded ghost sightings than any other country in the world because English people stopped praying for the dead at the Reformation, and retained a residual guilt for this betrayal of their dead friends and relatives. On the other hand, Protestant reformers confidently predicted that once Protestantism triumphed over Catholicism, people would stop seeing ghosts because all ghost stories were made up by Catholic priests trying to convince people to believe in Purgatory. They were to be disappointed, because people carried on seeing ghosts.

Some Protestants responded angrily to these continuing ghost sightings by declaring that ghosts were not the souls of the dead at all, but evil spirits who had come to seduce people back to Catholicism, by pretending to be ghosts. There was a problem for Protestants, however, who depended on their faith entirely on the Bible, because there is a ghost in the Bible. In Chapter 28 of the Book of Samuel, King Saul visits a woman at Endor with special powers, hoping that she will tell him whether he will be victorious in battle. The woman raises the spirit of the Prophet Samuel. Some Protestants thought that this was genuinely Samuel's ghost, some thought that it was a special miracle by God, and some thought that the devil created a simulation of Samuel's ghost to lead Saul astray. Either way, there was always a division of opinion on ghosts among Protestants.

Ordinary people were less interested in this dispute between Catholics and Protestants, and seeing ghosts was an everyday fact of life in sixteenth- and seventeenth-century England. As in the Middle Ages, ghosts always came for a purpose; they revealed murderers, uncovered the location of hidden treasure, and made sure that people discovered wills they had secretly altered before death, and ensured that their relatives honoured bequests made to charity. Indeed, it was almost as if ghosts at this time were a kind of control mechanism to ensure that people honoured the wishes of the dead; without the fear of exposure by a ghost, people would just spend the money on themselves. But ghosts also appeared to prophesy the future and reveal more important information. In 1678, a London magistrate called Sir Edmund Berry Godfrey was gruesomely murdered. His ghost appeared to several people shortly after, declaring not only that he had been murdered by Catholics, but also that there was a vast Catholic conspiracy reaching to the heart of government. This fed the most popular conspiracy theory of the time, that Catholics wanted to take over the country and start a persecution of the Protestants and produced a hysterical and bloody campaign against Catholics that lasted several years (the Popish Plot).

The English Civil War in the mid seventeenth century produced many of Britain's best known historic ghostly apparitions. In 1642 the Battle of Edgehill was fought in Warwickshire, the first serious engagement of the conflict. After the battle was over, night after night, local people could hear and see the battle re-enacted in the sky; many people visited the area and witnessed this phenomenon. Thomas Wentworth, Earl of Strafford, is supposed to have appeared to King Charles I on the eve of the Battle of Marston Moor in 1644, to forewarn him of his defeat. Strafford's death in 1642 had marked the beginning of the power struggle between King and Parliament. It was almost as if the trauma of the Civil War, in which brother was turned against brother, was reflected in the way in which people experienced ghosts and apparitions. However, the Civil War was also a time when strange new religious sects sprang up, and some of these denied the idea that the soul could survive after death at all. Towards the end of the seventeenth century, an Oxford scientist named Joseph Glanvill published a book called *Saducimus Triumphatus* ('Saducism Defeated') which amassed a huge dossier on the supernatural to prove the existence of a spiritual world and an afterlife. It is in this collection that we find the famous story of the Tedworth Drummer, the drum that played itself after a magistrate confiscated it from a wandering player.

However, the eighteenth century saw a change in the way that people talked about ghosts. The idea that ghosts existed was questioned by some scientists, who adopted a view of the world that focused on a rather narrow definition of experimental proof. Many writers insisted that it was only ignorant and uneducated people who saw ghosts; seeing ghosts and believing in them was a sign of superstition or a weak mind. Ghosts became a staple of comedy, regularly appearing in cartoons and comic plays. However, while it was fashionable to laugh at ordinary people for believing in ghosts, there was a huge amount of interest in ghost sightings from fashionable people in eighteenth century England. There were dramatic cases like the Cock Lane ghost, which Dr Samuel Johnson famously endorsed as genuine before it was proved to be a hoax. The Georgian attitude to ghosts was two-faced; on one hand, the only culturally acceptable public attitude to ghosts was contempt, but on the other people remained as keenly interested in phenomena of this kind as they had ever been. Most importantly, the late eighteenth century saw the appearance of gothic fiction, in which ghosts played a crucial part.

In the nineteenth century, talking about and seeing ghosts became intensely fashionable. Under the influence of gothic literature, such as the novels of Mrs Radcliffe and Horace Walpole and the poetry of Lord Byron, people became very interested in medieval ruins. For the first time, stories about black monks, brown friars and grey nuns began to appear. However, these stories were not entirely new. The link between ghosts and the Reformation is an abiding feature of the history of English ghosts. In the early seventeenth century, a historian named Henry Spelman had argued that any family that purchased or inherited lands that Henry VIII took from the monks would be punished by the curse of childlessness, with the heir to the land often dying in a particular manner. The curse on the Brownes of Cowdray in Sussex, for example, meant that the first born heir would always drown. In the nineteenth century, these old curses began to be accompanied by the appearance of a monk or friar, to forbode the death in the family rather like the Irish banshee. The Victorians were also much preoccupied with the idea of secret tunnels and recesses, some of which existed and others did not, and the discoveries they made behind walls and panels often inspired ghost stories of their own. For example, the tradition of screaming skulls, mysterious human skulls in some old houses that will not allow themselves to be removed, is first recorded in this period.

The Victorians wrote down more ghost narratives than anyone before them, which is both good and bad. Bad, because we cannot be sure that these really were old narratives, or whether they dated from the Victorian period. I have investigated one particular case in detail, which shows the sort of change that ghost stories can undergo. One night in 1807, a servant at Coldham Hall in Suffolk was carrying a tray to his master's bedroom, and had to pass through the great hall. At the far end of the great hall were the portraits of two nuns. As the servant was on the stairs, he saw two strangely dressed women advancing out of the portraits across the hall towards him; he was so frightened that he dropped the tray and ran upstairs. The owner of the house, Sir Thomas Gage, commissioned an engraving of the apparition based on the servant's description. Only one known copy of this engraving survives, hidden deep in an archive. In 1869, Coldham Hall was sold, but for some reason these portraits were not dispersed with the rest of the contents and remained in the house, although they were moved from the end of the great hall to the stairs. In the 1950s the then owner of Coldham Hall reported that when he attempted to remove the portraits of the two nuns from the stairs for cleaning, the house experienced poltergeist-type activity. The owner concluded that the portraits were cursed and then on they were never moved from their position. There is no evidence that this later owner had any direct knowledge of the earlier story from 1807.

In 2002, Coldham Hall was brought by the supermodel Claudia Schiffer, who still lives there. She brought in a medium because she felt troubled by the portrait; however, the pictures have never been moved and remain in position. This is an interesting case because it proves that modern stories can sometimes have a much older origin, and are not always just recent creations. However, it also shows that a process of 'Chinese whispers' goes on with ghost narratives: in this case a story of an apparition seems to have given way to a story about a curse, whereas in other cases the process is the other way round. Ghost narratives have to be treated carefully: they should not be dismissed as fabrications out of hand, although there are no doubt some cases in which stories have been created for commercial gain in a country where having a ghost in your pub or hotel attracts custom. On the other hand, ghost narratives should not be accepted automatically as a true record of what a person believed they experienced. People have a tendency to borrow the ghost narratives of others, and sometimes they will come to believe quite genuinely that they are their own experiences. On occasions, stories will become displaced in time and place, or two ghost narratives will be merged into one. I remain convinced, however, that at the core of most ghost narratives lies someone's experience, and it is a role of the critical historian to get as close to that core as possible.

Dr Francis Young holds a PhD from the University of Cambridge and is the author of many books including *English Catholics and the Supernatural, 1553–1829* (2013). He is a Fellow of the Royal Historical Society and Volumes Editor for the Catholic Record Society.

SEVEN

WHAT IS A GHOST AND HAUNTING?

Stories of 'ghosts' have quite literally haunted our imagination for hundreds if not thousands of years. But what exactly are they? Are they, as some people believe, discarnate spirits of the dead? A telepathic communication? Recordings of images from the past? A slip in time? Or a psychological hallucination? No one knows for sure, but one thing we can be certain of is that these experiences do happen. They are reported across a broad range of cultures and societies across the world also with different belief systems.

The first recorded ghost encounter occurred in Athens, Greece a century before the birth of Christ. A man by the name of Athenodorus, a philosopher, rented a haunted villa. The rent was preposterously low, so Athenodorus decided to move in and check the stories of a haunting for himself. On the first night Athenodorus heard a rattling of chains and a grey figure of a man materialized, manacled in chains, which beckoned to him. His appearance was so horrifying that a past resident of the villa had died of shock. As the apparition made its way towards Athenodorus it was moaning and clanking its chains. The philosopher continued to stand still to see what would happen. At last, the ghost gave up, moved to a corner of the courtyard and disappeared. As soon as it was morning, Athenodorus hurried to a magistrates and returned with workmen who started digging at the spot where the figure had vanished. It did not take long for them to unearth a skeleton of a man bound in rusty chains. The philosopher ordered a proper burial for the body and the apparition was never seen again.

A ghost or haunting is different from an apparition in the sense that a ghost seems to be an image that seems to be non-intelligent; in other words, it does not communicate with a living person and re-plays over and over again, doing the same thing it did when the person was alive. Ghosts in haunted locations are known to have certain phenomenological characteristics associated with such phenomena. These range from apparitions being seen, to noises being heard, cold spots and psychic breezes being felt, movement of objects being seen, doors opening and closing, music being heard, unusual fragrances being smelt, voices being heard as well as other unusual phenomena such as footfalls.

As a parapsychological researcher, people ask me from time to time, 'Do you believe in ghosts?' My answer to them is a plain and simple yes, but I have found no evidence *per se* to prove they are discarnate entities of the dead. Instead, I have found the evidence leads to what is commonly referred to as the Stone Tape Theory or hypothesis, or more commonly known as a Residual Haunting. This is where a building or a location is said to record a massive output of psychic energy from an individual or event that may, or may not be, have been traumatic in nature. This energy field contains visual or auditory information that then gets 'imprinted' on the environment for all time.

It is theorized by believers in this hypothesis that due to some unknown natural factors, the images or sounds replay themselves back to an individual. Whether the individual happens to be in the right place at the right time or is more perceptive psychically than others, or whether some external atmospheric phenomenon triggers the replay, are a matter of conjecture. Most natural stone contains magnesium silicates (silica), more commonly known as quartz, which has many applications in its uses. Silica is a substance used in CDs, DVDs, Blu-Rays, vinyl records and also the old VHS video tapes, as well as the microchips that are used in the machines that they are played back on. Silica used in these formats helps store electronic information such as visual imagery and audio tracks, so in theory it may be possible that building materials such as granite and limestone containing magnesium silicates may actually store psychic visual impressions and auditory sounds. It has been said that the sound of a potter's wheel has been recorded in the fine grooves of pottery. Perhaps a person under extreme anxiety or emotional content releases an enormous amount of psychic energy which somehow the building (or the location the building has been built on) absorbs and stores, only for that psychic information to be re-played back under the right environmental and atmospheric conditions. On this reading, a ghost really is an echo of the past. This really is only a theory and only anecdotal at best, however. For it to be a scientific theory it would need to be a testable hypothesis and unfortunately, with today's science, it is currently untestable. What is known is that consciousness plays the biggest role in this phenomenon as well as in all psychic phenomena in general, and without it psychic phenomena could not exist.

Many examples of what a ghost is can be drawn from the annals of psychic research. At Treasurer's House in York in 1953 a young apprentice plumber by the name of Harry Martindale was working in the basement of the house, when he heard the sound of a horn. He was then startled in horror when all of a sudden a horse was seen to come through the wall along with a Roman soldier who was also mounted atop it. All of a sudden a whole battalion of Roman legionnaries followed the horse and rider through the wall, all wearing armour, helmets with plumes, carrying shields and spears. Harry reported that they looked disheveled and tired as if they had returned from battle. Young harry also reported that the legionnaries could only be seen from the knees up and that they paid no attention to him whatsoever. The battalion then disappeared into the opposite wall, never to be seen again. The cellar was later excavated and what was found a foot below the cellar floor was the remains of an old Roman road.

Anne Boleyn's ghost (the second wife of Henry VIII) is one of the most travelled ghosts in Great Britain. She has been said to haunt Hever Castle, Blickling Hall, the Tower of London, Hampton Court Palace, Salle Church, Windsor Castle and Marwell Hall. If ghosts are recordings of the past her ghost must be the most famous in Britain. In Marwell Hall she is said to be seen on Yew Tree Walk, where Henry VIII and Jane Seymour are rumoured to have strolled whilst planning their wedding. At Hampton Court she has been seen wearing a blue dress and been described as walking slowly with a mournful look on her face. At Windsor Castle, her ghost has been seen standing at a window in the Dean's Cloister.

On May 19 (the anniversary of her death) her ghost is said to return to Blickling Hall (her birthplace). A phantom carriage comes up the drive leading to the hall, drawn by six headless horses and driven by a headless coachman. The ghost of Anne sits inside, dressed in white and holding her severed head in her lap. When the carriage reaches the front doors to the hall, the ghostly coach and horses disappear and Anne's ghost goes inside to roam the halls until daybreak. At Hever Castle and on Christmas Eve, she has been seen crossing the bridge over the River Eden in the castle grounds. She has also been seen standing beneath the great oak tree, under which King Henry VIII wooed her.

Anne Boleyn's ghost has been seen in several places around the Tower of London's grounds, in the White Tower, the Queen's House, Tower green (site of the scaffold and site of her execution) and the Chapel of St Peter ad Vincula, where she was buried under the floor of the chancel in an arrow case. In 1817 a sentry patrolling the White Tower suffered a fatal heart attack after encountering the ghostly Anne Boleyn on a staircase. In 1864 a sentry standing guard outside the Queen's House reported seeing the white figure of a woman veiled in mist. She was wearing Tudor dress and a French hood; however, where her face should have been, there was nothing. The sentry then challenged the figure and when it did not reply and continued towards him, the sentry made a thrust at it with his bayonet. What happened next caused him to pass out. As he thrust his bayonet at the ghost, it passed through the figure, and a fiery flash ran up his rifle and gave him a shock. The sentry was court martialed for falling asleep on the job. He was found not guilty when several eyewitnesses told the court that they had also seen the headless woman on Tower green that night. One officer who saw the event from a window in the Bloody Tower testified that he had heard the Sentry yelling at the figure to stop, and saw him thrusting his bayonet through it. He saw the figure pass though the bayonet and then through the sentry as well.

By far the most spectacular haunting by Anne in the Tower takes place in the Chapel Royal of St Peter ad Vincula, where she is buried. In the late nineteenth century a captain of the guard noticed a light burning in the locked chapel late at night. Upon finding a ladder and placing it against one of the chapel windows, he was shocked at the scene taking place in the otherwise empty chapel: 'Slowly down the aisle moved a stately procession of Knights and Ladies, attired in ancient costumes; and in front walked an elegant female whose face was averted from him, but whose figure greatly resembled the one he had seen in reputed portraits of Anne Boleyn. After having repeatedly paced the chapel, the entire procession together with the light disappeared'.

Residual ghosts pay no attention at all to the witnesses they are seen by, and seem to carry out a predefined set of actions. When the ghosts which are seen to walk through walls in a building there is often found a wall which used to house a door which existed in the past. Some ghosts are seen floating or gliding several feet above the floor, it is then later discovered after historical research that there probably was a floor over where the ghost was seen gliding which now did not exist due to modern renovations.

If ghosts are the spirits of the dead and the soul survives bodily death, as some believe, how then does that account for technological apparitions? What about apparitions of cars, buses and planes? Not to mention phantom ships and trains. In 1936 a ghostly large red double decker bus was seen by dozens of people in the Ladbroke Road area of London, racing down an empty road in the middle of the night, long after the real buses had stopped running. It was claimed that the ghostly red bus had caused a number of accidents and at least one death. Some people believed that it was an omen that the borough council should straighten the dangerous bend where the accidents occurred. The bend turned out to be a blind corner at the junction of St Mark's Road and Cambridge Gardens where the real No. 7 bus ran earlier in the day, finishing around 11.00pm each night. Three hours later the phantom bus would appear. An eyewitness testified: 'I was turning the corner into Cambridge Gardens and I saw the bus tearing down towards me. The lights of the top and bottom decks and the headlights were full on, but I could see no sign of crew and passengers. I yanked my steering wheel hard over, scraping the roadside wall, and the bus just vanished'.

Another driver was less fortunate. He hit a wall head on and died in the crash. At the inquest, the coroner was told that the driver had been going down St Mark's Road: 'When suddenly this bus appeared, ablaze with light. The car swerved and smashed into the wall. The bus immediately vanished!' other witnesses startled the coroner with similar experiences. An official from the bus depot nearby had sworn he had seen the ghost bus draw up in silence in the middle of the night, and disappear. He knew that no buses had been scheduled at that hour, not even on a late night service. It was after the coroner's inquest that the council demolished the wall and widened the junction. When the danger had been corrected the phantom bus was never seen again.

The legend of the Flying Dutchman was well known to sailors. It has been said to have been seen off the Cape of Good Hope. The legend begins with a Bernard Fokke who was famous as a daring mariner in the seventeenth century. It is said that he strengthened the masts of his ship with iron, and made rapid passages to the East Indies as a result. Because of this it was said that he had made a pact with the devil and when his ship disappeared without trace, substance was added to the legend. It was on 26 January 1923 that the P&O liner, SS Barrabool, left Cape Town on her passage from Australia to London. At midnight, two officers, the quartermaster, and a cadet, took over watch on the vessel's bridge.

Shortly after, wrote the second officer,

> I distinctly saw the silvery appearance of a full rigged sailing ship. No sails were set, or in other words, the sails were bare; the only conclusion was that the vessel was a derelict and abandoned, when to our increasing amazement she simply vanished! The fourth officer, Mr. Stone, reported the incident: about 12.15am we noticed a strange light on the port bow; I may add here that it was a very dark night, overcast, with no moon. We looked at this through binoculars and the ship's telescope, and made out what appeared to be the hull of a sailing ship, luminous, with two distinct masts carrying bare yards, also luminous. No sails were visible, but there was a luminous haze between the masts. There were no navigation lights, and she appeared to be coming closer to us and at about the same speed as ourselves. When first sighted she was about two to three miles away, and when within half a mile of us she suddenly disappeared. There were four witnesses to this spectacle, the second officer, a cadet, the helmsman and myself. I shall never forget the second officers startled expression: 'My God, Stone, it's a ghost ship!'

Stone subsequently drew a sketch of the ship and said: 'Many people who have seen it wonder if she was the Flying Dutchman we saw that night'.

An earlier well-documented sighting of the Flying Dutchman is to be found in 'The Cruise of Her Majesty's Ship Baccante', a record of a Naval voyage undertaken in 1881 by Prince George of Wales, and later King George V, and his elder brother the Duke of Clarence. An entry in the prince's journal for one night aboard HMS Inconstant reads:

> June 11th, 1881: At 4.00am the Flying Dutchman crossed our bows. A strange red light as of a phantom ship all aglow in the midst of which light the masts, spars of a brig 200 yards distant stood out in strong relief … the lookout man on the forecastle reported her as close on the port bow, where also the officer of the watch from the bridge clearly saw her, as did the quarter deck midshipman, who was sent forward to the forecastle, but found no vestige or sign whatsoever of the ship was seen either near or right away on the horizon, the night being clear, and the sea calm … Thirteen persons altogether saw her, but whether it was the Flying Dutchman or what else must remain unknown. The Tourmaline and Cleopatra, who were sailing on our starboard bow, flashed to ask whether we had seen the strange red light. Some thirteen people aboard Inconstant saw the phantom ship, together with more aboard the accompanying vessels.

The Tay Bridge disaster took place at 7.45pm on 28 December 1879 when a violent storm caused the Tay Bridge in Aberdeen, Scotland to collapse with a train and six carriages, which fell into the River Tay in the Firth of Tay. All 75 passengers and crew and the train driver were killed in the disaster. It is said that on the anniversary of the Tay Bridge disaster, a ghost train appears where the tracks would have been and the screams of the passengers can be heard as they vanish in the middle of the bridge at the site where they would have plunged into the river Tay.

So what are ghosts really? Are they psychic energy that has been recorded in the environment in conjunction with geomagnetic or magnetic forces, together with subconscious or conscious psychic awareness, or is there something more? Psychometrists (psychics who claim to gain personal information from hand held objects) may also work in the same way a re-play haunting does. They claim that everything we touch leaves a mental imprint on the object touched, so it could be that the information being picked up on is already there and is read by clairvoyants, so that in reality they are not communicating with intelligent spirits but channeling information already recorded in there. As things stand, all of this remains theory.

EIGHT

APPARITIONS

As I mentioned in the preceding chapter, ghosts are different from apparitions insofar as it is thought that ghosts are 'recordings' of past events, while apparitions can be intelligent, able to communicate in some way and have a personality. It is thought by some parapsychologists that apparitions are a telepathic link from one person to another, so one person may see the apparition whilst another person will not, as the image is being transmitted by the sender and received by the receiver. Apparitions cannot just be seen physically. They can make themselves known by being heard, smelt, felt etc., depending on how the information is perceived psychically by an individual (depending on how strong each individual's psychic ability is). Psychologists theorize that the apparition, especially the crisis apparition, is a hallucination induced by our brains in the hope of lowering stress levels. Presumably the grief-stricken person would gain comfort from seeing a relative or friend they had recently lost and therefore their stress levels would drop.

Thus the brain takes control of a situation, developing and delivering a beneficial psychological result. Of course, many people do not accept this theory, as people claim to have witnessed apparitions of dead relatives and friends at times they were not grief-stricken or even upset. But the theories and incidents abound and intrigue us still. Crisis apparitions are said to be the most common form of apparition witnessed. They are apparitions of people that appear to family members or friends in a time of need or in great danger (hence the telepathic link). They are also said to materialize when a person is in the process of dying or has died, either at the time (during the process of dying) or several hours or days after, when they are categorically recognised as apparitions of the dead. They may be witnessed locally or hundreds or thousands of miles away from the location where that person is in great need, in grave danger or dying.

Crisis apparitions were some of the first cases investigated when Parapsychology was in its infancy, by the Society of Psychical research (SPR) when it first formed in 1882. The researchers concluded that most so called ghosts were phantasms of the living. Ghosts of the living are apparitions that are witnessed when no one is in great need or in grave danger or dying, but are apparitions of still living and healthy people (again a telepathic link might be inferred). They seem to be psychic telepathic images sent unawares by the person who has transmitted them; for example, the person could actually be thinking about a person because they have not seen them for a long time, and the apparition is then seen many miles away by the person they have just been thinking about.

There are many cases of crisis apparition accounts appearing in parapsychological literature. One well-known case concerns Vice Admiral Sir George Tryon. On the afternoon of 22 June 1893 the ship HMS Victoria was rammed by her sister ship HMS Camperdown in the eastern Mediterranean. The Victoria's hull was torn open and sank to the sea bed with the loss of 358 people including Sir George Tryon. The ship was rammed as a direct result of orders given by Sir George himself. In Belgravia, Lady Tryon was entertaining guests at her home at a late morning tea party. The many guests being entertained were wives of the Royal Navy's leading commanders. At about noon, Admiral Tryon was seen walking down the stairs and across the drawing room. He was attired in his full dress officer's uniform but appeared oblivious to his guests. Some accounts say that he was seen by some 300 guests.

In another account, Sir George Tryon is said to have appeared in the library of his London house in Bristol Square, where guests said they saw him standing behind his desk, his eyes riveted to his globe and his finger pointing to Tripoli on the Mediterranean. The guests greeted him, and he nodded absently and was trance-like in his movements. The guests told the happy news to Lady Tryon, but when she reached the library, it was empty; on the globe was a wet fingerprint, and on the floor was a damp footprint where Sir George Tryon had stood. The clock had stopped at 3.44pm, allegedly at the time of his death.

In the First and Second World Wars, there were accounts of crisis apparitions of soldiers dying on the battlefields and appearing to still living relatives hundreds of thousands of miles away. Mrs Dawson's account, recounted by parapsychologist Steve Mera, is another classic tale:

> During the last World War my husband was called away into the forces and sailed overseas in December 1941. One night as I lay awake in my bed there was a tapping sound on the window pane downstairs. I then heard a key being put into my front door and then footsteps of someone coming up the stairs … The bedroom door opened and my husband stood there looking at me. I didn't know what to say, so I just looked at him. He walked over to me and kissed me on the cheek. He then reached out and grabbed my hand and just vanished. I sat there amazed looking at my hand which only a moment ago was tightly grasped by my husband's hand. It was not until 1945 that I received the news that my husband had died in a prisoner of war camp in the Far East, and to my surprise died on April 14th 1942; the very same night he visited me.

I have conducted much research into the crisis apparition and here I relate two personal cases which have never before been published (one is also of an apparition of the dead case). One happened to my wife Sharon in 2010, who happens to be an Emergency Care Practitioner (ECP). In this case there was another witness who was no relation or friend to Sharon.

One day in October 2010, at approximately 6.30pm, Sharon was called to a small RTC (Road Traffic Collision) involving four occupants in one car which was hit by one occupant in another car. This occurred approximately two weeks after a double fatal road traffic accident around 400 yards away. Both cars were in the layby on arrival. Also in attendance was a police car with two police officers. Sharon was checking patients at the side of the road whilst standing next to one of the Police officers. Sharon states: 'A girl suddenly appeared and ran to the first car's driver and said, 'Just saying hello, I'm on my way to the pictures'. Sharon commented, 'The driver did not acknowledge this girl and she left. Both the police officer and I commented on how silly it was to stop and run across the road, as it was dark and the traffic heavy. Neither I nor the police officer saw where she came from or where she went. This was approximately 6.55pm. All the patients were dealt with and called clear'.

At approximately 7.10pm Sharon was immediately given another 999 call to another RTC. This call was about a mile and a half away, so she arrived very quickly:

On arrival we saw a car on its side with one female driver who was out of the car and sat on its side with one female driver who was out of the car and sat in the passenger seat of a passer's by car. I said: 'Oh hello, you never made it to the pictures then?' as this was the girl I had seen with the Police officer at the other RTC approximately 15 minutes earlier. Although shook up, she suddenly looked at me and said: 'How did you know I was going to the pictures?', to which I explained I had just seen her at the other accident where she spoke to the driver. This young woman was visibly in a state of shock, as she stated she left Worksop in Nottinghamshire approximately 30 minutes earlier, which her mother later verified. At the time I and the police officer had seen her, she was avoiding a rabbit on the road, causing the car to skid and flip over onto its side and crash into a tree. As I was checking the patient, the same two police officers turned up on the scene. The police officer who I was stood with at the first RTC said to the girl: 'So no pictures for you then!' I then verified with him that this was the same girl we had both seen and commented on.

Sharon also stated: 'However could it have been the same girl? She had never physically been there as she would have been crashing her car at the time we had seen her!' Sharon said that no persons were seriously injured in either RTC, although in the second accident serious injuries might have been expected.

So what are we to make of these accounts? Are they a person's spirit saying one final goodbye to their loved ones? Or are they subconscious telepathic links from the dying or injured person to their relatives or friends, telling the person that they are in mortal danger and need some help? As I have stated before, some parapsychologists suggest that crisis apparitions and apparitions in general, are in fact hallucinatory in nature and are induced subconsciously produced in the brain.

Grieving, particularly, results in huge stress levels and emotional upset which disrupts the normal psychological and physiological processes. The mind may induce the hallucination as a form of psychological protection, to ease the physical and psychological balances of the traumatized brain. This is one possible interpretation of what happened to me in the next chapter on Spontaneous Dream Visitations (SDV), accounting psychologically for my own experience.

Some parapsychologists say that it might not be a hallucination *per se*, but the most dramatic result of a telepathic link to the person's brain. It is known that the relationship between twins and also the close bond between parents and children can often result in a telepathic connection, e.g. the parent may think of something which the son or daughter then comes out with, or as another example, a person may think of someone they have not seen for a long time, then suddenly the telephone rings and it is that person on the line. It may be that the sudden trauma of dying or a person undergoing severe stress at the time releases a Psi energy, which materializes in the form of the person in danger due to their close blood relatives, so that person may seek help. In Tibet, monks have been known to mentally train themselves in Psi abilities to produce full visible apparitions of themselves. These are known as Tulpas. There is still a remaining 6% of cases that seem to be unassociated with stress or crisis. Some people have suggested doppelgangers, but these are apparitions that are associated with living witnesses.

Doppelganger is a German word for 'double walker' and there are many fascinating accounts of people who have encountered apparitions of themselves. The phenomenon itself is called bilocation, being seen in two separate locations at the same time. Seeing one's own apparition was said to be a harbinger of death, but this of course is just an urban myth. A classic case of a doppelganger (or bilocation) comes from the American writer Robert Dale Owen who was told the story by Julie Von Guldenstubbe, the second daughter of the Baron Von Guldenstubbe.

In 1845, when Guldenstubbe was 13, she attended Pensionnat Von Neuwelcke, an exclusive girls' school near Wolmar in what is now Latvia. One of her teachers was a 32 year-old French woman, named Emilee Sagee, and although the school's administration was quite pleased with Sagee's performance, she soon became the object of rumour and odd speculation. Sagee it seemed, had an apparitional double that would appear and disappear in full view of students. In the middle of class one day, while Emilee was writing on the blackboard, her exact apparitional double appeared beside her. The apparition precisely copied the teacher's every move as she wrote, except that it did not hold any chalk. The event was witnessed by thirteen students in the classroom. A similar incident was reported at dinner one evening when Sagee's apparition was seen standing behind her, mimicking the movements of Emilee eating, although it held no eating utensils.

The doppelganger did not always follow her movements, however. On several occasions, Emilee Sagee would be seen in one part of the school when it was known that she was in another at the time. The most astonishing incident of bilocation took place in full view of the student body (42 students in all), on a summer day in 1846. The girls were all assembled in the school hall for their sowing and embroidery lessons. As they sat at the long tables working, they could clearly see Emilee Sagee in the school garden gathering flowers. Another teacher was supervising the children. When the teacher left the room to talk to the headmistress, Sagee's apparition appeared in her chair, whilst the real Emilee Sagee could still be seen in the garden. The students noted that Sagee's movements in the garden looked tired while the apparition of Emilee sat motionless in the chair. Two brave girls approached the apparition and tried to touch it, but felt an odd resistance in the air surrounding it. One of the girls actually stepped between the teacher's chair and the table, passing right thorough the apparition, which still remained motionless. It then slowly vanished. Emilee Sagee claimed never to have seen the doppelganger herself, but said that whenever it was said to be seen she felt drained and fatigued. Her physical colour even seemed to be pale at those times it did appear.

Apparitions of the dead are a different kind of apparition. They are said to be intelligent discarnate entities, parts of consciousness that have survived bodily death and can communicate in a number of ways, from being visually seen, to being heard and smelt; they have even been known to touch a person. They are also known to communicate meaningful and intelligent messages to witnesses and are usually seen within 48 hours of a person's passing. Here is a personal case investigated by myself of an apparition of the dead. It is an account given to me by Sharon's (my wife's) cousins, Margaret and Susan. They state that around twenty years ago, their father was found dead in the kitchen by his good friend and neighbour. This neighbour contacted his daughters, Margaret and Susan, who quickly turned up at the address. Margaret told Susan she was not staying there on her own and made arrangements to go to Margaret's home in Mansfield Woodhouse. It was dark, and whilst driving back past Parliament Oak, both Margaret and Susan saw their father, dressed in his best grey suit with his hand in his pocket standing at the side of the road.

Neither Susan nor Margaret said anything to one another at the time, as they did not understand how they could have seen their father, as he had died that morning. Both sisters arrived at Mansfield Woodhouse, and it was only later, because of what they had seen, and because it had bothered them so much, that Margaret told her sister what she had seen. Susan then took a sigh of relief as she thought she had been seeing things, for she had seen the same thing. Both sisters said that, oddly, their father never wore a suit unless it was a very important occasion, and his best suit was grey.

If some apparitions are personalities of dead people, and are experienced in some haunted locations, then how are they able to communicate? Or physically move objects? This would of cause have to by PK, as apparitions do not have any physical bodies to manipulate objects such as hands or feet. They also do not have physical brain matter to transmit Psi effects (if indeed consciousness is localized in the brain). To transmit a meaningful message would also have to be by PK whether transmitted telepathically by the apparition to the medium in the form of clairvoyance or directly by Psi to the witness's brain in the form of a psychic illusion with regard to 'seeing' the apparition or just receiving information psychically.

In my view, if Psi comes from discarnate intelligences, it would be in its 'raw' state. In other words, no brain matter can now hold back consciousness, and any given Psi phenomenon from consciousness would unleash its fullest possible full potential. It would be 'no holds barred' Psi energy, so to speak. It could well be far more powerful in a discarnate intelligence than in a living human being. So when we see in poltergeist cases (addressed later in this book) and hauntings in general huge pieces of furniture such as sofas and tables being thrown about, it is possible that instead of a person's subconscious mind causing the phenomenon, it may actually be the 'raw' state of RSPK directed by the mind of an intelligent apparition (in some cases) making themselves known to an individual due to the frustration and anguish felt by the apparition because they have no other means to communicate to a living person.

Another class of apparition is the deathbed apparition. This type of apparition has been seen by people suffering from terminal illnesses or several days or hours away from dying. In most cases the apparitions are of close relatives and friends that are long gone. In rare cases, some are seen by not just the dying person but others in the room. It could be that these are just hallucinations by a dying brain, a psychological process that may help the terminal patient cope with death. But what is interesting is that the dying patients report that the apparitions have come to take them away, to the other side.

Wilma Ashby was involved in a car accident which pinned her lower part of the body beneath tangled wreckage. After being hospitalized in a critical condition, she continued to bleed severely and despite their best efforts, the doctors were unable to stop the haemorrhage. Relatives of Wilma were summoned to her bedside and told of her inevitable death. Wilma's twin brother, Willard, to whom she had been very close, had died a premature death just four years earlier. At 8.00pm and fully conscious, she had just finished a prayer of thanks that her family, who had been with her in the car, had been spared any injury. Wilma then stated:

> Suddenly, something compelled me to open my eyes. I was astonished to see the grey wall in front of me changing. In the middle of a beautiful purple mist stood my twin brother. He was smiling the same kind of infectious smile he used to smile when he teasingly called me his sin-twister. His arms outstretched, he moved slowly forward. I reached out my arms to embrace him. My brother had reached the foot of my bed and our fingers were about to touch, when my husband entered the room my twin instantly vanished. I began to cry. 'Willard was here but he left before I could touch him'. My husband looked amazed. 'When I opened the door', he said, 'it was as if an electric shock passed through my body'.

Wilma Ashby recovered; her doctor said it was a miracle. Similar accounts have been reported by many others like Mrs Ashby and have come to the very brink of death, but have not died. They are even more common just before an actual death.

NINE

SPONTANEOUS DREAM VISITATIONS

Another class of apparition, rarely researched, is what I call Spontaneous Dream Visitation (SDV) or 'dream apparitions'. Spontaneous dream visitation is a phenomenon in which an apparition of a deceased relative or friend visits a person whilst they are asleep, or in an altered state of consciousness. I myself had a personal experience of an SDV quite a few years ago which led me on a path to study Parapsychology and paranormal investigation scientifically, to try and find out whether there really is life after death. Although I had always been fascinated by everything ghostly beforehand, the experience would push me on a path I am still following, to find out what is 'really' going on.

In 1998 I lost my father Terry to mouth and throat cancer; he and I were always pretty close. Unfortunately at the time I was living in Nottinghamshire and my parents were in Bedford where he passed away. I felt guilty for not being there when he died; I did not know he was going to die, although he did have several bouts of cancer over a six-year period.

One night a year or so later (I cannot recall the exact date), I went to bed as usual and dropped to sleep. During the sleep, I was having a normal dream about something or other when my dream changed. I was in a house, but I did not recognise whose house it was; it was just an ordinary house. I was upstairs in the dark on the upstairs landing, when suddenly a door opened on the landing and out stepped a man. At this point in time, I could not make out who the man was as he had his back turned towards me and I could not see his face. He went down the stairs so I followed.

As we both got down to the bottom of the stairs, he turned around, and it was my father, Terry. He hugged me and then said goodbye. Then, all of a sudden, I woke up. When a person normally wakes from a dream, the person knows that it was a dream. But, on this occasion it felt completely different. On this occasion it felt like it was real. What shocked me the most was that after I woke up, the guilt that I felt for not being there when my father died, had gone! The dream was so vivid that it felt as if the dream had burnt itself into my memory which I will never forgot. I have never had a dream such as this before or since then.

After the experience, I began to wonder whether it was just a vivid dream or something of a paranormal nature. Was it my deceased father's spirit or my subconscious dealing with the guilt I had felt of not being there when he died – like a subconscious psychological defence mechanism being triggered? Either way, it was an experience that pushed me into studying scientific Parapsychology, ghosts, hauntings and life after death.

After the experience I began researching to discover whether people had reported similar experiences to mine. To my surprise they had, although some but not all of the experiences reported the same phenomenological characteristics. Some of the characteristics reported are:

1. Brightness and clear strong colour unlike a normal dream.
2. Knowing that the dream and the apparition is no longer alive in the earthly environment.
3. Hearing music.
4. Recognition of the apparition (i.e. deceased friend or relative).
5. Waking up afterwards with a clear and vivid recollection of the experience.
6. Simple messages being passed on such as 'goodbye', 'I love you' and 'I'm fine'.
7. Remembering the experience many years later as if it had just occurred.
8. Symbolism is common in such experiences, such as meeting on a staircase to indicate the difference between the spirit realm and earthly environment, such as the landing on the upstairs floor of the house (the spirit realm) and the staircase, which symbolizes the way down from the spirit realm to the bottom of the staircase, which is the earthly realm.
9. Sometimes the surroundings of the dream are very simple, such as two empty chairs in the middle of an empty room.
10. The inner knowledge that the experience was not a normal dream.

Some Parapsychologists and researchers suggest that when we are asleep and all external stimuli (the five processes of information) have been subdued in the hypnogogic sleep state, i.e. sight, sound, touch, taste and feeling, and we are in an altered state of consciousness, our capacity for extra-sensory perception (ESP) is activated. When we are in a relaxed state it has been known to promote psychic experiences such as telepathy, clairvoyance, remote viewing, precognition and apparitional experiences. All these phenomena (apart from apparitional experiences per se) have been successfully tested and recorded in a laboratory setting with above chance results. As mentioned previously, the Ganzfeld procedure is an experiment where the subject's normal sensory processes are artificially subdued to promote psychic functioning.

So was my spontaneous dream visitation just a very vivid dream? Or a guilt-ridden hallucination from my guilt-infested subconscious? Or was it really the apparition of my deceased father coming to say goodbye for the last time? To be honest, I am not entirely sure. As a parapsychologist I look for scientific answers before looking for paranormal ones. At the present time, the fact that I was asleep when I experienced it, combined with the fact that we all have vivid dreams point to a non-paranormal explanation, but at the same time a sense of inner knowing, an intuition that it was something inexplicable, sways me towards a paranormal origin. It is certainly an attractive idea that perhaps it was the spirit of my late father coming to say his final goodbye, and that there really is life after death.

TEN

TIMESLIPS AND APPARITIONS

Time travel is the concept of moving between different points in time in a manner analogous to moving between different points in space, either sending objects, or in some cases just information backwards in time to some moment before the present or the future without the need to experience the intervening period, at least not at the normal rate. Although time travel has been a common plot device in fiction since the nineteenth century, one-way travel into the future is arguably possible, given the phenomenon of time dilation based on velocity in the theory of special relativity, exemplified by the twin paradox, as well as gravitational time dilation in the theory of relativity. It is currently unknown whether the laws of physics would allow backwards time travel.

Any technological device, whether fictional or hypothetical, that is used to achieve time travel is commonly known as a time machine. Some interpretations of time travel also suggest that an attempt to travel backwards in time might take one to a parallel universe whose history would begin to diverge from the traveller's original history after the moment the traveller arrived in the past. Some theories, most notably special and general relativity, suggest that suitable geometries of space-time, or specific types of motion in space, might allow time travel into the past or future, if these geometries or motions are possible. In technical papers, physicists generally avoid the commonplace language of moving or travelling through time.

Movement normally refers only to a change in spatial position as the co-ordinate is varied, and instead we might consider the possibility of closed time-like curves, which form closed loops in space-time, allowing objects to return to their own past. There are known to be solutions to the equations of general relativity that describe space-time, which contain closed time-like curves, but the physical plausibility of these solutions is uncertain.

The theory of general relativity does suggest scientific grounds for thinking that backwards time travel could be possible in certain unusual scenarios. So, perhaps some of these scenarios are paranormal in nature, which may simplify time travel without the need for a hypothetical time machine. Some parapsychologists suggest that Psi phenomena could be limitless and precognition and retro-cognition may be examples. Gaining information psychically from the future or past, without the need for a technological or hypothetical time machine may be the answer we are looking for. If Psi can gain information about future or past events and be harnessed, can we even imagine the breakthrough for historical books and information. Furthermore, what if these loopholes or holes in space-time, occurring at random intervals and during certain quantum conditions, could allow a person to simply walk back in time without knowing they have just taken a path back to the past? In the parapsychological literature there are many accounts in which a witness or witnesses claim to have travelled back to the past to encounter solid apparitions of long dead people and environments.

Probably the most famous is the account which comes from 1901, near Versailles, near Paris in France. The account concerns Charlotte Moberly and Eleanor Jourdain and their visits to the palace of Petit Trianon, when they saw and apparently experienced apparitions of the 1700s. In 1901, the two ladies were introduced to each other to see whether they could work together at St Hugh's College. They were not that well known to each other when, on the 10 August 1901, they set out together to visit the Palace of Versailles.

It was 4.00pm when Miss Moberly suggested visiting the Petit Trianon, a small house and gardens within the estate of Versailles, presented to Queen Marie Antoinette in 1774 by Louis XVI. There were two structures, some distance apart, known as the Grand Trianon and the Petit Trianon, just northwest of the main Palace of Versailles. The ladies visited first the Grand Trianon. To have reached the Petit Trianon, they should have first turned down the Allée des Deux Trianons. However, they crossed this road and entered a small lane at right angles to it, not realizing that by doing so they were passing the Petit Trianon on their right.

Their route to the Petit Trianon was therefore fairly circuitous and took them around the gardener's cottage, the theatre and other pavilions. Both ladies experienced feelings of depression, dreariness and extreme quietness, a factor that occurs in many cases of experiencing time slips. Perhaps this is where a quantum time loophole opens up and forms a bubble around the participants that allows them a trip into the past? As they passed what appeared to be the Temple de l'Amour, they saw a man of repulsive appearance sitting on the balustrade surrounding the building. Suggestions have been put forward to who this person might have been, including King Louis XVI himself.

Another man directed them to the right and they came to the rear of Petit Trianon. Miss Moberly saw a lady in summer clothes sitting on the lawn below the terrace, though it appears that Miss Jourdain did not. Miss Jourdain came across a story that Marie Antoinette herself was often seen sitting outside the Petit Trianon on a certain day in August. Miss Jourdain even suggested that Miss Moberly had seen Marie Antoinette herself. On reaching the terrace, a young man directed them to the front of the house and walked around with them until they found the entrance of the Allee des Deux Trianon, when everything seemed to become normal again as inside the building, they followed a group of visitors on a guided tour and then returned to their hotel for tea.

Both ladies later went on to have more time slip experiences at the same location a few years later. Miss Moberly confirmed Miss Jourdain's suggestions that the topography was different, distances seemed shorter, the grounds were less ornate and some features were not visible. They later wrote up their extraordinary experiences in a book entitled *An Adventure*, published in January 1911.

Another incredible account concerns an incident that supposedly happened near Avignon, again in France, when in 1979, Geoff and Pauline Simpson decided to take a late summer holiday with their friends Len and Cynthia Gisby. They decided on a Spanish destination and planned to drive to Spain via France, stopping overnight en route. At the end of the first day, they left the main AutoRoute at Montelimar North and followed a sign for a local motel. Unfortunately, it was fully booked and they were advised to try some of the hotels along one of the smaller, less busy roads towards Avignon.

Cynthia noticed that, once they got away from the motel and began to navigate the smaller country roads, everything became extremely quiet and she recalls laughing at the quaint, old-fashioned posters advertising such things as a local circus. After a while, the road became nothing more than a cobbled track, by which time they had pretty much given up hope of finding a bed for the night. Then, they came across a long, barn like building. Len parked the car and went inside to discover that it was actually a restaurant. He went up to the old fashioned counter and asked the gentleman there if the restaurant had accommodation. It took some time to get him to understand Len's English, but eventually it turned out that they did have two vacant rooms. Pauline remembers that the bedroom she entered was weird; it had starched sheets, a thick furry bed cover and no electricity. The window had no glass in it, just shutters and there were no pillows, just a bolster across the top of the bed. The bathroom too was strange, it was reached by going down a long corridor and had a sunken bath and a spike on the wall which the soap was stuck on.

Cynthia felt equally odd downstairs in the dining room, where a woman in an old fashioned cap and dress was trying to ascertain what they wanted to eat. They were having language difficulties and could not explain their wishes. So, in the end, the ladies ended up with egg and sautéed potatoes and the gentlemen with steaks. The cutlery was also peculiarly heavy and basic in appearance. All in all, the evening was decidedly strange, but following their hearty meal and local ales, they laughed about how rural France was and about their adventure. They all retired to their bedrooms soon after dinner and slept soundly. Len remembers hearing only the sound of a distant train during the night, the road outside the hotel being strangely silent.

The following morning, the group decided to take some photographs to commemorate their night's stay in this peculiar place. After Len and Geoff had snapped a few frames with their respective cameras, they sat down to breakfast. The food was once again odd in taste and appearance. 'The bread was heavy and coarse', Cynthia recalls, 'It was sort of brown, like in war-time. and very sweet'. The coffee too was strange and described by the group as 'black and thick'. The breakfast was interrupted by the entry of two gendarmes (French Policemen) wearing dark blue uniforms with gaiters up to their knees. This seemed odd because the group had seen gendarmes the day before, dressed entirely differently to these two characters. They put it down to the old-fashioned charm of the place and thought no more about it.

The next player to enter this peculiar scenario was a young woman wearing a long purple dress and strange boots. She could have 'stepped out of a fancy dress party', Cynthia recalls, but at 7.00am, in this part of rural France seemed highly unlikely. Len decided to ask if there was a quicker way of returning to the main AutoRoute than the one they had taken to get there. He was convinced that, despite the language barrier, they had never heard of an AutoRoute and he left them slightly bemused before packing their luggage into the car and asking the innkeeper for their bill. Minutes later, he rejoined the group with a wide grin on his face. 'It was 19 francs!' he proclaimed. 'What, for the breakfast?' asked Geoff. 'No, for everything!' Len replied. The complete charge for two rooms, bed and breakfast for four people with dinner and drinks came to an equivalent of £2.50!

Following a fantastic sunny holiday in Spain, the holidaymakers decided they would spend another night in the theme hotel. So, they made their way off the same AutoRoute exit on their return journey. They found the big Montelimar Motel where they had been advised to take the road to Avignon. After driving up and down the road four times they were dismayed and somewhat perplexed that they could not find the hotel. After making a thorough search of the area, they came to the conclusion that the hotel simply wasn't there.

They were certain they were on the same road, for there were no other roads that led to Avignon from the Auto Route. They even located the old fashioned posters that they had found so amusing two weeks before and the layby where the hotel had been, but the hotel had simply gone: 'What struck us was the trees down the road had been small during our first visit and now they were huge! They put their experience down to tiredness and the heat and cast it to the back of their minds. But then, on receiving their developed photographs from the holiday, both couples were amazed to find that the photographs they had taken at the hotel had not come out.

There was no sign of them on the negatives either. It was as if they had never been taken! Research into the case revealed some interesting facts. The dress worn by the woman in purple and the uniforms worn by gendarmes both matched the same time period, the turn of the twentieth century. In fact a French friend of Len and Cynthia told them that the gendarme uniforms they described had not been used since 1905. Bizarrely, when checking the price of accommodation and meals during the early 1900s in that region of France, travel agents Thomas Cook said that the cost of dinner would have been about 19 francs. More local research into the area showed that there was a building on the spot where the hotel would have been, long in the past. Locals couldn't remember if it had been a guesthouse, but they did inform the group that there had been a local village police station next door, all about the turn of the twentieth century.

So what are we to make of these extraordinary accounts? Are they really loopholes in time that just happen to open if being in the right place at the right time? Or could it be that time slips are not fractures in time, but full manifestations of the of the Stone Tape Theory? If it was a manifestation of the Stone Tape Theory, how then can the apparitions witnessed in these accounts have interacted intelligently with the people who witnessed them?

We know that, if it was a recording type of apparition, then communication with these apparitions should not have been possible, as such apparitions are usually regarded by parapsychologists as audible and visible phenomena recorded psychically into the environment – or at least that is the current thinking. What about the group in the second account who experienced eating real solid food, drinking solid liquids and using solid objects to eat with? What about sleeping in real beds on real wooden floors, in a seemingly real building? It seems that these accounts are not just manifestations of the Stone Tape Theory on a grand scale, but could very well be actual time travel experiences that theoretically may be possible.

ELEVEN

POLTERGEISTS AND RSPK

Poltergeist phenomena are indelibly linked to hauntings but are usually classed as a separate phenomenon. Nowadays, parapsychologists generally agree that poltergeist activity is the result of RSPK or Recurrent Spontaneous Psychokinesis, first named by Professor William Roll. But is it the work of an intelligent entity? Or is it really possible that the human mind can produce a field or a force that can move and throw heavy furniture around?

The term 'poltergeist' is a compound of two German words, *polter*, which means making a noise by knocking, throwing things around and to rattle, and the word *geist* which means ghost or spirit. So the word poltergeist literally means noisy spirit. Poltergeist phenomena have been reported for hundreds of years. There are many famous cases such as Enfield (1977), the Bell Witch (1817), the demon drummer of Tedworth (1661), Pontefract (1966), and Rosenheim (1967), all of which will be explored later in the book. There are also many other cases for the researcher to study.

The famous psychical researcher Harry Price, who investigated the Borley Rectory case in 1929 (which will also be recounted later in this book), at the time considered Britain's most haunted house, once stated that whilst ghosts haunt, poltergeists 'infest'. The phenomenological characteristics differ quite considerably from general haunting phenomena. They encompass furniture like tables, beds and chairs being thrown about, cutlery being bent, crockery being smashed, knockings and scratching sounds being heard, footfalls, apportation and asportation phenomena, formations of water appearing on walls and ceilings as well as blood, displacement of object phenomena, doors opening and closing, electrical items such as televisions and radios turning themselves on and off as well as lights. Spontaneous combustion of objects has also been reported, as well as many other apparently inexplicable phenomena such as apparitional sightings, which are rare occurrences in these accounts but not entirely unheard of. Poltergeists have also been heard mimicking animals and appliances, as well as disembodied voices. Some people have also reported being attacked and scratched by a poltergeist.

Poltergeist outbreaks usually last a few weeks, to a few months to a year or so, but usually do not last longer than 18 months and then dissipate. A poltergeist outbreak begins subtly, such as with scratching sounds and knockings being heard. The phenomena seem to escalate with incidents such as cutlery bending and objects moving from one place to another, then they escalate again with beds and sideboards being thrown across the floor and electrical appliances being switched on and off. It seems that, as the witness becomes more anxious and frightened, so the phenomena magnify. The final escalation of phenomena might feature apparitions appearing, voices being heard and spontaneous fires occurring. Then it seems that the poltergeist has used up its energy, which begins to decrease and then finally dissipate.

In a poltergeist case an apparition is rarely seen, but there are exceptions to the rule. In the Enfield case in 1977, dark phantom shapes were sometimes witnessed and in the Pontefract outbreak, a ghostly monk was seen. So is a poltergeist outbreak really the product of the subconscious mind releasing powerful psychic forces manipulating the environment? Or an extreme haunting? It is well known that in the majority of poltergeist cases there is often a focus, usually a human agent such as (more often than not) a young adolescent, often a teenage girl at the centre of the disturbances (again, poltergeist cases can happen around an adult focus but with fewer psychokinetic effects). It is now generally thought by parapsychologists that the subconscious mind of the focal individual can somehow influence matter around them which causes physical effects in the environment. Parapsychologists call it RSPK, Recurrent Spontaneous Psychokinesis. It is thought that a person with untrained psychic ability and who is going through a traumatic period in their life, experiencing stress, anxiety, anger, hatred, frustration, somehow projects their subconscious innermost feelings psychically onto the surrounding environment around them, causing macroscopic psychokinetic events.

In physics, there is a theory called quantum entanglement. Quantum entanglement is when two particles are entangled (connected) and remain connected regardless of how far apart they are from one another, even across the other side of the universe. When an action is performed on one particle, the other particle also responds instantly; not at the speed of light, but as if they were the same particle. Furthermore, physicists know that the mental act of observation has the capacity to affect the results of experiments with quantum particles – a sort of mental imprint on matter itself. So it is conceivable that once a person leaves that mental imprint, it could be manipulated psychically, subconsciously or unconsciously, causing an object to move or be thrown.

During hauntings people report poltergeist phenomena as well as the classic haunt symptoms, so why is it that there is poltergeist activity reported at haunted locations if ghosts are residual? There are some theories that are thought to account for such experiences. The people who are experiencing a haunting generally become anxious, frightened, scared and fearful. All this emotion in itself could manifest as recurrent spontaneous psychokinesis in the haunted environment around them, causing the poltergeist-like effects which the witnesses attribute to the residual ghosts that may already be imprinted in the environment, when in fact it is the person's subconscious mind causing the phenomena.

Another theory is that, if there are discarnate intelligent spirits in a haunting that may want to make themselves known to living people by moving objects etc., then they would have to use psychokinesis themselves – whether by making use of mediumistic or sensitive individuals as conduits for such effects or using their own post-death consciousness to create RSPK (apparitions or spirits cannot physically move objects as they have no physical body to manipulate physical matter). If in some poltergeist cases apparitions do use RSPK, then I believe it may be due to what I have called 'raw state' psychokinesis. In this I mean that because consciousness is now free of its physical body and the physical limitations of the human mind (perhaps due to belief systems, sociological and religious dogma suppressing Psi). If Psi does indeed exist, then it now becomes free to have an unlimited potential. I am put in mind of the line in the film *Star Wars Episode IV: A New Hope*, when Obi Wan Kenobi confronts Darth Vader: 'You can't win, Darth; if you strike me down I will become more powerful than you can possibly imagine!' It may not all be sci-fi after all!

A different theory may account for poltergeist effects in hauntings. This is the timeline theory. According to this theory, the past and present merge together for a small period of time in a certain time and place. It may be that an apparition is manipulating an object in their own time, but the contemporary witnesses do not see the apparition but only the manipulation itself of a given object. It is also an intriguing possibility.

In laboratory-based parapsychological experiments, macroscopic psychokineteic effects are rarely performed under test conditions. This may be due to a person knowing they are under test conditions, as a consequence of which they subconsciously or consciously suppress their Psi abilities. Then again, if some poltergeist phenomena are attributed to intelligent apparitions, scientists cannot very well ask one of them to be a test subject! As I have already explained above, psychokinetic effects are studied more by statistical analysis and random number generators which study subatomic radiation decay off a given random particle whilst a person uses psychokinetic abilities.

In 1979, scientist John Hutchinson's life changed drastically when, upon starting up an array of high voltage equipment which he was using to investigate phenomena produced many years previously by Nikola Tesla, he felt something hit his shoulder. It was a piece of metal. He threw the piece of metal back to where it seemed to have originated and it flew up and hit him again. This was how he originally discovered how fundamental frequencies can shield gravity. When his Tesla coils, electrostatic generator and other equipment created a complex electromagnetic field, heavy pieces of metal levitated and shot toward the ceiling, whilst some pieces shredded and others simply bent. He found that objects such as metal, porcelain, wood and rubber were most affected. Upon analysis and thorough investigation, the Canadian government dubbed this phenomenon the Hutchison Effect while his complex equipment was popularly dubbed 'the poltergeist machine'.

Some scientists conclude that all poltergeist effects are caused by electromagnetic fields and powerful radio wave interference. The problem with this conclusion is that to produce these macroscopic effects, Hutchinson had a whole room full of complex equipment and computers to produce the fields to levitate fairly heavy objects. He could not, it seems, produce fields strong enough to lift heavy furniture and appliances, let alone cause the many other explicable phenomena reported during a poltergeist outbreak, so it seems there are other forces at work as well as electromagnetic fields. Whether RSPK from a living or discarnate intelligence is at work in conjunction with electromagnetic fields, only more laboratory and field observational research may give the answers parapsychologists are looking for. As William Shakespeare once wrote, 'There are more things in heaven and earth, Horatio, than are dreamt of in our philosophy'.

TWELVE

MEDIUMSHIP AND PSYCHIC FRAUD

Mediumship is the alleged psychic ability to channel supposed intelligent spirits in different ways. There are different classifications within the neutral term 'mediumship', such as clairvoyance (clear seeing), which is the ability to see spirits; clairaudience (clear hearing), which is the ability to hear spirit such as voices, sounds and words; and clairsentience (clear feeling), which is the ability to feel the emotions and feelings of spirits.

Mediumship and psychic ability have been around since the dawn of mankind but gained notoriety in the mid-1800s when there was a strong popular urge to learn how to communicate with ghosts and spirits, which became a fad. At this period it was known as spiritualism. It all began when the Fox family moved into a small two-storey wooden cottage in Hydesville, a village in New York State, in December 1847. Soon after they moved in, the family began to hear knocking sounds coming from the walls. Due to the unusual sounds they became curious instead of alarmed and discovered that they could elicit imitations of the clapping of their hands and even answers to questions.

Mrs Fox described the events of 31 March 1848:

> It was very early when we went to bed on this night – hardly dark. I had been so broken of rest I was almost sick. I had just laid down when it commenced as usual. The children, who slept in the other bed of the room, heard the rapping, and tried to make similar sounds by snapping their fingers. My youngest child, Cathie, said: 'Mr Splitfoot, do as I do', clapping her hands. The sound instantly followed her with the same number of raps. When she stopped, the sound ceased for a short time … I then thought I could put a test that no one in the place could answer. I asked the 'noise' to rap my children's ages successively. Instantly, each one of my children's ages was given correctly, pausing between them sufficiently long enough to individualize them until the seventh, at which a longer pause was made, and then three more emphatic raps were given, corresponding to the age of the little one that died, which was my youngest child. I then asked: 'Is this a human being that answers my questions correctly?' There was no rap. I asked: 'Is it a spirit? If it is, make two raps'. Two sounds were given as soon as the request was made.

Some of the neighbors were called in to witness the strange happenings. One of those was Chauncey Losey, who asked the entity about his own personal affairs, and closed his written deposition on his experience with the words: 'I think that no human being could have answered all the questions that were answered by this rapping'.

News of the alleged haunting spread and crowds of attention-seeking individuals came to see the happenings for themselves at the Fox family's home. John Fox, the father of the girls, claimed that the rapping ghost revealed that it was the spirit of a travelling salesman who had been murdered in the house. E. E. Lewis, a local publisher who investigated the alleged paranormal events, learnt that the previous occupants had also been disturbed by paranormal events and even claimed to have heard of the alleged murder, but there was no firm evidence found. Later reports suggested that human remains had been found buried in the cellar of the house, but this story was never substantiated.

Mrs Fox took her two daughters, Margaretta, aged 14 and Kate (Cathie), aged 12, to stay with a married daughter in Rochester, and there, in 1849 the girls gave their first public demonstration, following it up with many more psychic performances throughout the eastern United States. They created a sensation at the time, and their fame was unaffected by the suggestion of three distinguished professors from Buffalo that the raps were created by movements of the girls' knee joints, or by the allegation made later on that Kate had confessed to making the sounds by cracking her toes.

The Fox sisters turned professional mediums, and were the focus of numerous psychical research investigations, such as that of Sir William Crookes, who was impressed by the girls' performances. Others dismissed them as frauds. Their later careers were marked with tragedy. They suffered mob violence, sank into alcoholism and at last confessed to fraud, only to retract the confession later on. If the case happened in today's age, it would be categorized as a typical poltergeist outbreak and not a communication with a haunting entity, but it did begin the age of spiritualism, a religion that still has a big following throughout the world.

Most traditional Séance sittings opened with hymns and prayers, and on many reported occasions spirits chimed in with ghostly music and the creation of melodies through instruments like trumpets, horns and tambourines. The Séance is an alleged attempt to try and communicate with alleged discarnate spirits. The word Séance comes from the French word for 'seat' or 'session' or 'sitting' from the French word 'seoir', to sit. A dark room, sometimes lit by a candle or two, was the usual setting. Small to medium tables and chairs were usually used as well as a large spirit bell which sometimes would be hung from the ceiling over the Séance table, or smaller bells might be placed on the table instead. Pen and paper were also present for the medium, who might have an urge to perform automatic writing. This is another form of spirit communication, where the medium enters some trancelike altered state of consciousness, then starts to write uncontrollably. The medium then alleged that a spirit entity was writing through them. This phenomenon is termed trance mediumship. Another form of mediumship is physical mediumship. This is where spirits are said to temporarily occupy the medium's body in the hope of communicating verifiable verbal messages.

Some mediums used spirit balls. These were sometimes made of wicker and were placed on the table in the hope that spirits would move them around. The blowing of the horn or the ringing of bells were sometimes carried out in the hope that spirits would tune into the frequencies and also be encouraged to participate in the moving of the trumpet and tambourine or ringing of bells. The famous spirit boards or talking boards, better known as Ouija boards, were often used. The word Ouija is split into two words, *Oui* (French for 'yes') and *ja* ('yes' in German). Sitters in the séance place one or two fingers on the planchette (French for 'little table') which is in the middle of the board. The appointed medium asks questions to any spirits present to make themselves known, with whom they are trying to communicate. The moving of the planchette around the board, spelling out names, dates, times and other information was deemed a success and generally thought to have been a genuine spirit communication. Today it is used in paranormal investigations and is called glass divination. Instead of a Ouija board, the sitters use a glass such as a wine glass, bit of paper with letters and numbers, yes and no questions etc. the sitters then place a finger (usually the index finger) on the glass and ask out loud any questions to the spirits to make themselves known by moving the glass. Sometimes it is also common not to use any bits of paper, but instead ask the glass to move backwards or forwards, or side to side depending where the sitter wants the glass to move to.

Slates, tables and cabinets were also used. In the more old-fashioned séance, spirits trumpets were horn-shaped speaking tubes that were used to magnify the whispered voices of spirits to audible range. However, these horns came in many shapes and sizes, and eventually, over the years, they ended up cone-shaped. Spirit slates consisted of two chalkboards bound together that, when opened, were said to reveal messages written by alleged spirits. Séance tables were special lightweight tables which were said to rotate, float or levitate when spirits were present. Today they are commonly used in modern day paranormal investigation vigils. Called table tipping, table rapping or typology, sitters place their hands on the table with the tips lightly touching the table, sometimes with or without touching other people's fingers. The sitters ask out loud for any possible spirits to make themselves known by moving the table. After so long the table may vibrate, gently rock to and fro, then start rocking heavily. The table may then shift across the floor with hands still attached, making the sitters vacate their sitting position and follow the table where it wants to go. Eventually the table may move onto one side, one leg and may even levitate off the floor completely. Knocking and rapping sounds are sometimes heard to come from the table.

But is it really spirit moving the table? Or the collective subconscious of all present? It is thought by many parapsychologists that table tipping is the result of group psychokinesis. All the people's beliefs in spirit and the willing of it to move create a psychokinetic manipulation of the table, causing it to move. Furthermore, in psychology there is an artifact called the ideomotor effect. This essentially means that all those present around the table, due to suggestion and belief, subconsciously produce miniscule muscle movements in the hands and arms, causing the table or glass (in glass divination) to move.

Another old method which was used in earlier séances was the use of spirit cabinets. These were portable closets which the mediums would place themselves in. They were often bound with ropes, in order to prevent the medium from manipulating the aforementioned tools and to keep the sitters from touching the medium when manifesting alleged ectoplasm, as interruption of this event was said to be dangerous to the sitter and medium. The ectoplasm said to manifest came from different orifices of the medium, such as the ears or nose, but more usually from the mouth. It was usually found by investigators that the ectoplasm was not a real paranormal substance, but a fraudulent effect made of cheesecloth. Ectoplasm was a term coined by psychical researcher Charles Richet and denotes a substance or spiritual energy exteriorized by physical mediums. Ectoplasm is said to be associated with the materialization and formation of apparitions and was hypothesized to be an enabling factor in psychokinesis. Another fraudulent method of mediumship in its heyday was spirit photography. This was where a person would sit in front of the camera, whilst the medium would take a picture. The photographer would leave quickly then add a second image to the photographic plate before it dried out. In the final image it would show the person seated in front of the camera with a ghostly image to the side or behind them.

Unfortunately, mediumship is notorious for producing fraudulent mediums so they can make a fast buck. There are many methods and techniques in which the trickster medium can falsify paranormal claims. Cold reading is a way that a complete stranger can seemingly tell you everything about yourself without being psychic and without knowing anything about you. In essence the cold reader is providing a lot of words, and you as the sitter are providing the meanings to these words. The process relies upon a number of techniques. Linguistic tricks are used and unless you are aware of them, they are easy to fall for. These tricks can make you believe that the reader knows everything about your character and may refer to facts about your life they could not seemingly know about. The methods involved in mediumship demonstration are learnt by understanding the Barnum Effect. This is a type of subjective validation in which a person finds personal meanings in statements that could apply to almost any individual.

Another trick technique is the Forer Effect. The Forer Effect refers to the tendency of people to rate sets of statements as highly accurate for them personally, even though the statements could apply to many people. There are many tricks false mediums use to deceive the vulnerable person. Some use stooges; this is when mediums use their own people to find out meaningful information about people and their environment. They are also used in large gatherings (such as television audiences), and get picked by the medium and corroborate their so called 'meaningful' information, to the amazement of the captive audience.

Even during the old days of spiritualism, there were ways in which the so called medium produced psychic fraud. Materialized spirits were actually dummies or dolls or even real people dressed up as an apparition. Tables lifting from the ground were sometimes found to contain special mechanisms that lifted the table. Wires were connected to objects said to be floating around by themselves and lights had diodes in them which caused them to flash and fade. Even scratching and knocking sounds were sometimes found to be caused by special levers and switches. Falsifying psychic phenomena is nothing new, and it would be a great benefit if more paranormal investigators and parapsychologists better understood the conjuring tricks used by some so-called psychics to deceive the mind. Some professional parapsychologists do also practice magic and conjuring techniques so as to be able to detect psychic fraud. But not many do. The reader may be thinking that I want to condemn every psychic as a fraud. That is not so; I believe in Psi phenomena and there is hard evidence to suggest they exist. There are good mediums and bad mediums; I happen to use mediums in my parapsychological investigations and they are very good. The good mediums, I believe, are people who want to help others and not trying to make a fast buck, such as by trying to get their own TV shows etc., but are genuine people with a genuine ability, willing to help others for free or very little money.

THIRTEEN

THE SURVIVAL HYPOTHESIS

The Survival Hypothesis postulates that some part of the human mind, i.e. consciousness, the spirit, soul, or ghost can somehow survive bodily death and can account for a multitude of cases regarding ghosts, apparitions and hauntings. Or at least that is what some believe – but what evidence is there? As well as ghosts, apparitions and hauntings that allegedly account for the survival hypothesis, Parapsychology explores other areas which could perhaps prove that life after death does indeed exist after all.

THE NEAR DEATH EXPERIENCE

The Near Death Experience, otherwise termed NDE, is a phenomenon whereby a person at the point of death, or whose life is under threat from some traumatic illness or injury experiences what that person describes as an afterlife experience. Some of the witnesses have been pronounced clinically dead but have then began to respond to resuscitation techniques. Later on, they may describe experiences such as an overwhelming feeling of peace and wellbeing, including freedom from pain and suffering, the impression of being located outside their physical body, floating or drifting through darkness (which some people describe as a tunnel), becoming aware of a golden and intense light which can almost be blinding in nature, encountering and in some cases communicating with a presence described by some as a being of light, witnessing a rapid succession of visual images detailing their life up to that point and experiencing a world of beauty, contentment and an overwhelming feeling of love whilst meeting with their dead relatives and friends and communicating with them. In some cases they are then told by some voice that it is not their time to go and they are then sent back to their physical bodies.

Some of the experiencers report more of an Out-of-Body Experience (OBE), whereby a person feels separated from themselves and witnesses their own physical body undergoing medical treatment and hearing the conversations going on in the room. Some of the doctors researching the field have even placed certain artifacts in the room that can only be seen from a certain vantage point high up and are only known to the researchers at the time. The foremost expert in this study of Parapsychology is Dr Raymond Moody MD, who coined the term in 1975 in his famous book, *Life After Life*. Dr Moody also identified and investigated another near death phenomenon known as Shared Death Experience. This is where other people in the room have also shared their loved one's NDE and corroborated their loved one's experience, although this phenomenon is rare.

OUT-OF-BODY EXPERIENCES

The Out-of Body-Experience, termed OOBE or OBE, can be understood in conjunction with its counterpart phenomenon, the Near Death Experience, but it is essentially a different phenomenon altogether. The Out-of-Body experience includes the feeling of one's consciousness outside one's body, again not too dissimilar to the NDE, but it happens without life-threatening circumstances or danger to life. It has been known for practitioners to achieve an OBE at will and this is known as astral projection. The sensations that the person feels undergoing an OBE can be auditory such as a cracking or buzzing sound, vibrations and violent shaking at the start, followed by the lack of bodily control or body sensation known as catalepsy.

Experiencers have reported seeing their own bodies lying in bed or in other relaxed positions such as sitting in a chair. They have reported flying to far off lands and even to other planets. Again, this phenomenon could be synonymous with the phenomenon of remote viewing. Other people have reported seeing their 'parasomatic form' or astral form with a definite shape, attached to an 'astral cord' which seems to be or feels like it is linked to the forehead, solar plexus, or the back. It is often more felt than seen, and experiences often have the sensation of being 'tugged' back to the body. Some people believe that if the cord breaks, death is inevitable.

When the Out-of-Body Experience ends it is usually by an emotional reaction such as fear of being outside one's body or the physical body being touched by someone. The return is sometimes reported with a sudden and rapid jolt to the body, much like one feels when one is dreaming and about to hit the ground.

REINCARNATION

Reincarnation is a belief that the soul, spirit or some part of consciousness, under some circumstances, does not move on to the afterlife, but instead is transmuted into another body when a person dies. Some people believe that when one dies, perhaps due to dying younger than anticipated, before a person has learnt all of life's lessons, a previous incarnation is then transported into a new body to carry on learning. It is believed by some metaphysicists that the physical human body is just a container of our real selves, the soul or spirit which forever lives on in one form or another, and that if the body dies before physical learning is complete then the body is reincarnated into another physical body. Some believe that the physical body is just an organic tool to learn with, to prepare our 'real selves' for the afterlife.

Parapsychologist Dr Ian Stevenson was the major proponent of research into reincarnation and believed that reincarnation did indeed exist. The phenomenon has been known to start very young; it has been reported that the age at which people have started having reincarnation experiences is as young as between two and five years old. The child begins telling their parents that they used to live in a different time and place with different parents and knows the names of the 'other' parents. They sometimes give the parents the name of their previous incarnation and can tell them the way they previously died, even incorporating birthmarks which correspond to the injury or death that happened to the previous personality. The previous incarnation has been known in many cases to have died a violent death (hence the possibility that their life learning was incomplete, and that they have moved on to another incarnation to complete the life training?).

The spontaneous memories of the past lives seem to cease between five to eight years old, perhaps because the child's own new personality fully takes over and is no longer confused between the two, as the child has developed new learning skills and knows who they really are. But is it really reincarnation? There is another possibility to account for reincarnation experiences and that is the super ESP hypothesis. This is where a person can gain psychic information from around them or other people no matter the distance of time or space, and that ESP could be untestable and infinite in its nature. Some metaphysicists speculate that all information is stored in some sort of cosmic databank where all information about people and places from the past, present and future can be accessed psychically. This has been termed the Akashic Record. Either way, there is much evidence in reincarnation experiences to support the idea that an afterlife could indeed exist.

ELECTRONIC VOICE PHENOMENA (EVP)

Electronic Voice Phenomena (EVP) are recordings of unknown voices on a recording device that are not heard acoustically at the time of recording. The source of the voice is not accountable by anyone present during the time of recording and is not classified as human speech due to many odd characteristics. EVP has no currently agreed explanation but it is generally thought by parapsychologists that the voices are discarnate intelligences trying to contact the living. The voices termed 'Anomalous Speech' (Dr Ingrid Irwin) seem to have their own strange oddities of their own. They differ from their human counterpart voices in terms of tone, style and manner and are generally inconsistent in nature.

EVP is now generally termed Instrumental Trans Communication (ITC) because of the more recent advances in technological recording devices. The devices that can and have been used are: tape recorders, digital voice recorders, radio devices, mobile phones, computers, video imagery and television. Smartphones, tablets and equivalents are also now quite commonplace. There are many theories as to where these voices come from but no substantiated factual evidence has been presented that proves one theory is correct from another. These types of theories endeavour to probe into the supposed source of the phenomena, developing process-orientated ideas in order to establish who or what is behind these anomalous voices.

One theory behind these anomalous voices is that they could be caused by the recording person themselves by a psychokinetic effect, by which the person imprints the voices onto the recording device. Some other theorists suggest that the origin of the voices may be extraterrestrial or interdimensional in nature. The science of human speech and sound needs to be researched and studied in trying to figure out what these voices actually are.

There is much history in EVP research. Guglielmo Marconi the inventor of the wireless telegraph was experimenting with radio signals when unexplained code signals were picked up by him in 1895. Nicola Tesla, who invented the Tesla coil, was also interested in EVP. Thomas Edison is said to have designed and constructed an EVP recording device, and he himself wrote, 'If our personality survives, then it is strictly logical or scientific to assume that it retains memory, intellect, other faculties, and knowledge that we acquire on this Earth. Therefore, if we can evolve an instrument so delicate as to be affected by our personality as it survives in the next life, such an instrument, when made available, ought to record something'.

Raymond Bayless reported unexplained voices in his experiments that included clearly identifiable male and female voices. Some of the voices sounded rather mechanical and he found that the voices showed intelligence and responded to questions. In 1959 Friedrich Jurgenson, together with his wife and dog, made a trip to their country residence in Nysund, Sweden. He brought along a tape recorder with the intention of recording bird song. In actual fact as he recorded the bird song he accidentally recorded a male voice speaking in Norwegian. He wondered if it was a stray radio broadcast but felt it was too coincidental and he was miles away from anything in the countryside. He later recorded many other voices including his dead mother.

In 1965, Dr Konstantin Raudive, a Latvian psychologist, read Jurgenson's work and tried experimenting himself. In 1971, controlled recording experiments were conducted with Raudive by chief engineers of Pye Records. Equipment was installed in their sound laboratory to block out stray radio and television signals. Raudive was not allowed to touch any of the equipment. Raudive used one tape recorder, which was monitored by another control tape recorder and all he was allowed to do was speak into a microphone. The engineers taped Raudive's voice for eighteen minutes and none of the experimenters heard any sounds, but when scientists played the tape back, to their amazement they heard over two hundred voices on it.

George Meek, a retired engineer with a strong interest in the afterlife developed a device called the Spiricom and was alleged to have captured and recorded conversations with Dr George Jefferies Mueller, a deceased university professor and a former NASA scientist, who gave messages on how to refine the Spiricom device. It was reported that Meek recorded more than twenty hours of dialogue with Dr Mueller and many more with other discarnate voices.

Raymond Cass was interested in acoustics and ran his own hearing aid business in Yorkshire. He was considered one of the foremost researchers into EVP. Cass began experimenting and recorded many voices that gained worldwide attention. Cass produced 'polyglot' voices. These are voices that produce a sentence and elements of foreign languages. Cass's voices were studied by various institutions such as the Bio Energetic Institute in Osaka, Japan, the Parapsychology Unit of Olivet College, Michigan, USA and the Parapsychology Unit at Freidburg University.

Scott Rogo and Raymond Bayless published a book in 1979 called *Phone Calls from The Dead*. The book was a result of a two-year investigation into ghostly phone calls and describes many accounts of people who have received telephone calls from deceased loved ones and friends. Rogo and Bayless proposed three theories to account from telephone calls from the dead. One was that they were indeed communications from the dead to the living. A second was that Extra Dimensional Beings (EDB) were manipulating the phone system; the third was that the effects were caused by psychokinesis and that it was in fact the living unconsciously projecting their unconscious thoughts through the telephone system.

In 1982 Sarah Estep founded the American Association of Electronic Voice Phenomena, whose name was recently changed to The Association of TransCommunication in 2010. Sarah had a strong interest in Parapsychology after reading Dr Ian Stevenson's work on reincarnation, and she developed her own method of recording anomalous voices. She used 'white noise' in the background to help produce her recorded voices. She wrote two books entitled *Voices from Eternity* (1988) and *Roads to Eternity* (2005).

In 1985, Klaus Schreiber began his experimentation into EVP and obtained many remarkable voices including visual images of deceased people, including his two dead wives and his deceased daughter, Karin. His original images were blurred, but he later refined his method and his images became fairly clear. Since then there have been many people who have researched EVP and have obtained some remarkable results.

Where exactly these voices come from is still a matter of debate. Many people report hearing unusual voices in their recordings but most are very faint or unintelligible. Some are indeed very clear, but some are down to audio pareidolia, where a person thinks they hear human voices and sounds, but they are in actual fact due to one's own interpretation of the alleged voices and suggestion from other people. The reader might like to try it themselves and see what results they get.

*

So, is parapsychology a science worthy of study? Should it be classified as a 'real' science and not 'pseudoscience'? I believe the answer to both questions is yes. After conducting personal research into this enigmatic field of study for the last twenty years, I believe this science, Parapsychology, is the future of science. It is the science of the human condition with the potential to unlock the mysteries of consciousness. And should we unlock the secret of psychic abilities in the near future, it could very well be the next crucial step in human evolution.

PART TWO

PARANORMAL CASE FILES

ONE

INVESTIGATION PROCEDURE AND EQUIPMENT

In this section I will not go very deeply into investigative procedure with regard to Psi phenomena, as this book gives a general account of a wide variety of topics. However, I will cover basic investigative procedures that should be used by people wishing to conduct their own paranormal investigations. Understanding of investigative procedures and methodologies comes with patience and practice, and develops over time. There are other books and courses that delve more deeply into the investigative procedure of hauntings, such as Lloyd Auerbach's *Hauntings and Poltergeists* and his other good book, *Ghost Hunting*, as well as Dr Andrew Nichols' *Ghost Detective*. The first stage of an investigation into ghosts, hauntings, apparitional experiences or poltergeists is the interview stage. This is when an investigator or researcher interviews the witness to the alleged phenomenon. It can be done face-to-face or over the telephone. The telephone has its advantages as the investigator can decide whether or not it warrants an investigation in the first place and eliminates the need to travel for miles. The investigator can establish whether the person over the phone is embellishing facts to fit their own beliefs or is telling the truth. An on-location investigation is not always necessary, as it can be established that the so-called paranormal incident may in fact just be a case of mistaken identity or natural causes.

If the researcher feels like the phenomena warrant a face-to-face interview, then they will meet the witness in person, just so long as the investigator and the witness both feel comfortable with this arrangement. When interviewing witnesses the investigator should always take along an recording device, pen and writing pad and also a video camera to film and audio record the interview session. The investigator should not forget to ask if the witness is happy to be recorded on video, audio or both, as videoing or recording someone without their authorization is illegal. The investigator must also take along questionnaires and report forms.

The background of the person or family involved should be checked out during the interview, such as a history of such occurrences, their religious beliefs, beliefs regarding the paranormal, their social upbringing, the psychological profile of the witness, health issues, mental health issues, substance and alcohol abuse, sexual abuse or child abuse, marriage problems and many other types of relevant questions may be asked. If there are other witnesses to the same phenomenon or other paranormal incidents, whether past or present, they too should also be interviewed, preferably separately so that witnesses do not contaminate each other's reports. When asking questions, the investigator should be open-minded, objective and, above all, tactful. The investigator should not let their own beliefs regarding the paranormal affect the interview. All reports by witnesses should remain private and confidential unless authorized by the witness and should remain to hand for writing up finished reports and for later use or research.

When the interview has been completed, the investigator should conduct historical research into the background of a location or building. They should find out if there have been reports of any previous paranormal occurrences, discover if anybody has died or been murdered in the location, who were the people that lived there before, any births, marriages or deaths, etc. These can be found (if any records exist) by using libraries, local historians, the public records offices, the internet and other sources. The investigator could also try asking local people about the past and present people associated with the alleged haunted property; they may be more willing to help. Common sense should be used and the investigator should not go on other people's property without first obtaining permission, as this is trespassing.

The next stage of an investigation (if it warrants it) is a pre-visit before a full-fledged investigation. The investigator should walk around the building, making notes of any extraneous sounds coming from the property or locale; drawing a map of the building may also help. They should look for any noises, such as pipework, faulty electrical wiring etc. that may account for alleged paranormal incidents. They should also take baseline readings such as electromagnetic field readings that may indicate faulty wiring. In one case I investigated recently I was contacted by a man saying he was having all sorts of paranormal problems. The family were experiencing the feeling of being watched, getting dizzy, feeling nauseous, having headaches and seeing things as well as auditory noises. They said that as soon as they left their house, such as to go shopping, they felt better again until they returned to the house. The man also had previous mental problems, such as twice trying to commit suicide and he also said he was a sensitive. So he had some stability issues in the past.

After walking round the house with an EMF (electro-magnetic field) meter and a tri-field meter I was getting extremely high readings on both sets of instruments. The readings were profoundly strong and were coming from upstairs more than anywhere else. After checking where the readings were strongest, I found a cupboard at the top of the stairs, opened it up and there was a huge electrical box humming away. I knew straight away what was happening. The family were not experiencing a paranormal occurrence but a case of electromagnetic field hypersensitivity. This is where a person or persons are subjected to high levels of electromagnetic radiation over a given period of time, which then has a physiological effect on the human biological system and may also affect the temporal lobe of the brain.

The person may start to feel sick and dizzy and feel like they are being watched; the hairs on their arms stand up (static electricity) and they may begin seeing and hearing things. No one really knows if such huge amounts of radiation can permanently damage one's health, but research in this area is ongoing. What we do know that is that being subjected to such powerful electromagnetic fields over a long period of time is not good for you! The family was due to move house in a few weeks after our visit and I stated that once they moved house, I was sure that they would start to feel better and things would get back to normal. I did not hear from them again!

Another piece of equipment I like to use on a pre-visit is a good, reputable medium. A medium is always useful for taking round on a pre-visit or investigation to see what information they can pick up psychically. The information they give to the investigator may prove important, especially if it can be verified later on by historical records, staff workers at the location or by other means of research. If a pre-visit cannot be authorized, then just a main investigation at the location will suffice.

On the main investigation, the number of investigators should be kept to a minimum as extraneous sound must be kept down as much as possible. The investigator should think about the size of the location being investigated. Too many investigators running round a small location might cause all manner of noisy disturbances. If it is a private house, I suggest keeping to just two or three investigators. Furthermore, the investigators should remember that this is somebody's home and not a circus; the people who are experiencing the disturbances are putting their trust in a person or persons they do not know. Investigators should do everything they can not to upset the home with breakages and interference with people's personal belongings.

Regarding investigation equipment, I like to use EMF meters, Natural Tri-Field and normal Tri-Field meters, digital voice recorders, Ion Counters, walkie talkies, torches and, above all, human objective testimony. The best equipment to use in an investigation is perception and the human brain. Without the human condition we have no legitimate phenomena to explore or investigate. If it is a building that is being explored, the investigators should walk from room to room, spending between 30 minutes to an hour in each. They can remain quiet in a vigil or ask out questions for any intelligent spirits to make themselves known by asking them to do something to show their presence, but investigators should remember that when asking out they should try to be quiet as possible, as there may be other vigils going on elsewhere in the building. Investigators should try to remain in one position for the duration, whether standing or sitting. If using a digital voice recorder, the investigator should make a note of the sounds around them, such as someone breathing, moving about, whispering, clearing their throat, stomachs making a noise, cars passing by, electrical appliances making noises, heating and pipe system noises, etc. If the investigator hears any of these, they should make a note of it on the voice recorder as this can eliminate natural occurring sounds when analyzing audio footage for EVP anomalies.

Investigators should take a break between vigils, at least 15 minutes every two hours, as the process can become very tiring and energy levels may become low; food and drink is a must, especially on long investigations. Investigators should try different experimental techniques, such as trigger object experiments, table tilting and glass divination as well as creating their own unique ways of trying to provoke phenomena to manifest. If asking out questions, investigators should be tactful and must not use foul language. They should be professional and try not to provoke spirits (if they are alleged to exist and are indeed intelligent) negatively. If spirits exist, these were once people too and may still have feelings. Spirits may be confused about where they are. Do they know that they are alive? Do they want to stay where they are now? Do they wish to move on? What are they looking for? Do they want to communicate? Or do they wish to be left alone? There are more questions than answers in this field.

Investigators should take readings with their equipment every so often to see if there is anything in the atmosphere or environments that have changed since their last readings. They should try to validate one piece of equipment's 'hits' with another piece of equipment, logging any anomalous readings or phenomena with times, dates, and the nature of the incidents that occurred, either by pen and paper or with the digital audio recorder. The lead investigator should make sure no one goes off to do a lone vigil, especially for health and safety's sake. It is wise to take out public liability insurance before an investigation in case of an accident to an investigator or for any breakages. When taking photographs throughout the investigation, an investigator should shout 'flash' as a prior warning to others so they do not temporarily blind other investigators. Also when taking photographs in cold conditions, the investigator should make sure they hold their breath for a second, as breath and smoke can show up as a misty form on the photograph; for the same reason, investigators should not smoke during the vigil, and only during breaks. On many occasions I have caught what I believe may be genuine anomalies by adhering to these guidelines.

At the end of an investigation, investigators should make sure they take all their equipment away with them. They should check and double check to make sure they have all their equipment with them before they go home. They should tidy up after themselves and make sure they move everything back to exactly it was the way it was before they got there. If an investigator cannot investigate a location personally, they should ask if they can set up equipment running overnight, or longer if necessary, without anyone being there. This is called blanket monitoring and may be useful if an investigation is not warranted.

The pre-visit and main investigation are just the beginnings of a full investigation. After the investigation is over, the investigators should make sure they fill in any report forms from the team or any other observers while the investigation is still fresh in their mind. It is best to have as many details as possible, with dates, times and reported phenomena logged. These can be used later for future reference.

The investigator's next task is to analyse and collate the data collected from the investigation, such as photographic evidence, audio and video footage and any other data gathered. Photoshop is a good tool to use to analyse photographs. It can be used to highlight, brighten and enhance photographs to better see the image. When looking at photographs the investigator should eliminate any photographs containing so-called orbs. These can appear as small white blobs in the picture and can appear in many shapes and colours. Orbs are notorious in the paranormal community, as many people believe them to be some form of manifestation. This is not so. What they are in fact is dust particles, water droplets, insects and lint. The closer a camera lens is to the flash, the more 'orbs' it will capture. This is because a particle close to the lens will reflect light off the flash back into the shutter, acting like a small mirror, capturing a bright blob on film. For audio I use Nero Wave Editor. This tool is suitable for looking for EVP (Electronic Voice Phenomena). When listening to audio footage, the investigator should note any normal/natural sounds within the footage. They should also take note of any unusual voices, breathing sounds and answers to questions which have not been logged in audio footage. These may become important in making a conclusion to the report on the investigation, and may in fact be true anomalies.

When looking at video footage, whether through camcorder or CCTV, the investigator should make a note of any movement of objects, shadowy forms that cannot be accounted for, etc. They should also take note of anybody who may accidentally have been caught on camera and who should not have been there whilst recording; otherwise these appearances could be misleading and may lead to a false conclusion. This is where notes come in handy: was everyone accounted for? Were they here at this time? The investigator should not forget to take a break when analysing video and audio footage, as this can be a long, tiring and tedious process, especially going over hours and hours of footage. The investigator may want to be fresh when analysing this footage as they do not want to miss anything. It might be a tedious process but it is a necessity.

After these tasks have been completed the investigator needs to write a full report on their findings and conclusions. A copy should be sent to the owners of the property under investigation, and another should be later filed for future reference. Confidentiality should be assured, unless the witnesses have agreed to waive this.

TWO

CASE FILES OF THE OFFICE OF PARAPSYCHOLOGICAL STUDIES

CASE FILE: PLEASLEY VALE MILLS, MANSFIELD, NOTTINGHAMSHIRE

In 2005 The Office of Parapsychological Studies and guest medium Barry John were invited to conduct a paranormal investigation of Pleasley Vale Mills outside of Mansfield, Nottinghamshire. The site is renowned for its haunted history. This was our very first investigation for the team.

In the nineteenth century William Hollins, with four other respected business men, decided that Pleasley Vale would be an ideal place to construct a cotton mill. The textile industry was in its infancy at this point, but the partnership knew that it was about to grow. William Hollins also built a village store, a school, a mechanics institute, a reform church and a bathhouse for the employees of the cotton mills. The company that operated the mills closed in 1987 and the buildings fell into disrepair. Bolsover District Council declared the Vale a conservation area and the site is now home to many thriving businesses.

Many staff on these premises have witnessed striking paranormal activity over the years, including the sounds of trolley carts being pushed along, unexplained feelings of depression, the sounds of children playing in the woods, the apparitions of two young children in the lake where they were said to have drowned, and the apparition of a man who is claimed to have been murdered in the lake nearby and is often seen standing outside next to an abandoned forklift truck outside the mills. He is often seen by lorry drivers who have come to drop off their loads, who then find out that it was a ghost. Other apparitions include a woman named Annie who is said to have murdered somebody, and there are also the infamous haunted toilets, near where I had a strange encounter.

I and my wife Sharon (who is also one of my investigators) often visited the mills, conducting our own investigations in the hope of capturing some legitimate phenomenon that substantiated the claim that the mills were haunted. In one incident, while we were in the corridor leading from the haunted toilets to a large derelict room, I heard what sounded like a man's groan. I did not tell Sharon what I heard, but just after I heard it, without me saying anything, she said, 'Did you hear that?' I asked 'What did you hear?', and she repeated what I had heard. As I walked into the room I suddenly felt what I can only describe as an unpleasant atmosphere envelope me. From then on I felt I had to leave the room. On returning later to the room, the feeling had completely dissipated.

On another vigil, high up on the fourth floor landing, we conducted a table tipping session. While asking out questions to any spirits to make themselves known to us, we allegedly came into contact with a spirit called Fiona (a medium was present during the session but not involved with the table tipping). Whilst asking her questions, the table would tip onto two legs in response to questions. It felt as if an energy came up through the table's legs and moved. On some occasions the table would drag itself across the floor and we had trouble keeping up with it.

While the table was tipping towards me in response to questions, on one occasion it tilted up onto just two legs then just stopped. Then it would not budge, and just lifted back down. On another occasion, while walking around the mills and going down a corridor I suddenly walked into a cold spot. The cold spot felt as if I had just walked inside a refrigerator. I asked one of the guides who was with me at the time if there were any air conditioners on that floor that were turned on. He stated that there were no air conditioners installed on the floor. The windows were also shut. Some of the photographs taken by us on numerous investigations at the mills showed numerous strange mists and dark shapes that seem to show something genuinely anomalous. Video footage taken has shown strange lights that seemed to float just in front of the camera. These were more than likely just dust particles and insects.

During our investigation with Barry John not much really occurred. But due to our other personal experiences here at the mills and with a long history of paranormal activity occurring here I would have to say there is something definitely unusual taking place at this site

CASE FILE: ANNESLEY HALL, ANNESLEY, NOTTINGHAMSHIRE

Annesley Hall was built in the twelfth century and is reputed to be the most haunted building in Nottinghamshire and one of the most haunted in Britain. Annesley Hall also has connections with the great Lord Byron. Annesley Hall is located eight miles northwest of Nottingham, close to the Derbyshire border. The Annesley estate came into the hands of Lord Chaworth, an Irish peer, by one of his ancestors' marriage to Alice de Annesley in the reign of Henry VI. Up to this time, it had been held by the Annesleys, the family who gave the estate its present name.

By the Chaworth/Musters marriage, it passed into the hands of the Musters family, who assumed the additional name of Chaworth and have held it since. The Chaworths continued as lords of the manor until the beginning of the nineteenth century. One of the family, William Chaworth, who was born in 1726, died after being wounded in a duel with Lord Byron in 1765. The Chaworth line continued until 1790, when George Chaworth died, leaving his only child Mary Ann as heiress to the lands. They were conveyed to John Musters, the squire of Colwick's son, on his marriage to Mary Ann in 1805.

The family took the name Chaworth-Musters and made Annesley their home. John C. Musters took over the property in 1859 and made extensive changes to the land around the hall. In particular, he took down the houses which mainly comprised Annesley village and turned the lands into gardens for the hall. The hall finally passed out of the hands of the Chaworth-Musters family in 1973, when they sold the property to live at nearby Felly Priory. The hall since then has had a major fire and fallen into disrepair.

There are many ghost stories associated with the hall, due to its long history and tragic tales. Black magic and witchcraft were also said to have been practised at the hall. Ghosts that are said to haunt the old building are: an old man, a young girl, a haggard woman, a ghostly monk, an angry old man, a rather dapper man in a hat who haunts the breakfast room of the house, a maid in a flop hat as well as a young girl's restless spirit, who is thought to have fallen pregnant by one of the landed gentry and hanged herself at the top of the stairs in the laundry room. There is also a female ghost who is said to climb out of the well that is now filled in and is seen wandering Annesley's grounds as if looking for something.

On 12 November 2005 we were invited to conduct an all-night vigil at the old hall. It proved to be one of the best investigations we have conducted. Before the main investigation, I and my wife Sharon met Dick Starr, who was Annesley Hall's main historian and who in his younger days worked at the hall. He showed us around on a pre-visit giving us a talk while we took baseline readings in the old building. During the fascinating tour of the old hall, whilst down in the cellar, we heard what sounded like a man's deep sigh. No one said they made a sighing sound at the time and it is reported to be a regular occurrence. The man is said to be the ghost of William Chaworth, who was said to have been a rather nasty character; he is also said to have been interested in the occult and to have conducted black magic in the cellar. His ghost has also been seen in the cellar as a dark shadow, standing in the corner.

The night of the evening's main investigation started off very quietly, with guest mediums picking up on names connected with the property. Outside in the stable blocks Sharon and her group heard what sounded like a door shutting in the clock tower, although there are no doors left in the building. The group also heard the entrance gates rattle, although upon investigation, no one was there. Sharon also said that she distinctly witnessed an apparition of a woman that seemed to be dressed in Victorian clothing walking across the lawn in the bright moonlight. She was the only one in the group who witnessed this; it corresponds with past reports of witnesses seeing the same thing in the same place. A security guard at the hall whose office was opposite the lawn also reported seeing the figure of a woman who passed his door to the office in the daytime. This shook him greatly at the time. Another member of Sharon's group reported that he had heard distinct whispering in his ear ten minutes earlier in the same area.

Inside the hall itself, I picked up a high EMF spike on the meter at the exact time that guest medium Lindsey picked up the vision of a woman standing between me and Lindsey in the doorway. The spike fluctuated then dissipated. It was interesting as there are no longer any electrics inside the property. Later a photograph taken by our friend Neil Clarke picked up a large light anomaly between me and Lindsey at the exact time my EMF meter fluctuated and she reported her vision.

In the main hall, investigator Gemma Palmer felt what she described as 'a gushing cold wind pass me, and I felt all tingly'. Upstairs in one of the main bedrooms, we tried a glass divination experiment which produced no results. Whilst upstairs, and about to take a photograph, I witnessed what seemed to be a dark, shadowy (possibly hooded) apparition move into the middle of three archways separating what used to be two large bedrooms. The form appeared to be that of a large, broad shouldered man with a collar sticking up. There were no distinct facial features. Our friend Joanne Clarke and Gemma also saw it as well at the same time. Initially I thought it was a shadow cast by a torch from one of us and then projected onto the wall so I tried to replicate what I saw. It seemed similar, but the figure had seemed three-dimensional although I saw it for just a few seconds. I am still not convinced that it was an apparition rather than a shadow cast by a torch onto the back wall, which seems more logical. However, Lindsay did state that people have reported these shadow apparitions at the hall before, so who knows what I saw?

Next, Neil and I went down into the cellar to conduct a vigil. While asking out questions to provoke some sort of activity, we both heard what sounded like footfall on the stairs and shuffling sounds. Upstairs in the main hall, Sharon, investigator Scott Warrener and his then wife Kelly Warrener distinctly heard a little girl's voice say, 'Come play with me Grandpa, come play with me'. Meanwhile, upstairs in the bedrooms, flashing light anomalies were reported on a number of occasions.

It was also upstairs that an unnerving alleged temporary possession took place involving one of the female guests. It seemed as if some external influence was trying to take her over. She was genuinely frightened and was crying, but I remain skeptical about this incident. I firmly believe that hysteria and suggestion were to blame, due to the night's progressively escalating activity, although later an incident similar to this happened on another investigation at Annesley. During the alleged woman's cleansing, a horrific woman's scream was heard by me that seemed to come from downstairs in the main hall and which was also captured on video. Neil and another investigator, Matthew Palmer, came running in from outside to see what was happening and although I asked my wife Sharon 'Who is screaming downstairs?' she replied, 'No one!'

Near the end of the investigation we decided to conduct a séance in the cellar downstairs. As the mediums were trying to contact the spirits at the hall, Matt and his brother, together with fellow investigator James Palmer reported extreme pains in their sides. Matt had to leave the cellar due to his suddenly feeling ill and the severe pains he was experiencing. As the group packed up and left for the night, Neil and I stayed behind in the cellar to pack up our cameras and equipment. All of a sudden the temperature in the cellar dramatically dropped and the atmosphere in the cellar changed considerably. It was almost electric as the hairs on both of our arms and neck stood up. Just then we both heard a man's deep moaning sigh. I asked Neil if he had made that noise and he said no; he thought that I had also made the noise, which of course I did not. We sat there to see if anything else occurred, but unfortunately nothing else did. This brought an end to the first investigation at Annesley Hall.

During our second investigation at the Old Hall, we was invited by a group of mediums who wanted a parapsychologist there to see what was going on. Nothing much occurred on this investigation apart from one incident that shook me and Sharon to the core. While she was chatting away and being led from upstairs to the downstairs main hall with a security guard, they both felt a sudden cold breeze brush passed them and then down the stairs. A bit later on during the investigation, while Sharon and I were sitting down, Sharon became suddenly quiet and transfixed. She then would not respond to anything I said to her. I knew something was wrong so I asked a couple of mediums, including Lindsey, to have a look at Sharon, as she looked very ill and did not say anything. One of the elder mediums stated that she felt as if something was attaching itself to her, so they then began a cleansing ritual to rid her of this alleged 'unwanted guest'.

As they were cleansing Sharon she began to cry uncontrollably and her eyes were rolling back into her head as the mediums placed both their hands next to her head. What was fascinating about this ritual was that as the mediums were moving her hands back, whilst supposedly drawing the spirit attachment out of Sharon, her head was moving back in relation to the mediums' hands moving back without her hands actually touching her head. This was quite fascinating to watch, but also deeply unnerving since my wife was involved. After the cleansing Sharon had no recollection at all about what happened to her. My wife is very level-headed, scientifically minded, logical and holds a bachelor's degree in paramedic science. Whatever happened to her unnerved me and I thought back to the incident with the guest being supposedly 'taken over' by a spirit attachment. What if something really did try to influence my wife and take her over? I still do not know what to think about this episode, but what I do know is that I got me and Sharon out of that place as fast as I could, and it was a real terrifying experience that she still does not remember. This has not happened before or since that time at Annesley Hall.

Next to Annesley Hall, on a small hillock overlooking the old building, lies Annesley Church which lies within the Annesley estate. The old church is in ruins and is hundreds of years old; it is also said to harbour a ghost. The apparition is said to be dressed in a monk's habit from the distant past. Some people think it is the ghost of James Annesley who would often stroll about the churchyard, but this seems unlikely. The ghost has been seen in the day as well at night and is seen to jaywalk on the busy road then walk up to the hillock and then into the churchyard. He has been seen wandering amongst the ancient gravestones of the old ruined church.

CASE FILE: ROSE COTTAGE, RUFFORD, NOTTINGHAMSHIRE

The Rose Cottage pub and restaurant in Rufford, Nottinghamshire has had a long reputation of being haunted. There are not many records about what the pub used to be, or when it was actually built. What is known is that it also used to be tearooms and, before that, a nursery many years ago. The original and oldest part of the pub is thought to be several hundred years old. It is also located near the well-known haunted Rufford Abbey. Rufford Abbey and its surrounding forest is said to be haunted by a white or grey lady and also a ghostly monk which has been seen wandering the Abbey grounds. Rose Cottage is thought to have several ghosts. An old man has been witnessed as well as the apparition of a little girl. Poltergeist activity is also a regular occurrence at the pub.

The pub has gone through many landlords and landladies over the past years, and still is. Whether it is down to ghosts that are said to frequent the pub or just because the pub trade is dying in the UK is another matter; no one really seems to know. On our first investigation at Rose Cottage some unusual incidents were reported. A trigger object experiment set up with coins had proved most fruitful. Several of the coins had apparently moved on the paper by several millimeters. My wife and fellow investigator Sharon reported that as she went to go into the toilet, a male voice said, 'Get out!' She thought that the previous landlord, Lee, was in there, but in actual fact nobody was in there at all. Subsequently, when we went to meet the next landlord and landlady to arrange a second investigation, a number of strange occurrences took place. Whilst talking among ourselves about ghosts in general, a picture frame fell behind the bar face down, which we found quit amusing.

The displacement of chairs was also reported. The landlord stated that when the restaurant area of the pub was closed, all the chairs were placed neatly towards the tables. When we went to investigate, several of the chairs had moved as if they had been pulled away from the table. When we placed them back in and walked out of the restaurant area, the same thing happened again. But it seemed to be the exact same chairs that moved before.

In July 2007 we went back to Rose Cottage to conduct a second investigation. Again, it had another new landlord and landlady, Richard and Emma. The night did not disappoint. After taking initial baseline readings, which proved normal using EMF and temperature equipment, we started the vigils. Investigator Brent Whitworth reported battery drainage on his video camera. This is thought to precede the occurrence of a manifestation.

We sat in the bar area to conduct a vigil and started asking out questions to see if any intelligent apparitions would make themselves known to us. Almost immediately we established communication by a series of two knocks for yes and one for no. We allegedly established that it was the supposed spirit of a little girl which had been reported and seen to ascend the stairs on numerous occasions. During the night, voices in the toilet were reported again. We moved onto the table to conduct a glass divination session. This is where a spirit is alleged to move the glass on the table while investigators ask questions. What ensued was a fascinating conversation using the glass.

Whilst using yes and no for answers on the table, we established that the little girl's name was Martha and that she was grounded spiritually with her family, Emily, William and Tom. Martha stated that her mother died at childbirth and had moved on, whilst the rest of the family had not as they remained grounded. Asking why they were grounded, Martha said that they had lived at Rose Cottage in the 1700s or the sixteenth century. Allegedly, she and the rest of the family were convicted of witchcraft and burnt at the stake for heresy. Martha said she was ten years old at the time. She said it was the monks from nearby Rufford Abbey that had condemned the whole family to death. After bringing forward the supposed spirit of a monk, the monk said that they did not want to condemn the family to death, but were given orders from someone above them. The monk said they were burnt at the stake at Rufford Abbey.

During the séance, other phenomena were beginning to manifest. Footfalls were heard in the bar area, two loud knocks were heard behind Scott and several rappings were heard. One of the strangest and quite disturbing elements of the phenomena manifesting was the landlord's dogs barking and growling while we were conducting the séance, especially while communicating with the monks. When Martha came back to the table the dogs remained quiet, but every time the monks were brought forward, the dogs became unsettled again, barking and growling. When we asked Martha if this was the monks causing the dogs to become unsettled, she said yes.

Was the ideomotor effect at work the cause of the glass divination communication? The ideomotor effect is where subconscious/unconscious thought causes miniscule muscle movements in the arms to manipulate the glass. This effect, in association with belief and suggestion, could have brought about the effects we observed. Brent's battery drainage could have been caused by not charging the batteries properly; but again, battery drainage in all types of equipment used on paranormal investigation is a common phenomenon reported. On the pre-visit, the picture frame behind the bar that fell could just have been down to coincidence, and the appearance that the chairs had moved away from the table may have been just a misperception.

Unfortunately there are no records suggesting that a family was burnt at the stake for heresy at Rufford Abbey by monks. But it was interesting all the same. There were too many incidents that I could not explain. To say Rose Cottage is not a haunted building would be wrong; there was objective evidence reported by all the investigators which was backed up by video and audio, and I do firmly believe that some form of paranormal activity is at work at Rose Cottage.

CASE FILE: TUTBURY CASTLE, STAFFORDSHIRE

Not much remains of this once large castle, and not all the ruins are genuine. The tower on top of the mote is an eighteenth century folly. The original castle was built in 1071 for Hugh d'Avranches, but it was almost immediately transferred to Henry, Lord of Ferrers and Chambrais in Normandy in 1174. William Ferrers came into conflict with the crown, causing Henry II to lay siege to the castle and to subsequently to order it to be demolished. The castle was rebuilt, but in 1263, Prince Edward, the future King Edward I, also attacked the castle, again causing great damage. In 1265, Henry III gave Tutbury Castle to his younger son Edmund, created Earl of Lancaster in 1267. It has remained in the hands of the Earls and Dukes of Lancaster ever since (the Queen is now the Duke of Lancaster).

In 1362, John of Gaunt, second Duke of Lancaster, gave royal permission to repair the castle and over the next century, new walls, towers and buildings were added. However the castle was in a poor state of disrepair when Mary, Queen of Scots was imprisoned at Tutbury in the late sixteenth century. In 1646, during the Civil War, the castle fell to Parliamentarian forces after a three-week siege and was again ordered to be destroyed, leaving the ruins now visible today. The only building left mainly standing is the Great Hall. Mary, Queen of Scots is the most famous resident ghost at Tutbury and was seen by at least forty people whilst on a tour of Tutbury several years ago.

Our investigation started at 7.30pm on Saturday 4 August 2007. We were met by a number of castle staff when we arrived. Sharon, one of the tour guides, took us on a tour of the castle before the vigils began. After the tour, we had a drink whilst discussing what we were going to do for the main investigation. We split into two teams and my team undertook a vigil in the Great Hall, while the second team took the ruins including the North Tower. We began taking EMF readings but the meters were useless due to the extraneous high levels of electromagnetic fields from wiring and a large generator downstairs, so we had to resort to other equipment.

We sat down in the Great Hall and started asking out questions to see if any intelligent spirits would make themselves known to us. At this point no anomalous experiences were reported except for a couple of odd bangs which seemed to come from the King's Bedroom. This room is said to be the most paranormally active room in the building. I and investigator Andy, investigator Brent Whitworth and another guest, Brent, sat down on the floor in the King's Bedroom. We asked out questions to see if we would get a response but no communication was reported. The only thing that happened was that, whilst in the room, I distinctly heard a woman's moan. This was also captured on video. I was not sure if I heard it in the room or just outside the Great Hall, but this was interesting nonetheless.

From here we went back into the Great Hall and started asking out. Nothing happened at first, but after a while rappings started coming through. They sounded as if they were coming from the floor. The floor was wooden with a large carpet in the centre. We started conversing with intelligent raps as answers to our questions. We communicated by two raps for yes and once for no. We found out through the raps that the spirit was a woman who was allegedly imprisoned in the castle. After some communication with the supposedly intelligent entity, we were quite astonished to find out that we were allegedly in communication with Mary, Queen of Scots! Whether it really was Mary, Queen of Scots was a matter of debate but the experience was fascinating nonetheless.

From here we decided to have a break to talk about the events so far in the night. After this, I took my team to the outside ruins and the North Tower. We started off conducting a vigil in the dungeon and whilst there, we heard somebody walking around the gravel path. I looked outside and nobody was there; we were completely alone. This is another supposed haunt of Mary, Queen of Scots, where she has been seen walking outside the North Tower where she was imprisoned. We asked out to see if we would get a response, but no phenomena were reported. We decided to conduct a vigil in the North Tower but the only thing we could hear in the North Tower was the wafting in the wind of the Union Jack flag on top of the tower. Team two reported trigger object movement with coins, but I did not get a chance to see the coins before the investigation finished, so I could not comment. This vigil brought an end to a fascinating investigation at Tutbury Castle. It was now 6.00am and we were all extremely tired and fatigued.

Tutbury Castle was a fantastic location to investigate but I could dispute the interpretation of some of the phenomena experienced. The rappings in the Great Hall with the alleged spirit of Mary, Queen of Scots was one. Although the rappings sounded intelligent and seemed to respond correctly to questions being asked, I cannot dismiss the possibility that the raps could have a natural explanation such as the expanding and contracting of the wooden floor boards as the air outside cooled down. But I also cannot fully dismiss the possibility that this was indeed some form of intelligent communication with the famous Tudor queen. The King's Bedroom was said to be the most paranormally active room in the castle; we found no real substantial experiences associated with this room apart from a guest experiencing a feeling of unsteadiness. I put his experience down to the old uneven floorboards and low level light conditions in the room itself.

CASE FILE: ENGLAND'S MOST HAUNTED HOUSE? THE ANCIENT RAM INN, GLOUCESTER

The Ancient Ram Inn, in Wooton-under-Edge, Gloucestershire is thought to have been built around 1145, and has been suggested that the workmen who built the parish church opposite were lodged here. It served for a period of time as a priest's house before it was converted to an inn. It was also used as a makeshift mortuary for a time. Satanic and sacrificial worship is thought to have taken place here; the building is known to be located on a criss-cross of Leylines, and water is known to run underground under the building. Murders have been known to occur as well as several suicides here. Later, as an inn, The Ancient Ram poured its last pint in 1968. Once it had closed for business its single sole occupier, John Humphries, purchased the building from the brewery.

He has been battling to save the property ever since, irrespective of the endeavours by former residents to interfere as much as possible. As John Humphries opened up the Inn as a Bed and Breakfast, he noticed something strange. People were leaving in the middle of the night and no one would stay, so one night he decided to stay in what is now the 'Bishop's Room'. This was the last time he stayed in the room. As he lay in bed asleep, he was yanked out of the bottom of the bed by his feet by an invisible force and he had to crawl out of the door. He now sleeps downstairs in a freezing cold room surrounded by pictures of Christ and crosses that adorn the room.

The moment you enter the old building an aura of dreadful foreboding envelopes you: it is as if you know something is not right with the building. The bare walls, creaking floorboards, steep old stairs and old world appearance are enough to send shivers down your spine. There are many ghost stories from this building's mist-shrouded past that can chill the blood of the most steadfast sceptic. As one visitor put it, 'The atmosphere was awful, I can only describe it as pure filth, dark and heavy'.

The first room that greets visitors is the 'Men's Kitchen'. This room reputedly stands on the site of an old pagan burial ground, and the disturbing sound of a baby has been heard here. As you make your way into what used to be the 'Bar Area', there is an open pit with a stuffed crow above. This is where two skeletons of children were unearthed along with a sacrificial knife that was found alongside them. This is where it is rumoured that they were murdered, due to either pagan or satanic worship.

People ascending the steep staircase up to the first floor have been thrown up the stairs by an invisible force, which then leads to 'The Beaufort Room', otherwise known as 'The Witches' Room', this is where reputedly the ghost of a witch called 'Elspeth Grant' haunts the room with her cat. Across the small upstairs landing is the Ram Inn's most haunted and terrifying room, 'The Bishop's Room'. A medium pushing its door open was once lifted off the floor and flung to the ground. The atmosphere inside this room is more oppressive and disturbing than anywhere else in this inn.

A ghostly cavalier has been known to materialize by the dressing room table, stride purposefully across to the opposite wall and disappear. Two phantom monks have been seen shimmering in the corner of the room. Witnesses have heard the terrifying screams of a man who was said to have been murdered here by having his head thrust into the fireplace. A phantom shepherd and his dog have been seen near the door. The spirit of a young boy is said to inhabit the room, as well as allegedly the demonic entity known as either an incubus or succubus. The entity is said to have sexually assaulted John Humphries on many occasions, but this is just conjecture as John is best described as an eccentric individual.

Climbing the now crumbling stairs into the attic, and crouching beneath the old wooden timbers, a feeling of intense melancholy appears to hang in the air. An innkeeper's daughter is said to have been murdered here by a highwayman in the early 1500s, and people attempting to sleep in 'The Bishop's Room' below often hear the sound of footfall and of something heavy being dragged across the floor above their heads.

On the 6 October 2007 the first in a series of investigations by me and what is now The Office of Parapsychological Studies took place at this allegedly most haunted house. We were not to be disappointed. It began with the arrival of a team of investigators: myself, my wife Sharon, Brent, Scott and Kelly. We also brought along psychic medium Nicky Bryant and her partner Richard. We arrived around 7.30pm with John already there to greet us. John took us around on a tour of the rickety old building with some fascinating stories about the history of the inn and the ghosts that were said to haunt it. The tour took us around and hour and a half. We had a short break, then started the investigation.

I and investigators Brent and Scott started by taking EMF and temperature readings around the whole building, which proved to be normal. Scott reported being stroked on the head in the 'Witches' Room'. We then took Nicky Bryant, our medium at the time, around the Inn where she picked up on many different characters said to haunt the old building. We went into the 'Bishop's Room', said to be the most haunted room in the inn, where she said she picked up on a bad spirit called John, who was said to have committed murders and sexual offences in its dark historic past, and a demonic spirit (to much conjecture) said to be an incubus or succubus that had been known to molest and attack people in the room whilst they slept.

We went into the 'Witches' Room' and Nicky said she picked up psychically a spirit of a woman in the room. After we finished taking Nicky around the inn, we split into two groups. I, Brent, Scott and Richard investigated the upstairs floor, while Nicky, Kelly and Sharon investigated downstairs. My team started by going into the 'Bishop's Room' with three camcorders and sat there while asking out to see if there were any alleged spirits wishing themselves to make contact with us. This lasted for around half an hour and proved to be very quiet.

Next we went into the 'Witches' Room' and started asking out. Due to the thin walls and floorboards, we asked the team downstairs to sit for half an hour in the quiet as well as upstairs due to the extraneous noises that can be heard around the old building. As yet there was no response. I tried an experiment to see if any intelligent entity would communicate with us by shutting down all recording equipment to see if any intelligent spirit knew it was being filmed. We secretly kept the audio recording going instead.

With the equipment shut down, we again began asking questions. All of a sudden we began hearing shuffling along the floor as if somebody was walking around on the carpet. We were all seated in chairs at this point. We asked more questions and the shuffling of feet continued as well as rapping sounds in response to questions. We used two knocks for yes and one for no. We allegedly found out through a series of raps that the so called spirit we were in contact with was Elspeth Grant and that she was the 'witch' said to haunt the room.

We also found out allegedly that she was married to a soldier called Robert whose spirit was said to be with her. He was also said to be communicating with us by the sound of shuffling feet and a series of raps. We found out that he allegedly died in the Battle of Nasby in Leicestershire and died of a wound to the chest. Because of the constant activity we seemed to be getting, we asked the second team downstairs to join us upstairs and sit with us whilst we continued to ask questions. This would bring us more objective witness testimony to hear what we were experiencing.

The second team also witnessed the sounds of shuffling feet and rapping sounds. While Sharon sat on the bed next to Nicky and me, she let out a blood curdling scream which would have put an old Hammer Horror actress to shame. She said that she had felt her pony tail tugged hard at the back of her head. We asked out if this was Elspeth that tugged her and the alleged spirit said yes, so we asked if she would be kind enough not to touch anybody else again. This was enough for Sharon as fright got the better of her. She was quite distraught at this point and she went back downstairs with Nicky and Kelly. She never moved from downstairs for the rest of the investigation.

My team concluded our investigation in the 'Witches' Room' and moved back to do another vigil in the 'Bishop's Room'. We sat down and turned off all the lights and started asking out questions again. As we were filming, again, there was no response, so again, I asked my team to turn off all video equipment but kept the audio recorder going. We started asking out questions, and all of a sudden the sound of footfall and the loud shuffling of feet now started again, but in this room.

This time the alleged spirit was named John, and it seemed to be the same character that Nicky picked up earlier on. The shuffling of feet continued and so did the sound of small raps and knocks. We asked John if he was alone and he said he was not, by the shuffling of feet. We asked if this second spirit was the alleged malevolent entity said to haunt the room, which said yes by very loud shuffling of feet. Some of the questions asked seemed to antagonize it. All of a sudden an almighty boom occurred in response to a question asked. We all jumped out of our seats with fright. It seemed the alleged malevolent entity had come forward.

We turned on the lights whilst calming down. We then resumed the vigil by turning off the lights again and we sat back down. We started asking out more questions and asked if it was a non-human spirit. 'Boom' was the sound in response to the question, startling us all again. I asked if it was born from witchcraft and sorcery; there was no response. I then asked if it was born from pagan worship, 'Boom' was the response again. I then asked if it was known as a demon (again to much conjecture), then there was the loudest of all 'Booming' sounds in response to questions. That was enough for us: we turned on the lights and went back downstairs for a drink to calm down.

The booming sounds sounded as if someone was stomping their foot as hard as possible on the old creaking floorboards. You could feel the whole floor vibrate with the force of the bangs. Brent stated that the bed that brushed his leg whilst sat down was being lifted and then dropped with force which seemed to account for the booming sounds. He also said that he felt as if he had been touched. Whatever it was that was causing those booming sounds was utterly unnerving.

After another break, I and my team went back upstairs to the 'Bishop's Room', although much to our dismay, and we started again. This time we tried a table tilting experiment, but to no avail. We went back to our original plan by asking out questions to any alleged intelligent spirits. Again, the sound of shuffling feet occurred in response to our questions. Richard asked the alleged spirit what 'it' wanted. All of a sudden, Richard said it would be best if we stopped what we were doing and retreat from the room as he wanted to leave. He said he had his answer to the question.

We thought this as odd, so we wrapped up the vigil in the 'Bishop's Room' and went back downstairs. We asked Richard why he wanted to leave so suddenly, and what he meant by he had his answer. He said that in response to the question he asked 'What is it that you want, demon?', he said a voice in his head say, 'I want your souls!' (although I am very sceptical on demons in general and of this particular statement). We did decide not to return to the 'Bishop's Room' for the rest of the night.

Next, we decided to investigate the 'Mayflower Barn' which is said to be very active. I, Brent, and Scott went into the barn and again started asking questions while the cameras were rolling. Again a pattern seemed to be emerging; there was no response to our questions while the cameras were recording, so we switched them off yet again. It seemed as if there was intelligence behind the activity taking place. This time I asked any alleged spirit to manifest itself by whistling in response to my questions. To my astonishment it did! And 'it' continued to whistle at us in response to questions.

While we all heard the whistling, the sound of footfalls was heard yet again, making their way towards us. Brent said that he felt as if his ear had been pinched and also his trouser leg tugged. The whistling continued as we moved into the hallway at the foot of the stairs. We asked out some more questions and then heard two distinct bangs come from upstairs in one of the rooms, although nobody was up there. We also heard the whistling again.

From the hallway, we decided to conduct a vigil in what used to be the bar area. As we sat down in the bar area I started asking out questions. All of a sudden, we heard a sound as if a stool had moved across the wooden floor. We got out of our seats as it had made us jump. We switched on a torch and found that a stool had indeed moved. We sat back down again and asked out, and the sound of another stool being moved occurred, scraping along the wooden floor.

Richard came in and said that Nicky, our medium, wanted to close us down psychically as they were leaving shortly. As if in retaliation, a loud crashing sound was heard. We switched on the torch and a stool had been literally picked up and thrown to the floor on its side. We all still saw it rolling from side to side from being thrown. Richard decided to join us for this vigil, so we all sat back down.

We started asking out questions again and whistling was heard in the bar area with us. All of a sudden, a small round table in front of me moved and was still shaking from side to side as I quickly switched on my torch. I asked another question, and a glass that was on the table in front of me slid into my lap, followed by the small round table, which I felt being tilted and pushed between my legs whilst I was sitting down in a pew, trapping me in my seat. I switched on my torch and I saw it move back into position.

I switched off my torch again, and asked out another question; we heard the sound of a candlestick moving across the barrel it was sitting on. I switched on my torch again and it had indeed moved across the top of the barrel. I couldn't believe the poltergeist activity we were witnessing. Although it was fascinating it was unnerving all the same. We wrapped up this vigil and decided to do our last investigation of the night in the reputedly haunted attic.

We went upstairs into the attic and sat down in the small bedroom. We started asking out questions, and almost immediately the sound of shuffling feet was heard as well as scratching sounds. We did not attribute the scratching to rats as it seemed to respond to our questions. By this time we were all getting extremely tired and wrapped up the night's investigation around 4.00am.

This location was one of only a few where I can honestly say that genuine paranormal phenomena occurred. The phenomena I experienced on this first and on subsequent investigations at this infamous inn were unprecedented compared with anything we have investigated before or since, especially at this level. On the analysis afterwards, although no video footage of anything paranormal was recorded, all the footfalls, raps, and loud bangings were recorded on audio plus also a most fascinating EVP was captured in the Bishop's Room.

Whilst I left the camcorder and audio recorder running in the room, on the analysis afterwards I caught the voice of a little boy saying 'Why do you scare me?' This was as clear as it could be, and although I went through both the audio and video footage playing at the same time, the voice was only recorded on the Dictaphone and not the camcorder. This must have been due to the voice recorder's microphone being more sensitive to noise than the camcorders. This EVP would later have significance regarding an alleged spirit of a young boy we were supposedly in contact with later during other investigations at the inn. Nothing was captured on photographs either.

On 12 January 2008, we returned to The Ancient Ram Inn for a second investigation. Again this proved quite eventful. This time the team consisted of me, Sharon, Brent and guests Andy Hill and his friend Brent. We also had with us another couple of guests who we invited. We arrived at John Humphries' home just after 8.00pm. John took the people who had not been before on a tour of the inn, while I and Sharon brought in the equipment for the night ahead. After the tour, Brent and I took EMF and temperature readings throughout the inn with a Tri-Field meter and thermometer, which proved normal apart from the attic, which had off-the-'scale EMF readings. The readings were not down to paranormal phenomena manifesting but due to the loose and unshielded wiring around the attic roof, so using EMF and Tri-Field meters would be useless around the inn. After taking the baseline readings, we split into two teams. Team one was to investigate the upstairs floor and the attic and team two to investigate the downstairs area and barn. My team started off in the 'Witches' Room'. We sat down, with our video cameras and other equipment to hand.

We started asking out for any spirits to make themselves known to us, communicating by two knocks for yes and one for no. Again, as in our previous investigation, nothing would respond while the cameras were running, so as before, we switched off all electrical equipment and just kept the audio recorder running. We asked out questions again. Almost immediately, and as in the previous investigation, the shuffling of feet was distinctly heard many times and a series of responsive raps to questions were heard.

A small piece of glass which was on the table in the room beforehand and photographs taken of the table proved that it was there; this had seemed to have been thrown as we found it on the floor, although it could well have been knocked off accidentally while we were sitting in the dark. Whilst we sat down in the room, we heard movement come from upstairs in the attic. No one was up there at the time, as team two were investigating the downstairs areas. To see if I could make something happen, I asked out loudly; 'If there is anybody up there in the attic, could you walk across the floor?'

To my astonishment, we all heard distinct footfalls walking across the attic floor as if someone had boots on. We also heard 'ting' sounds, as if crockery was being flicked or tapped. We normalized this incident due to finding out that the blustery conditions outside would simultaneously 'ting' some ornaments on the window sill, due to the window pane banging against the ornaments.

From here we decided to conduct our next vigil in the Bishop's Room. Again, as in our previous investigation of the room, nothing happened whilst the cameras were recording, so yet again we switched off all the equipment. We asked out questions and in return, on a number of occasions, the middle bed (there were three in a line with a foot or so gap between each) sounded as if it were picked up or dropped, making loud booming sounds as it hit the floor, startling us all.

Other instances in the room were the shuffling of feet on the carpeted floor in response to questions and two instances where a cuddly stuffed gorilla toy and another soft toy were thrown to the floor, While guest Neil Clarke sat on the bed with his legs stretched across to the middle bed, he said he felt as if somebody had sat down on the bed next to where his legs were. This was the bed which seemed to have moved or dropped. Neil's other incident in the room was that as he sat next to the door to the room, he sat up startled. He said that he felt as if somebody had blown in his ear twice. The strange thing was that Sharon downstairs did ask something to happen to Neil while we were all upstairs. Whether this was in the correct time period we did not know for sure, but thought it probably was. A natural explanation could have been a draft from the door, but two bursts in quick succession? He did say that it was definitely somebody human blowing in his ear.

In the Bishop's Room we all could hear creaks and rustling noises coming from the bed Brent had sat on, so I went over to sit with Brent on the far side of the bed and found that the covers next to Brent had been pulled back as if something had sat next to him. I sat on the bed and asked out. We all heard distinct intelligent raps to questions, but they seemed to be coming from under the bed. The bed also seemed to be trembling.

From the Bishop's Room we all needed the toilet, but just as the light was switched on and we were leaving the room, the walking stick which is left outside the room and with which John knocks on the door to the room (which he said he does so the spirits allow us to enter the room or, so he says), was thrown to the floor. Personally, I think the stick just fell to the floor as it was leaning near the door to the Bishop's Room beforehand.

From here we decided to conduct a vigil in the haunted attic, so we climbed the old crumbling stairs one by one and sat in the small bedroom which is built into the attic. We asked out but no responses were heard. We asked spirits in the room to move something a number of times and a number of strange things happened. A one penny coin was thrown from the dark attic space and hit the bottom part of Brent's jeans and landed at his feet. I threw it back into the attic and asked it to do it again whilst making sure there was no money lying in the room beforehand. Shortly after, a five pence piece was thrown and this time it hit Brent's jacket and fell at his feet. I threw that coin back. Next a ten pence piece was thrown into the middle of the room, so I threw that one back into the darkness. It again was thrown back and landed at Brent's feet. I felt this really unusual. On the humorous side, every coin that was coming back was of a greater amount than the one thrown: I was hoping that they would start coming back in pounds! I was not so lucky, otherwise I could have made a fortune by the end of the night. I tried throwing a ball into the blackness of the attic, but that did not move.

For the next vigil we went into the Mayflower Barn, where in our previous investigation we all heard distinct whistling in response to questions and also where we heard the shuffling of feet. On this occasion in the barn, nothing unusual was reported. From here we went into the bar area, where on the previous investigation we experienced high levels of poltergeist phenomena. Again, on this occasion nothing anomalous was reported. The only strange thing we heard was a lot of unusual clicking. To me this could be explained as expansion and contraction of the old wooden interior and the blustery conditions outside.

Next we continued our investigation with another vigil in the Witches' Room. The only strange thing that occurred on this occasion was that a small candle nightlight was thrown near Andy and landed near his feet. From here, we went back into the Bishop's Room where we all settled down under blankets due to having no heating in the building whatsoever and the freezing temperature outside.

I asked out for anything to come forward and make itself known. Allegedly the spirit of a monk seemed to come through. We used a series of two knocks for yes and one for no. through very distinct knocks and raps we seemed to establish that the monk's names were Albert and his best friend Edmond. They were said to have come from a church near the inn in about the 1700s. They said that they used to drink at the inn when it used to be a tavern and meeting place for the monks. They said through a series of knocks that they both died in a fire at the church that was set deliberately. Albert said he was 57 and Edmond was 45 when they died.

I asked if there was a priest hole at the inn and he said yes, and that it was set two feet behind the fireplace which actually extends ten feet behind the old bricked up fireplace in the Bishop's Room. I asked if this is why it was called the Bishop's Room and he knocked for yes. He said that the remains were brought back to the inn (his favourite meeting place) to be buried behind the fireplace. Albert knocked that the remains remain undisturbed and he is still happy visiting the place he loved so much in life. He said he cannot rest properly because his remains still remain undisturbed.

I asked how many spirits were said to haunt the inn and he rapped out seven. He said five are grounded to the location and two who visit (himself and Edmond). The other five other grounded spirits he said are the highwayman, the cavalier, the witch Elspeth Grant and an alleged negative entity. I asked Albert about this so called demonic entity and he said that Elspeth Grant conjured it up from performing pagan worship and not witchcraft, but it became too powerful for Albert and Edmond alone. But they said that, combined, they can keep it at bay.

I asked if Elspeth Grant was an evil person and he rapped out yes but that she likes us (investigators) and that is why she has not done anything malicious towards us. Albert said that he was protecting us and that our investigator Andy Hill reminded him of a friend of his and said that Andy was a monk in a previous life. Andy reported that he felt his ear was hot. Albert said that it was him affecting him.

We decided to conduct our last vigil of the night back in the bar area downstairs. A number of strange things happened on this occasion. Brent said the chair he was sitting on was dragged back twice, which we all heard. A small table shook from side to side as we put our torches on it and still saw it shaking. Brent's hands were between his legs so we knew it was not him doing it. It moved once more and I got Brent to sit next to me. While he was still sitting next to me, the chair in front of us was dragged on two occasions. We were all now very tired and had a long journey ahead of us. It was 5.00am and we ended the investigation.

It proved to be a fascinating re-investigation and a lot of strange phenomena did seem to occur. Some of the same phenomena were reported as on our previous investigation and some different phenomena were witnessed on this investigation. We also established a natural explanation for a number of reported incidents. Again, a lot of the phenomena seemed to centre upon Brent. I do not believe he was fraudulently creating the phenomena; there does not seem to have been any logical reason for him to do so. To me, he seemed genuinely scared of what was happening around us on both investigations. Could he subconsciously/unconsciously be affecting the environment, by RSPK for instance? Could some entity be feeding off his fear and anxiety from his unique energy field and manifesting in some way? Or is he a powerful untrained medium?

The Office of Parapsychological Studies arranged for a third investigation at this very active location. I decided on limiting the number of people on this investigation to see what impact it would have on the location psychically. This time only I, Scott and Brent arrived at the location. We arrived around 9.00pm, where we sat talking for half an hour with John Humphries about any new strange happenings at the inn.

The only part of the investigation we could not conduct was the throwing object experiment in the attic as the attic on this occasion was closed due to the crumbling old stairs. At around 9.30pm we started setting up some experiments. In the bar area we drew around stools, specifically around all four legs of the stools using chalk to see if any of the furniture would move as in the previous investigations. We also covered a table with a light dusting of flour to see if any ghostly prints would be left in the flour.

We set up trigger objects in the Bishop's Room and also the Witches' Room, as well as a small room just off the top of the landing, to the right of the stairs. The rooms that we locked off contained cameras and outside the room were beam breakers (motion detectors) to make sure that if any trigger object movement was reported, we knew that nobody could have entered the rooms.

We started the investigation by conducting our first vigil in the Witches' Room. As normal, we started asking out for any spirits to make themselves known to us. This time Robert, the alleged cavalier came through to communicate by a series of two knocks for yes and one for no. To our surprise not many raps were heard on this occasion but Robert would communicate by making other noises vocally such as gasps or breaths which could be distinctly heard. The strangest aspect of the audible phenomena occurred when I asked him to communicate with his voice and he would respond by making popping sounds, such as the one made by putting the index finger inside the cheek, and clicking sounds.

During the vigil, we asked if he could walk across the floor and all of us heard the sound of footfall and the shuffling of feet as if someone was moving about the room. Whilst in the room, Scott with the audio enhancer and Brent with the ultrasonic detector picked up the sound from downstairs as if furniture was moving. We went downstairs and passed the bar area and checked on the stool and flour experiment. To our surprise one of the stools and a chair had indeed moved. The most amazing part of the experiment was when we looked at the table with the light dusting of flour on, we saw in the flour, what seemed to be a finger mark that had been dragged through the flour. Specifically the finger mark seemed to be that of a young child. We then took photographs of the scene.

From here, our next vigil was in the most haunted room at the inn: the Bishop's Room. We sat down and asked out. Almost immediately, knocking noises were emanating around the room. I asked if this was Albert, the monk said to haunt the room. He said yes, whilst using the usual two knocks for yes and once for no. After a brief conversation, another alleged spirit came through: this was the dark entity said to inhabit the inn. This time the knocking and pounding sounds were loud and more pronounced and seemed angry in nature. I asked specific questions again, questions similar to our first encounter with this so-called entity on our first investigation at the inn. We asked many questions of the entity and again, it would pound and knock very loudly.

We asked if the so-called spirit would knock five, ten and twenty times to see if there seemed to be a definite intelligence behind the knockings, which it did immediately and correctly. Furthermore, footfalls were reported from this room as before. Another alleged spirit that came through was that of a young boy aged five or six years of age. The spirit communicated by a series of two knocks for yes and one for no. During the rapping communications, it became clear that the negative entity said to inhabit the room apparently keeps the young boy's spirit close by it for which its purposes remain unclear. During the communication we did establish by a series of raps that he was allegedly murdered in 1847.

After this vigil, we went into the Mayflower barn where on our first investigation footfalls and whistling were heard. This time, however, no activity was reported from the barn. From here we conducted another vigil in the bar area, but on this occasion no activity was recorded. Next, for the first time, we conducted an investigation on the landing area, which is at the top of the stairs between the Witches' Room and the Bishop's room. The landing area looks more like a room than a landing. We sat down and started to ask out. We all heard footsteps walking slowly up the stairs and move into the landing area with us. This was very eerie and I was almost expecting to see somebody appear around the door frame but, unfortunately, nobody did. What we did hear was very pronounced footfalls and the shuffling of feet.

We were all getting very tired at this point and decided to conduct one last vigil in the much haunted Bishop's Room. Again allegedly, the dark entity came through, but did not seem as strong with the knocks and sounds as it made before, but we could hear and feel as if something was with us in the room. After this vigil we decided to call it a night on this investigation and started to pack away our equipment. We checked on the trigger object experiments but no movement was recorded.

The most fascinating part of this investigation was the flour and stool experiments where we seemed to capture a finger having been dragged through the flour and also the stool movements with chalk. The only sceptical thing I could say about these experiments is that John could have moved the stool himself and used his own finger to mark the flour, but he never interferes with the investigation and usually goes to bed to leave us to it. As stated before, the finger mark looked like a child's finger mark rather than an adult's.

On Saturday 18 October 2008 we conducted our fourth investigation at The Ancient Ram Inn. We arrived at around 8.30pm and the team members on this night's investigation were me, Scott, Brent and Charlotte Farrah. After a short chat with John Humphries, we began setting up trigger objects in all rooms, including the flour and table experiment in the bar area where, on the previous investigation, we had success.

For the first two and a half hours we split into two groups of two. Scott and I took the Bishop's Room, while Brent and Charlotte took the Witches' Room. We sat down and asked out to see if any spirits wished to communicate with us, but nothing was reported from our vigil in the Bishop's room. But whilst in the Witches' Room, Brent and Charlotte reported movement from around the bed and a small candle was thrown.

Next, both teams swapped rooms; we took the Witches' Room, while Brent and Charlotte took the Bishop's Room. We reported no occurrences from the room but Charlotte and Brent reported faint whistling coming from theirs. We had a break and talked about our surprise at the lack of phenomena from the investigation so far. We decided to stick to one group of four and conducted another vigil in the Witches' Room.

This time phenomena began to manifest. Whistling in the room began to be heard frequently, as well as the heavy footfall of some invisible entity walking around the room. Extremely loud banging raps began manifesting in response to questions. Apparently it was the spirit of Robert the cavalier making himself known to us by stamping his feet in response to questions.

We tried using an experiment using telepathy and also our fingers in the darkness to see if the alleged spirit could read our thoughts and also count by rapping how many fingers we were holding up in the pitch black, especially if the so-called spirit could see us. We could not see anything in the room. Unfortunately each count the spirit gave us was wrong: was it deception? Or the spirit playing tricks? Possibly.

From this vigil we conducted our next one back in the Bishop's room. This time the usual raps in response to questions was heard. The communications were allegedly from our ghostly monk friend, Albert. We took a break and then started some vigils downstairs, namely, in the Mayflower Barn and the bar area. No phenomena were reported from these areas.

We decided to conduct two more vigils before wrapping up the night's investigation. Once again, one in the Bishop's Room and the other in the Witches' Room. In the Witches' Room nothing else was reported, but in the Bishop's Room rappings in response to questions began again. The communications came from the alleged spirit of the boy in the room. Because of the unusual lack of phenomena on this investigation compared with our other previous investigations at the inn, we decided to provoke a response from the so called negative entity. Brent began to swear and mock the entity. All of a sudden, while it was all quiet, an almighty bang occurred, startling all of us. The door to the bedroom had been hit or kicked ferociously from outside the room and opened.

Brent took off out of his seat and sat in the middle of three beds. Nobody was outside the room. This had not happened before on our investigations at the inn and was very unsettling. We decided not to mock the entity again. Shuffling from the bedclothes and movement on the floor was also heard in the room on this vigil. Another incident that happened which was intriguing was the shifting of the bed near the door, which was seen by me, Brent and Charlotte, as the light from the EMF gauss meter illuminated the bed. The bed moved to the left. After this occurrence all became quiet. After another eventful night we called a halt to this investigation.

On Saturday 23 May 2009 we yet again arranged for another re-investigation at The Ancient Ram Inn. On this investigation I was lacking investigators due to other commitments, so instead, I brought along some guests. For this investigation the team members were me, Glynn Sparkes and Charlotte Farrah. Other guest investigators such as Matthew Yarwood and Chris

Berry also came along. We arrived around 9.00pm and I took the associate members around for a tour of the old building (these had never been to the inn before) and told them of the phenomena and stories associated with the ancient inn. After the tour I split us into two teams. My team decided to conduct our vigils on the upstairs floor, whilst the second team investigated downstairs.

My team conducted our first vigil in the Witches' Bedroom, but unfortunately on this occasion, no phenomena were reported in this room during the entirety of the investigation. I set up a natural Tri-Field meter and Dictaphone in the room and the meter did spike many times in most parts of the building, which may suggest to some a possible presence in the rooms, although the fluctuations are yet to be substantiated as having been caused by paranormal phenomena, they remain interesting nonetheless.

During the vigil Chris did report feeling very disorientated, but this could have been down to the old uneven floors in low level light conditions, in conjunction with fatigue from the long distance he drove to get us there. From this vigil our next room to be investigated was the infamous Bishop's Room. Surprisingly, again there was no activity reported except for one vigil in the room later on during the investigation. As I was asking out for any intelligent entities to make themselves known to us, I heard for a brief time some shuffling towards the door to the room and a stomp on the floor as if somebody stomped their foot down and I could feel the vibration.

From here we conducted our next vigil in the now re-opened attic bedroom. Again surprisingly, nothing was reported from this room either, except as we were making our way towards the attic by the staircase. One guest reported what sounded like footsteps making their way down the stairs. As I confirmed this with another guest to see if there was anyone moving downstairs, she and the others reported what sounded like footsteps coming down the stairs whilst they were in the bar area downstairs. As we were making our way towards the attic bedroom, Glynn reported hearing a deep breath and also a tug on his top as he was making his way upstairs into the attic bedroom. Unfortunately, this investigation was the first time we hardly reported anything from the location. It was at this point that I began to wonder if one person was missing from this investigation, someone it seemed the phenomena centered themselves upon.

On 18 February 2012 we arranged another investigation at The Ancient Ram Inn. The team on this night consisted of me, Chris Berry, Glynn, Charlotte and new investigator Rob Jacklin and other guests. Although, yet again, not much phenomena was recorded or reported from this investigation, some phenomena were experienced. Whilst in the Witches' Room, several taps which sounded unusual were heard, but these could have been normal environmental extraneous sounds. When we were conducting a vigil in the Bishop's Room, we heard a loud thud which seemed to come from where the Witches' Room is situated. We do know that we were all together and alone at the time. While conducting a vigil in the bar area, we heard movement and footfalls which seemed to come from under the stairwell and also the sound of walking up or down the stairs as well as a voice reported by a guest, which said 'Yeah' in response to a question.

The second group also reported a latch on a door being moved while they were investigating the bar area downstairs. This could have been due to the latch slipping off its hook when the door was not secured properly. When my group was investigating the Mayflower Barn, we reported hearing footfalls near the doorway to the barn. We asked Glynn, who was leading the second team, if they had been moving about. They reported that they had but only briefly, so we tried to replicate it by asking them to move again. We did indeed hear them moving around and this could well have been them, but to be fair the sound we heard did sound closer than we thought, but it also could have been a normal sound, so has to be dismissed.

Our most recent investigation at the inn, on 13 December 2014, did not produce any personal observable and recordable phenomena at all during the course of the investigation. Some investigators think that because it has been investigated by so many people and paranormal groups over the years, the phenomena are like a battery and that all the psychic energy has been drained from the place. Personally, I think it is down to being in the right place, at the right time, with the right people, psychic or otherwise. One of those people I believe is either very psychic or a perfect candidate for RSPK.

What I will say is that my fellow investigator Brent Whitworth seemed to be at the centre of the disturbances at this location. Most of the phenomena centred on him or near him. Some of my investigators began accusing him of fabricating phenomena on later investigations at this location. I do not believe this to be the case, as he was genuinely terrified at what was happening near him. If he was hoaxing phenomena, he would have had to be a member of the Magic Circle in London! What we were experiencing, without anyone being caught out, was not logical. Common sense also needs to be applied.

What I believe was happening was that Brent was an RSPK (Recurrent Spontaneous Psychokinesis) agent, although he was not aware of it. Sharon and I knew he was having problems in his life. His own business as a mechanic had collapsed, he found out that his wife was having an affair and he was not allowed to see his daughter. We also found out later that he had been in trouble with the police over some issue. All this emotion and turmoil I believe played a significant part in the investigations by his subconscious mind, affecting the physical environment around him psychically. This, in conjunction with a residual haunting and possible intelligent apparitions inhabiting the place, combined with suggestion, all played their part in the RSPK projected by Brent.

CASE FILE: BELGRAVE HALL, LEICESTER

Belgrave Hall in Leicester is a Queen Anne style house built in 1709 in the middle of two acres of walled gardens. The hall was opened to the public in 1936 as a museum. Today, Belgrave Hall shows the contrasting lifestyles of an upper class family and domestic servants in Victorian society. In 1999, Belgrave Hall became famous across the world when two ghostly figures were recorded on security cameras outside the hall. The site is still of interest to ghost hunters and psychical researchers.

The ISPR (International Society for Paranormal Research) examined the footage and decided the image was environmental in nature rather than paranormal. Sceptics have said that the image depicts only a leaf. I have to agree with this conclusion as I also believe it is some kind of leaf or debris caught in front of the camera, but there is still much debate regarding the footage. If it was an apparition, states the ISPR, it would have to have been over ten feet tall.

There have been ghost sightings at the old hall for many years. Gardener Michael Snuggs said he encountered an apparition in a red dress that was seen walking down the stairs. He said that it paused to look out of the window, then turned, smiled and walked through to the kitchen where it then vanished. Another ghost which has been heard rather than seen is 'the Victorian Lady' which has been heard by staff members at the hall as it walks around on the upstairs floor. The house has also seen visits from a 'Green Lady' and a ghostly 'Grey Lady'. Also the smell of cooking also permeates the building from time to time, despite the fact that the kitchens are museum pieces and are never actually used.

Our investigation of Belgrave Hall began when we left our home at around 5.30pm. After getting lost somewhere in Leicester we mistakenly ended up at a sewage treatment plant; this was not the wanted beginning of a paranormal investigation. We got back on track and arrived at the hall finally around 6.45pm where we met medium Lee Gilbert and three of his own team members. We waited for two people to arrive and, when they did, we were taken on a tour of the house. Belgrave Hall was always a place I wanted to investigate. After the tour we split into three teams to cover the entire hall. My team incorporated me, Brent and Scott. We took with us EMF meters, laser thermometers and night vision camcorders attached to tripods.

We started off on the middle floor while the other two teams investigated the ground floor and third floor. We started off in the Master Bedroom. Both EMF and temperature readings proved normal, so we started asking out into the environment for any intelligent spirits to make themselves known. No phenomena were reported. We next went into the Colonel's Room and heard strange footsteps above our heads, but we believe this was the other group above us in the room directly overhead.

We did catch on video a large orb shape materialise near a chair in the room, float slowly down past the stationery video camera before dissipating. This was not dust, lint or other debris caught on camera, but something I believe was truly anomalous. Next, we moved into the Ladies' Parlour. EMF and temperature readings again proved normal. The only thing that was unusual was that the security breakers in the parlour (we were not allowed to step over the cordoned off areas, because of the museum pieces and artifacts). The breakers started setting the alarms off before we settled in the room, while Brent was in the room, and he stated that while he was sitting down on the floor, the security breakers went off. What was unusual was that to break the beams, he would have had to step over the security barriers in the room to trigger the alarms but he was sitting on the floor. Had something invisible triggered the alarms? These occurrences of security alarms going off around the house were reported regularly by staff members.

We settled down in the room started asking out questions to the atmosphere. Nothing happened at first but all of a sudden, rappings started to occur. Thus began our alleged intelligent communication with the ghost of a past lady of the house. We communicated by a series of two knocks for yes and one for no. We were also filming at the time the rappings were occurring. There were also creaks of the floorboards next to the fireplace in the room as if somebody invisible was moving around the room. The alleged spirit we were in communication with was said to be one of the Ellis sisters who used to live in the house.

From here we headed up to the third floor where we investigated the Nanny's Quarters and the Nursery. The EMF and temperature readings in this room also proved to be normal and no unusual activity was reported from these rooms. Next we investigated the kitchens of the house and the Multicultural Room. As we were walking and talking from the house's kitchens to the Multicultural Room, with were suddenly pelted with small stones that were thrown from an unseen assailant. This was an intriguing phenomenon and the stones continued to be thrown at us while we entered the Multicultural Room. The strange thing was it seemed as if the stones had come from outside the house.

On the second floor one of the other two groups also reported stone throwing. There then followed an incident of fraud by one of the guests from the other group. Sharon discovered that one of Lee Gilbert's so-called investigators had a small bag of stones in her handbag.

Nevertheless, our experience with the stone throwing seemed genuine as nobody barring me, Brent and Scott were on our floor and all the other folk were on the upstairs floors conducting their vigils.

We made our way into the Multicultural Room, closed the door behind us and sat down. Nothing else was reported from this room, until we left. The only thing that occurred in the room was the sound of a couple of thumps, and Brent said that he felt as if a sign in the room had moved against him and he jumped out of his seat. To try and provoke something to happen (something we do not normally do), Brent started to swear and insult the unseen, stone-throwing assailant who we were told was Edmond Craddock. We were mocking this so called Edmond Craddock and making fun of his name, calling him Eddie and Ed to see what the response would be. As we left the Multicultural Room and were slightly frustrated as nothing else had happened in the room, an almighty crash occurred.

We turned around and saw to our astonishment that a metal chair had been thrown to the ground. This bemused us a little and the other groups came rushing downstairs to see what was going on as they all heard the crash. It seemed Brent had provoked a response after all. Although it may have been unscientific, it worked! Was a poltergeist responsible for the stone throwing? And the chair being thrown to the ground? It did seem to be the case, as it followed a pattern for poltergeist activity. Yet again though, Brent was at the centre of activity. The author will have to make up their own mind as to whether this was a haunting or another case of RSPK.

Next we went for a walk around the gardens with cameras and night vision goggles but nothing else anomalous was reported. We finished a last vigil with everybody in the Multicultural Room, but nothing untoward happened except that Lee was allegedly taken over by a so-called spirit. This I believe was nothing but fraudulent entertainment for the naïve, the sort of thing that gives mediumship a bad name and hinders people with genuine psychic gifts. We said our goodbyes and headed home.

CASE FILE: YE OLDE TRIP TO JERUSALEM, NOTTINGHAM

On 16 February 2008 we had the chance to investigate one of Nottingham's most famous haunts, Ye Olde Trip To Jerusalem. The inn dates back to 1189 and is carved into the sandstone rocks below Nottingham Castle. The inn is said to be the oldest in England and is known throughout the world. Many people from all walks of life and from all countries come to visit this quaint old place.

The year 1189 was the year of accession to the throne of King Richard I, also known as Richard the Lionheart, and one of his first acts as king was to crusade against the Saracens who at the time, occupied the holy land of Christian religion. Nottingham Castle was a stronghold favoured by the king and legend has it that the brave knights and men at arms who rallied to his call rallied to fight in this third crusade. The soldiers gathered at the castle to rest before journeying to Jerusalem. Legend also has it that these crusaders stopped off at the inn at the foot of the castle for welcome refreshments.

In the Middle Ages a 'Trip' was not a journey as such, but a resting place where such a journey could be broken. This is where the inn gets its name. The resident ghost said to haunt the inn is an old tenant called Yorkey, who also used to drink there on a regular basis. Other legends at the inn consist of a cursed galleon, and if it is ever cleaned, the person is said to die. Allegedly three people have died in unfortunate circumstances and it is now covered with about sixty years of dust. The galleon is contained in a lighted glass case that nobody can touch because of the curse. That is, if you believe in such things. Also in the same bar is an old wooden chair. If a woman sits in that chair she is said to become pregnant. I have a friend who sat in that chair and several weeks later, she did indeed find out she was pregnant. Coincidence, perhaps?

Our investigation began with our team consisting of me, Sharon, Brent, Scott, Kelly, Nicky and Richard. The investigation began at 12.30am as it is still a working inn and we had to wait until all of the punters had left. We split into two teams. Team one consisted of me, Brent and Sharon, which took the main part of the inn, and team two comprised Scott, Kelly, Nicky and Richard, and they took the inn's cellars and network of sandstone caves.

We started our vigils in the Rock Lounge and took with us video cameras, EMF meters and audio voice recorders. Unfortunately no phenomena were reported from this room. We next headed into the Museum Room. Again, no anomalies were reported. Richard reported later in the night that whilst he was in the Museum Room, he felt disorientated, light headed and did not like the room. I debunked this experience as there is a generator near the room which would give off high levels of electro-magnetic fields. Some people call these rooms that give off high levels of EMF 'fear zones'. This means that being exposed to such high levels of EMF over a given time period can cause disorientation, nausea, dizziness, the feeling of being watched and the hairs on the arms and neck standing up (static charge). So I feel this was the most likely explanation of his discomfort.

We next moved into Yorkey's Lounge where paranormal activity has been reported. Again no anomalous activity was reported from this area. We stopped for a short while in the lounge where we met up with team two, who also reported no activity except for a few bumps they said they heard in the cellars. After the break, I and Brent went down into the cellars whilst Sharon stayed upstairs in the lounge. Whilst down in the cellar we distinctly heard what sounded like a shuffle along the concrete floor. Three stones were also thrown against the metallic beer barrels on three separate occasions which made a distinctive metallic 'ting' sound. We asked the landlord, Richard, about these incidents and he reported that there is small sand fall that happens (the cellar's roof is made from sandstone rock), but it normally leaves small pockets of sand on the top of the barrels. The strange thing was that the pebbles thrown were clean pebbles with no sand on or around them at all. The throwing also coincided with us asking out for any spirits to make themselves known to us. We can put this down to either debris falling from the ceiling or poltergeist activity.

Another incident that happened in the cellar was that Brent reported that a bottle of cleaner left on the rock wall apparently began to shake. I turned around to see the liquid in the bottle still vibrating as if the bottle had moved. We also seemed to feel a presence in the cellar, as if we were being watched or followed. Apparently the apparition of Yorkey has been seen down in the cellars on a number of occasions and is known to play pranks on its unsuspecting victims. We heard a number of individual banging sounds, but we put these down to the pulling of the pumps in the cellars. On the second occasion we visited the cellars, we heard two distinct bangs in succession on the metallic barrels, but nothing else was reported. We finished the investigation off in the Rock Lounge and Museum Room, but no more activity was reported.

CASE FILE: THE GUILDHALL, LEICESTER

The Guildhall, Leicester was built around 1390 as the meeting place of the Guild of Corpus Christ; the guild was a group of businessmen and gentry who had religious connections. The Guildhall was used for banquets, festivals and as a home for a priest who prayed for the souls of Guild members in the nearby St Martin's Church. The corporation of Leicester bought the Guildhall by the end of the fourteenth century. It is believed that Oliver Cromwell visited here several times, and it is reputed that William Shakespeare performed here. It has been used as law courts and was the home to Leicester's first police force and contained cells for criminals.

The Guildhall is reputedly Leicester's most haunted building and is said to accommodate at least five ghosts. The most famous, said to wander the old hall, is the ghost of a white lady and she has been seen on numerous occasions. Other ghosts said to haunt the old hall is a grey monk said to haunt the library. A tormented apparition of a cavalier has been seen in the Great Hall, and a phantom policeman and a ghostly dog have been seen in the Courtyard; a phantom black cat is seen in the Great Hall, and at least one witness claims to have been shocked to see a pair of legs materialise from the portrait of Henry, Earl of Huntingdon, hanging in the Mayor's Parlour.

On Saturday 7 June 2008 we had the opportunity to investigate the much haunted Guildhall. After getting lost, we arrived at the building around 7.00pm. We were met by Lee Gilbert, investigator and medium, and he took us on a fascinating tour of the old hall. As he took us into the Mayor's Parlour, and whilst he was talking, we all heard the latch on the door move. Sharon went to try the latch, but found it was quite hard to elevate or drop and there was no one outside.

When we got to the Jury Room, and whilst talking, a number of strange taps and creaks were heard, as if somebody else was with us in the room. After the tour, Sharon took Nicky, our group's medium, on a walk around to see if she could pick up any other relevant information about the place psychically. I and Scott set up some trigger objects with coins and crucifixes around various places in the building. After we set up the trigger object experiments, I, Scott and Brent took some EMF and temperature valences, but no anomalous readings were recorded and all proved normal.

We then took a walk around the old hall whilst conducting an EVP session to see if we could record any inaudible voices on the Dictaphone. After a brief chat and drink, we broke off into two groups. My group consisted of me, Scott, Brent and our other medium, Glynn. We started our first vigil in the Jury Room. After setting up our camcorders on tripods we began filming, then sat down and I started asking out if there were any intelligent spirits that could make themselves known.

While we were asking out during this vigil, we all kept hearing footsteps, taps and bangs. They also seemed to be coming from underneath the table where we sat. This proved strange but fascinating nonetheless. Whilst we were in the Jury Room, we also kept hearing the sound of furniture being dragged around, which we thought was coming from downstairs. But, after asking Lee later, it turned out that he thought it was us moving things around. We were sitting quietly in the Jury Room at the time. Where this sound emanated from we do not know, but it was strange and both groups of investigators heard it.

We conducted our next vigil in the Mayor's Parlour, said to be the most haunted room in the Guildhall. After starting our cameras rolling, we sat down at a table. All of a sudden, we did not feel alone; we kept hearing something as if it was creeping around the room. Scott kept reporting that he could see shadows moving around. Whilst we were still sat at the table, the table felt as if it was starting to vibrate,;we all felt it and so we decided to conduct a table tipping session.

When we began asking out if any alleged spirits could make themselves present, the table started to move slowly, then get more powerful, until it began to vibrate and shake violently from side to side, all the while whilst the cameras were filming what was happening. The table felt as if it was being lifted from the floor by an unknown force and being shaken from side to side. It gradually diminished in strength, then finally stopped. It proved to be a superb vigil which seemed to indicate we were experiencing some remarkable paranormal activity.

Whilst all of this was still happening, Sharon had to leave her group as she said she kept feeling angry for no apparent reason. She also had a glass thrown at her whilst filming her table and glass experiment in the cells area. The team also reported that the table jumped to the left and then the right. The incident spooked her and she remained in the canteen area for the rest of the investigation. Later, I, Scott and Brent went to view the trigger object experiments. The crucifixes hadn't moved, but when we went to check the coins in the Mayor's Parlour, some of them had moved, pictures of which we took beforehand then afterwards, which do indeed show coin movement. After a break, we headed off into the cells area and again sat around a table in a corner of the room.

Again, we tried another table tipping session, and again, the table began to vibrate and jump accordingly in response to questions being asked out. Glynn picked up two names, Joseph and Marwood, who he says haunt the cells area. The table movement seemed to be genuine paranormal phenomena and the movements of the table were also recorded on video. The only explanation for the table tipping experiments conducted at the hall would be the psychological phenomenon called the ideomotor effect. This is where subconscious/unconscious thought such as belief and willingness causes miniscule muscle movements in the arms that move the table unknowingly. From a paranormal explanation, it could be a spirit manifesting in such a way that it moves the table, or RSPK due to belief in spirits and willingness which actually causes the table to rise, move or levitate psychokinetically.

From here, we moved from room to room trying to find any more psychic activity before we left. We went back into the Jury Room where, once again, we heard anomalous tapping sounds and also footsteps that sounded as if they were running. These seemed to come from outside, but on checking no one was there. We went back into the Mayor's Parlour and started asking out. This time an incident occurred that stunned us all and made us quite wary.

Brent said that he felt a quick sharp pain on top of his head and when I switched on the torch, we saw that his head was trickling with blood; something had taken a small chunk of skin away from his head. Lee said that it was perhaps the spirit of a surgeon who he believes haunted the old hall. Brent said he did not bang his head due to low level light conditions and he also said he did not catch himself with his own hand. We looked at his hands and there was no blood on them and his nails were short. It was an intriguing occurrence. This ended an incredible investigation.

CASE FILE: MARGAM CASTLE, PORT TALBOT, WALES

On 15 November 2008 my organization had the pleasure of investigating Margam Castle, in Port Talbot, Wales. The castle itself does not look like the normal castle most people think of, but is in fact a massive gothic mansion that, if it is not haunted, certainly ought to be! It looks like the classic haunted house.

The castle itself stands on the site of what was once a Cistercian abbey, founded in 1147. The only surviving building of the abbey is the nave which is used as the parish church. The present castle was built in 1840 by the Talbot family who made a fortune from industry using coal in the Welsh valleys. Before the arrival of the Talbots, the Mansel family owned the abbey who forced the monks from the abbey to leave. One of the monks who was forced to leave apparently placed a curse upon the place which seems to have been fulfilled. The castle is now a romantic shell said to be haunted by an apparition known as the white lady. She has been seen to descend the large gothic staircase that leads from the top floor of the house. A phantom monk is seen flitting about the ruins of the abbey, and the ghostly voices of children have been heard. Dark shadows have also been observed in the castle.

My team arrived at the fantastically lit castle at around 9.00pm, where we were met by Yolande, Geraint and Sharon of Ghost Watch Wales. My team consisted of me, Scott, Sharon, Brent, Nicky, Richard and Glynn. After introductions with one another, we made a base of operations for ourselves. We were then taken on a tour of the castle by Geraint or, as we were told to call him, Grant, as most people could not pronounce his name. Geraint was also a medium and a lovely man to talk to.

During the walk round whilst on the top floor, we all heard what sounded like a man's whistle. We asked everybody present if they had whistled, to which they all replied 'No'. I asked out to see if whoever or whatever whistled could do so in reply, but unfortunately no one did. After a short break, we began the vigils. We were all led out of the Chapter House which is all that is left of the old ruins of the abbey which was a short walk from the mansion. We asked out if any spirits could make themselves present before us, but unfortunately nothing was reported except that a couple of my investigators reported seeing a shadow cross what was left of one of the abbey's windows.

After a short walk back to the castle, we split into two teams. Team one consisted of me, Scott, Brent and Glynn. We took the upstairs floor, whilst Sharon's team consisted of Nicky, Richard and Glynn, and they took the Great Hall, the downstairs floors and the main staircase. Armed with night vision camcorders, audio recorders, digital cameras and natural Tri-Field meters, we moved from room to room on the upstairs floor asking out to see if any spirits wished to make contact. Although no knockings or rappings were heard, what we did hear was quite astonishing.

On three occasions in an upstairs room where the apparition of a white lady is said to manifest, we all heard very distinct footsteps with the sound of swishing clothes, which sounded like the noises a dress would make if it was rubbing against the floor with its hem. The footsteps seemed to be moving towards us through a doorway in the next room. Although we were expecting someone to enter our room, no one did. On three occasions we chased through the rooms to see if anyone had gone walkabout from the other team, but no one had. The door we entered through was still locked from the inside, which we forgot about.

Other noises we did hear we found a natural explanation for, such as the wind and rain which battered the building while we were there. When we were in the Nursery at the other end of the mansion, both mine and Scott's audio recorders were drained of battery power and switched off. They both had new batteries in them. A strange feeling of dread overcame the room, which we all felt, and the natural Tri-Field meters we set up in the corner of the room began to whine. We asked out to see if any intelligent entities wished to communicate, and the meter spiked again and again in response to questions. This seemed compelling as nothing should trigger the Tri-Field meters, as they only fluctuate due to any natural electromagnetic fields they pick up.

The natural Tri-Field meter, when calibrated correctly, can also register the weak electromagnetic field of the human body. It also eliminates all Alternating Current (AC) fields. So, is it possible that if consciousness does survive bodily death and it leaves a residual weak electromagnetic field, it is conceivable that the natural Tri-Field meter would pick up the trace of an apparition (if indeed the apparition is a case for survival). Or could it have been due to an electromagnetic field being produced from the storm and rain outside? It did seem that no matter where we placed the meters in the castle, they would spike and whine in response to questions and also to the sound of footfalls we were hearing.

Other strange occurrences we heard upstairs in the rooms were whispering, which Scott heard, and the faint sound of what seemed like a dog barking, which has been reported here before. To me it sounded like a woman laughing, but we all heard something. We also tried a table tipping experiment. Although the table did vibrate, it never actually moved. Sharon from the second team reported a whimpering sound upstairs and whilst downstairs, she reported being stroked on the back of her neck. Others reported that a gruff voice which shouted something like 'Carol' or 'Karen' was heard, and also that the big entrance door slammed shut, which locked some people outside.

When we took to investigating the Great Hall and other rooms including the staircase, no other anomalous experiences were reported except for, yet again, the spiking of the natural Tri-Field meters in response to questions. Is it possible that intelligent spirits were using the devices as a means of communication? Or did it have a natural explanation? When we conducted some more vigils again upstairs, this time we also took two sets of beam breaking security devices, to see if the footfalls we heard could set off the alarms. The strange thing was although we heard again the footfalls, they did not set off the barriers. The natural Tri-Field meters spiked again and again.

We asked Geraint to conduct a séance upstairs, but nothing occurred except the sound of movement near the doorway and the meter again whining in response. We went for one last vigil in the Nursery, but nothing untoward was reported. The spiking of the natural Tri-Field meter stopped, but did start again whilst we were talking before wrapping up the night's fascinating investigation.

CASE FILE: THE LANGWITH POLTERGEIST

On Saturday 20 December 2008 my organization were invited to conduct an investigation of the disturbances at a residential address in Langwith, Nottinghamshire. We originally met the family at a lecture and investigation back in October, where we met Sheena Cooper who told us about the disturbances they had been living with for quite a number of years. I arranged for our psychic medium, Nicky Bryant, to attend in the afternoon to see what she could pick up psychically. She telephoned me with her results and told me that she picked up on an active spirit of a woman that went by the name of Eve, Evvy, or Izzie. We jotted down her findings so that our evening's investigation could get underway.

The night's investigation team consisted of me, Sharon and Brent. We arrived around 8.30pm where we were welcomed into the home of Sheena and Paul. We began the investigation by interviewing Sheena and Paul about the disturbances which plagued their home. She told us about some fascinating experiences they had undergone over the last few years, including the apparition of a woman seen clearly in the kitchen and also the incident of a perfectly formed pyramid made out of baby rice on the cooker top. She also told us about an incident where a picture had been thrown from the small bedroom and then taken apart without being broken and perfectly laid out in a horizontal position side by side, incorporating the glass front, the picture itself, the backing and the front and back frames lined up, lying flat on the floor side by side.

The family said these incidences could not have been done by human hands as nobody was upstairs or in the kitchen when they took place (unless they could have done these themselves?). Other strange occurrences they reported were audible sounds such as voices calling out to members of the family and also footfalls on the upstairs landing. Sheena also reported that she was once hit with a twenty pence piece and Paul kept finding his cigarette lighters disappearing, as well as other odd incidents.

Sheena told us some history of the house and its previous occupants. The house itself used to be an old pit house and two occupants in particular we took notice of. Sheena said that they knew the previous occupants of the house very well and that they were Mrs Evelyn and Mike Searson. Mr Searson had died in the house and Evelyn Searson had succumbed to breast cancer in hospital. After a brief drink and a chat, we began the evening's investigation. We began by taking baseline readings with the EMF meter and temperature devices which proved normal during this and the rest of the night's investigation. We also took a photo shoot with the digital camera to see if any photographic anomalies could be picked up. I set up a locked off camera in the bedroom which had a large doll's house and a rocking horse.

Downstairs we turned off all the lights in the house and began asking out questions to any intelligent spirits that may haunt the house. Also in hand we had a digital voice recorder running and Sharon had the ultrasonic detector amplifier. We also had a natural Tri-Field meter calibrated ready and waiting. We started off in the living room, but no responses to questions were heard. We did hear several bumps and knocks, but they were down to the refrigerator and other appliances running in the kitchen.

From this, we conducted a glass divination session in the dining room, but nothing occurred here or in the kitchen area, so thereafter we set up the video camera in the kitchen and moved upstairs to what was allegedly the most active part of the house. Upstairs we split into two teams consisting of my team with me, Brent and Paul, and the second team consisting of Sharon and Sheena.

Just as we got upstairs, Sheena shouted for us to come into the bedroom as an incident with a pen seemed to have occurred. Sheena stated that a pen, which had been on the side of a small table next to one of the beds in the room, had moved onto the bed lying perfectly vertical, just below the pillow. I was sceptical of this incident as one of them could have placed the pen there before, but she swore that the pen had earlier been on the table and Paul corroborated this.

After this incident we took to conducting a vigil in the bedroom with the doll's house and the rocking horse, whilst Sharon and Sheena took to conducting a vigil in the bedroom where allegedly the pen had moved. Just as we sat down in the bedroom and were getting ourselves comfortable in the room, we suddenly began to hear shuffling sounds coming from around the bed. We moved position, and kept very still so as to eliminate any natural movement sounds.

I began asking out to any spirits to make contact. We again heard the shuffling of feet and footfalls coming from around the bed. Intelligent rappings began to be heard. I asked if it could knock and shuffle its feet, three, five and ten times and it would respond in kind, which absolutely fascinated us. We also asked the alleged spirit to rap to questions by two knocks for yes and once for no. By the series of knocks, we got a story saying that the so-called spirit we were in communication with was Evelyn. She said she did die of breast cancer and that she did not want to move on because she loved family life and being around children.

We asked if it was her that was moving the cigarette lighters and if she had moved the pen onto the bed, to which she replied by two knocks. We also asked her if her husband was with her, but she said that he was not and that he had moved to the other side. During the vigil, we also asked Sharon and Sheena to join us in the room. Sheena began asking out, and just as she did a box behind Brent moved. We were not sure if it had been Brent that accidently caught the box and moved it, as he was sat straight in front of it. It was also pitch black inside the room and he said he could not be sure that he did. To me it did not seem as if he did, as he seemed startled by it when it moved, but unfortunately we cannot be sure so we have to remain sceptical about this incident.

When Sharon and Sheena joined us in the room, the activity seemed to die down. They did hear the shuffling of feet, but no more intelligent rappings were heard. We went into two other rooms, but no other activity was reported in any of them apart from the bedroom where the pen had moved. We heard again the sound of shuffling feet but that also died off. We decided to conduct another vigil in the bedroom with the doll's house. Again, we got more knockings and footfalls. After this we were getting extremely tired and decided to wrap up the night's investigation and thanked Sheena and Paul for their kind hospitality. We asked if we could return at a later date to conduct another investigation, as we were convinced some form of paranormal activity was taking place.

On Saturday 13 June 2009 I arranged a re-investigation with Sheena and Paul to see what and if any further disturbances had developed and if they were still going on – which they were. As we arrived at Sheena and Paul's home we were greeted yet again with their kind hospitality. On this occasion I brought in my investigator and medium, Glynn Sparkes, as I was interested in what information he could pick up psychically at this location. On the previous investigation, I had brought in Nicky and was impressed with the information she picked up on, so it was with great interest that I waited to see if Glynn would pick up on the same information or something entirely different.

After a drink and chat together, we took Glynn around on a tour of the house to see what information he could pick up. He said that the main centre of the disturbances was upstairs and especially in the master bedroom (where the rocking chair and doll's house were situated) and where we experienced activity on the previous investigation. Glynn picked up on a little girl which had been seen and which Nicky also picked up on in the previous visit. Glynn stated that the little girl's name was Emily, that she was around ten years of age and that she was quite mischievous. He also picked up on someone entirely different. This person was male, was quite stocky in stature, liked a drink, and was very short tempered but protective. Sheena and Paul substantiated that they knew this person before he died and that he was married to Evelyn who Nicky picked up on on her visit, and whom we seemed to have communicated with before. But Glynn did not pick up on Evelyn at all.

After the tour around the house, we decided to concentrate the investigation upstairs where the activity before took place. We split into two small groups of two. I and Paul took the master bedroom and Glynn and Sheena took their bedroom and the small room next door. I set up and calibrated the natural Tri-Field meter net to the bed on the floor and also set up a voice recorder running.

While we were asking out for any intelligent spirits to make contact with us, the Tri-Field meter began spiking strongly to certain questions, especially when asking for Emily. We also heard random knocking sounds as if they were moving around in the next room. I asked out if the knockings were made by Sheena and Glynn, but they replied that it was not them. They thought the noises came from us. It was strange, as we could not fathom where the noises actually originated, as we thought they were coming from the room next door and Sheena and Glynn thought they were coming from the landing or from downstairs.

After this vigil we went into the bedroom next door. This was the room of the previous pen incident. As we made our way in, Sheena reported hearing a whistle coming from the farthest bed she was lying on. Glynn and Sheena got up and made their way into the master bedroom. I lay down on one bed and Paul lay down on the second one. Just as I lay down and switched off the table lamp, Paul and I both heard a whistle. This came from exactly the same place as where Sheena had heard it. I began asking out and we both heard footfalls that sounded like shuffling coming from near the door.

During the vigil and while we were still asking out, Paul got the shock of his life as a box toppled over near the bottom of his bed. 'Jesus!' he said, scared out of his wits. I thought he had moved to get up from the bed and that he caught the box as he was getting up, but he was still on the bed in the same position, but this time more rigid from fright. I immediately got up and examined the box. I stated that it was entirely possible that the box could have just fallen over, but Paul stated that the box had been in the same position since Christmas and had never moved before. Was this just extreme coincidence that the box toppled over just as I was asking out for a spirit to make itself known? Also in the room Paul reported hearing a moaning sound, but I did not hear it as I was talking about the box incident at the time.

While Glynn and Sheena were in the master bedroom they reported hearing what sounded like a growling sound, and what sounded like a dog yawning. Sheena had felt herself lifted up and Glynn had felt something move through his hair. Sheena was quite disturbed by this and decided to take another break. Afterwards we decided to conduct another vigil in the master bedroom while Glynn and Sheena took the room next door with the two beds. Again whilst asking we heard some random knocking noises as if someone was moving around, as well as seeing spiking in response to questions from the Natural Tri-Field meter. This brought the intriguing investigation to an end as we had to be up early the next morning.

Several months later we arranged to conduct another investigation at this property but unfortunately Sheena and Paul had fled, and we arrived at an empty house. Did they flee because of the poltergeist activity they experienced? Or did they just move out? We do not know as we have not heard from them since.

CASE FILE: WYGSTON HOUSE, LEICESTER

On 14 March 2009 The Office of Parapsychological Studies arranged to conduct an investigation at Wygston House, Leicester. Not much history is known about the building, but what is known is that it has a chequered and speculative past. Wygston House was certainly built in the fifteenth century by a cotton and textile merchant. He was the uncle of the better known William Wyggeston, who was the mayor of Leicester and also of Calais in France. It is thought that, although Roger Wygston was married, he had a mistress. The house was probably saved from development by virtue of the fact that an impressive Georgian house was built in front of the old wattle and daub original. Wygston House was then unnoticed for many years. Eventually it was acquired by the City Council and operated until comparatively recently as a museum of costume. The main ghost said to haunt the house is that of a little boy dressed in an Edwardian outfit. Although he has been seen, he has most often been heard. Poltergeist activity has also been reported in the cellars underneath the house.

We arrived at Wygston at around 7.00pm. The team consisted of me, Sharon, Nicky, Richard, Brent and Glynn, with two guests. We were met by medium and investigator Lee Gilbert, whom we knew from previous investigations at Belgrave Hall and Leicester Guild Hall. After a brief chat, Lee took us on a walk round of the house telling us of its little known past and of its alleged haunted inhabitants.

We began the night's investigation by most of us conducting a vigil in the cellars underneath the building, where alleged poltergeist activity has manifested. During the vigil we took in a Natural Tri-Field meter, audio recorder and a night vision camcorder. We began by asking out if any spiritual presences could make themselves known to us. Some of the group began to say that they felt as if they were being touched and stroked. Suddenly a screw took off and hit Richard on the jacket. I went into another room in the cellars by myself to see if anything anomalous occurred. Unfortunately nothing did, but the other investigators reported more screws being thrown at them in the room next door. When everybody had left the cellars, I locked off the video camera in the hope of capturing some poltergeist activity on film and also set the audio recorder running.

After a quick drink, we split into two groups of four people. My group consisted of me, Sharon, Brent and Glynn, and we started off investigating all the rooms downstairs, while group two consisted of Nicky, Richard and the two guests, and they began investigating the upstairs floor. My team began in Room One, which is said to have been an illegal abortion clinic many years ago. We began by asking out to any intelligent spirits who might be in the room with us to make themselves known. As we did this, the Natural Tri-Field meter started fluctuating in response to questions. Sharon took over the questioning due to her excellent knowledge of medicine, and during the questioning and using the meter as a possible communication device (although not scientifically proven), we established that the spirit was female and that she was a nurse in the 1890s.

After this vigil, we moved into Room Two. Sharon asked out and the Tri-Field meter again started spiking and whining in response to questions. Then, all of a sudden, we heard four distinct noises that sounded like a guitar string being plucked. After we heard this again, we found the source. It was a computer on standby – mystery solved! After this vigil, we moved into the Georgian part of the building and then to the Main Hall and staircase leading upstairs. Nothing anomalous occurred. When team two came downstairs, I set the Natural Tri-Field meter up for them, but it never fluctuated once. We moved into the upstairs room and begun a table tipping session.

All four of us placed our hands lightly on the table using just our fingertips and we started asking out. All of a sudden, the table began to vibrate. This happened for at least twenty minutes without the movements getting any stronger. We tried a glass divination experiment instead. Glynn began by picking up the presence of a former owner of Wygston House. We seemed to establish that Roger Wygston was present in the room with us. We used the glass for yes and no questions, and it moved quite violently to some of the questions asked.

We decided to try another table tipping session and it was Sharon this time that asked out. She asked out for the spirit of Roger Wygston to move the table. This time, the table started to vibrate harder and harder. When we asked the supposed spirit to pull or shift the table in a certain direction, it would pull or twist in the direction we wanted (towards us, away from us, side to side and in diagonal twists). The session proved a great success. Was it our subconscious minds that actually moved the table? Or something else?

At one point during the vigil, Sharon saw a dark shadow cross the room by the window in the room next door. She got up to investigate, but nobody was there. After this, we went into the Main Hall upstairs and sat in chairs. We heard a couple of taps but nothing significant. Nothing else was reported from this vigil. Next we moved back into the cellars downstairs, but this time without Sharon.

The three of us headed downstairs into the cellar, sat down and asked out. On several occasions we did seem to hear footsteps and shuffles come from the floor, but nothing else was reported. We went back upstairs for a break and afterwards headed back down into the cellars, but this time with Lee and several others. Whilst we were in there, the phenomena began to escalate. A very loud bang occurred which startled us all, coming from behind the bar in the cellar. We established that either a drawer had dropped onto the counter or the large board behind the bar had moved.

Next, a stone seemed to have been thrown which hit Lee on the head and a bar and bell, which was being used as a trigger object, took off from the bar and landed several feet away. But the most impressive incident occurred to me while in the dark cellar. At one point during the vigil, Richard switched on his torch briefly, to illuminate the bar area. During those few brief seconds I saw a shadowy form I took to be that of a man. At the time I said nothing, considering the possibility that it could just have been my eyes playing tricks.

Lee asked Richard to put the light on again as he said that he had seen something over in the corner behind the bar. So without saying a word I asked Lee to go over to where he thought he saw something. When he stopped and said 'It was here', I was astonished; he stood in exactly the same place where I saw the shadowy form. He said it looked like a person stood there. Only I and Lee saw it. Did I witness an apparition? I am not sure, but it is a possibility and I cannot explain what I saw. I tried to replicate the circumstances to find an alternative explanation. I failed. This experience brought an end to the night's investigation as we were all getting tired. This was an exciting investigation, especially for me.

CASE FILE: THE HAUNTED GAOL HOUSE, THE GALLERIES OF JUSTICE, SHIRE HALL, NOTTINGHAM

In 1155 King Henry II gave a charter to the town of Nottingham. The town was to be forever separated, divided and utterly exempt from the county. Nottingham was to be a county itself. The King's Hall was the County Hall or Shire Hall and stood on the site of the present structure. Assizes and quarter sessions were held here and the knights of the shire were selected to serve the county in Parliament. The dungeons, deep below the hall, date back to the very early years of the original Saxon settlement and were in use well before the Norman Conquest.

The rebuilding of the Shire Hall began in 1770 and the hall has occupied the site for nearly five hundred years and has seen many changes. It was used as court, men's prison, women's prison and place for execution. Today, it is known as the National Centre for Citizenship and Law and serves as one of the City of Nottingham's leading tourist attractions.

There are said to be many ghosts that haunt the building. In the courtroom there have been rapping sounds, groaning sounds and a dark shadowy apparition seen walking about on the balcony above the Main Courtroom. Down below, in the County Gaol, in an area known as the Pit, an oppressive feeling overcomes people, as well as the feeling of people being touched by some invisible entity. Stone throwing has also been reported here and also in the Chapel. In the County Gaol itself, which is below the courtroom, dark shadowy figures have been witnessed as well as footfalls being reported along the corridors. There have also been reports of moans, groans and breathing which unnerves visitors, and also reports of heavy cell doors slamming shut and becoming solidly jammed. In the Women's Prison and the Laundry Room, the ghost of a woman has been seen.

The Entrance Hall is said to be the home of three placid spectres which have been witnessed over the years. One is a man seen wearing a military type of uniform, another is a petite lady and also an apparition of a person in Victorian clothes. In the Exercise Yard where some executed prisoners are buried there is a mock up gallows where one originally stood. A dark figure has been seen moving about the yard. The steps outside the yard which lead into another entrance to the Men's Prison are reputedly haunted by the ghost of a young boy which has been seen from time to time.

On 20 March 2009 we were invited to conduct our first (and one of many) investigations at the Galleries of Justice. The team for the evening consisted of me, Sharon and Brent. We were also met by Apparitions Anonymous Investigation Team leader, Lee Gilbert, whom we had met on three previous investigations. Lee conducted his investigation with his team, and we conducted ours with mine.

For our first vigil, we had with us a Natural Tri-Field meter, camcorder, digital audio recorder and digital cameras. We headed down into the County Gaol and as we were walking around in and between cells, a deep breath of a man was heard by us all. The breath was caught close to the video camera as well as the audio recorder. Whilst we kept walking around and asking for any alleged spirits to make themselves known more breaths were heard as well as moaning sounds. Again, these too were not only objectively witnessed, but were all caught on video and audio.

After this vigil, we made our way into the Main Courtroom. As we were walking up the stairs from the County Gaol to the courtroom, I forgot to shut the door behind me, so I asked Brent to go down to shut it for me. As he went down the stairs and leant around the corner to pull the door to, he saw, standing in the corner, a dark shape which frightened him to the point that he bounded back up the stairs. He was visibly shaken and said that it did not look like a reflection of his shadow. Unfortunately, with the video in hand and due to the fright he received, he did not think to try and film it.

After this incident and in the courtroom, I sat in the chair where the county judge would have sat and Brent placed himself in the conviction cubicle; Sharon sat below me around a table where evidence would have been given. In here I set up and calibrated the Natural Tri-field meter and then started asking out questions. During the vigil several taps and raps were heard, but this could have been down to expansion and contraction of the wooden witness pews etc. in the courtroom, as there was a cold breeze coming up from the County Gaol and blowing through the courtroom. The only strange occurrence that happened here on this night was the fluctuation from the Natural Tri-Field meter in response to certain specific questions. After these vigils, we went back upstairs to have a break and a chat about the investigation so far.

After the break, we headed back down into the County Gaol for another vigil. Again, whilst walking around the cells that occupy the gaol, more breathing and deep sighs were heard. In one instance in the Condemned Cell (actually this cell was not the real condemned cell as it was really an isolation cell – the real condemned cell was further along the corridor), as we were walking out, a loud deep breathing sound was heard between Brent and Sharon. This provoked quite an amusing response as both of them ran out of the cell!

Sharon went back upstairs and we continued our vigil in the County Gaol. Again, whilst we were walking around, we heard choking and gurgling sounds as if somebody was be choked to death coming from around us. This proved quite unnerving. We went into the real Condemned Cell. This is where the guilty prisoners were held before their execution on the gallows. This cell contained a single bed. We sat down on the bed and started asking out questions to the atmosphere in the hope of gaining a response. We heard footfalls almost instantly and it sounded as if someone was shuffling their feet across the concrete floor. It would respond to the questions we were asking. This phenomenon was also recorded on video. Breaths were also heard in the cell during the vigil and, in one instance, as we got up from the bed to leave the room, a loud man's groan was heard, sounding as if it was meant to scare us. This startled Brent to such an extent that it made him cry out. Again, this was caught on video and audio.

From here we made our way into the Pit, the Laundry Room and the Women's Prison, but unfortunately nothing anomalous occurred. We also went outside into the Exercise Yard and the Dungeon where an old oubliette can still be seen to this day. A couple of strange sounds were heard, but nothing spectacular. From here, we went upstairs for another break and then back downstairs into the County Gaol for one last vigil. Sharon went into the Juvenile Courtroom. This courtroom is a smaller one inside the building and was used to convict young offenders.

Whilst we were conducting our last vigil in the County Gaol below, footfalls were again reported from the Condemned Cell with the single bed. As we were asking the alleged spirit to make itself known, it would respond in kind by shuffling its feet, but as we heard the footfall and kept saying 'thank you' it would respond every time to 'thank you' by shuffling its feet twice in response. We could not help but laugh at this incident as the alleged spirit seemed to be having a laugh with us. The faster we said 'thank you', the faster the shuffling.

During several vigils in the Gaol, metallic sounds seemed to manifest. Could this have been the Gaolers' keys that have been heard on several occasions in the past? Just before we left the vigil, a long drawn out breath was heard next to my ear. Brent also heard it. This cell seemed to produce louder audible phenomena than anywhere else in the Gaol. Unfortunately this one was not recorded as we had just about packed away our equipment. This brought about an end to a fantastic investigation that produced the best evidence to date. It proved to be the perfect case, with objective witness testimony backed up by video and audio.

Although we have been back to the Galleries of Justice several times since, the amount of activity we had experienced the first time has not been experienced again. We have had a few interesting EVPs and a few sounds, but nothing like what we had the first time we investigated. On the most recent investigation (20 November 2014) we had some very interesting experiences to recount. During an incident in the dark isolated cell, Sharon heard three distinct knocks over our laughter in the cell. These were caught on audio also.

Also in the cells area, towards the second exit/entrance to the courtyard outside, Scott reported that the heavy wooden door moved two feet on its own accord as he entered the room. There was no breeze and the door could not budge without applying a good amount of force to it.

It was also held in place by a door wedge. However, the most satisfying experience that occurred on this investigation happened in the main Courtroom.

As we sat down at different places within the Courtroom, creaks and taps were heard in a pew in front of us as if somebody was moving about. Other bangs, knocks and raps were also heard around the Courtroom. I started asking out to any spirits of any condemned prisoners to make themselves known to us. We were not disappointed. What we did experience was alleged communication between us and a former prisoner called Arthur (whose name Glynn picked up on). We used two knocks for yes and one for no. We established that he was found guilty of a crime he did not commit and wished to move on. He was hanged for his crime.

The raps were intelligent in nature and they were not the expansion and contraction of wood in the Courtroom. They were definite intelligent responses which would only respond to me. I asked if Arthur wished to be moved on, he agreed and Glynn helped him move over to the other side. After this, the vigil became flat, no more communication was reported and no sounds. Beforehand in the Courtroom, we had a few issues with certain members of staff so we were discussing our issues in the Courtroom. It is quite possible that the anger etc. fuelled the atmosphere with negative emotional energy which helped manifest the phenomena reported (RSPK). Again, this was another interesting investigation at the Galleries.

CASE FILE: THE GOLDEN FLEECE, YORK

The City of York is said by some to be the most haunted city in England. Some would dispute this claim as others claim it is either London or Edinburgh in Scotland. Either way, York has an impressive reputation for all things ghostly. The Golden Fleece public house in York is allegedly the city's most haunted inn. There is a reference to it in the York Archives as far back as 1503, when it was owned by the Merchant Adventurers. It was their role as woollen traders that resulted in the name of the inn, which was licensed as far back as 1668. It became a popular coaching inn during the early part of the eighteenth century, when it was under the ownership of John Peckett, the Lord Mayor of York.

The Mayor's wife, Lady Alice Peckett, gave her name to the yard at the rear of the pub and the street that accesses the yard and is now also known by her name. Her ghost has been seen on a number of occasions, usually in the early hours of the morning. Another female ghost said to wander the inn's corridors, attired in Victorian dress, vanishes through the wall into the shop next door. A Canadian airman who came to a violent end by falling or committing suicide out of a bedroom window has been witnessed from time to time. A number of people claim that they have felt the ghost of a small boy pulling at their legs when they have been sat down. The ghost of One Eyed Jack, dressed in sixteenth- or seventeenth-century costume, has been seen as well as the ghost of another woman, dressed in black which has been witnessed in the St Catherine's Room.

On 4 April 2009 we arranged to conduct an investigation at the Golden Fleece Pub. We arrived at the inn around 6.00pm. The team to conduct the night's investigation was me, Glynn, Brent and two guests. We set up base in the Function Room and we started the evening's investigation by setting up trigger objects in the St Catherine's Room, the Shambles Room, Peckett's Room, and the Minister's Room. Each room contained a golf ball numbered one to four which was placed in each room in the middle of the bed with the exception of a crucifix, placed on paper that was also in Peckitt's Room. This room is allegedly the most active room in the inn.

We started out by conducting a glass divination and table tilting session in the Function Room. I also set up the Natural Tri-Field meter in the room. As I began asking out questions, the Tri-Field meter started fluctuating as if somebody was present in the room with us. We did get some movement from the glass in response to questions (although I am sceptical of glass divination as a paranormal means of communication with spirits), but no other anomalies were witnessed or heard except for the table vibrating in the table tilting session.

After this vigil, we took a short break and then split into two teams. The first team consisted of me, Brent and Glynn and the second team consisted of our two guests. We decided to conduct our vigil in St Catherine's Room and team two took Peckett's Room. Whilst in St Catherine's Room and whilst asking out questions for any spirits to make themselves known to us, we did hear a few creaks and knocks which did not seem like expansion or contraction of wood. They seemed to come from the area around the beds.

I decided to lie on one of the beds in the room and as I lay there I saw to my left a dark shadow which moved quickly down past my left side. A couple of minutes later Glynn reported a dark shadow cross the window in the room down the right hand side. Had we seen the lady dressed in black that has reportedly been seen in the room? I tried to replicate what I had seen but to no avail. In the room, the Natural Tri-Field meter was also spiking as if something was in the room with us. We decided to conduct a table tipping session in the room, and whilst asking out, we heard a number of rappings that seemed to respond to our questions by using the method of two knocks for yes and one for no. Brent at this point started to feel sick and extremely tired and I asked if it was a spirit affecting him this way to back away.

The rappings continued and we decided to use a mug instead of a glass to try and get a response from the table. The mug started to move in response to questions. The alleged spirit we were in communication with said it was Alice Peckett, and that it was her shadow we had seen in the room with us. She said she was grounded in the Golden Fleece and that she had committed suicide because her husband had been violent towards her. She did not want to move on to the other side because she was scared that she would meet her deceased husband on the spirit plane. She said she was also scared because suicide is believed by some to be a sin and she may go to hell. She said that she was using Brent's energy because he reminded her of her husband Jack. At this point, we decided to wrap up the vigil as Brent was feeling extremely unwell at this point.

After a break, we decided to conduct a vigil in Peckett's Room and team two conducted a vigil in the St Catherine's Room. Whilst in Peckett's Room and whilst we were asking out, we did hear some scratching and movement around the bed, but the strangest thing we heard was what sounded like someone making clicking, popping or clucking noises with their mouth. The only other time we heard this was in the Witches' Room at The Ancient Ram Inn in Gloucestershire. This happened on several occasions and was really strange. Nothing else was reported from later vigils in this room. At one point the bed began to vibrate slightly whilst we were sitting on the bed, and Glynn felt he had been poked in the side a few times during the course of the night.

In the Shambles Room and the Minister's Room nothing was heard or experienced during the night's investigation except the occasional creak on the floorboards. This could easily have been expansion and contraction of floorboards as the inn began to cool down in the course of the night. Team two reported nothing much at all except a few noises etc. After another break, we decided to conduct vigils in the bar area, but nothing anomalous was reported. We decided to conduct some more vigils in the St Catherine's Room, Peckett's Room and the Function Room. No more personal experiences were reported. As it was 3.30am, we decided to call it a night at this fascinating location.

CASE FILE: BODELWYDDAN CASTLE, DENBIGHSHIRE, WALES

On 14 November 2009 we arranged to conduct an investigation at the reputedly very haunted Bodelwyddan Castle in Denbighshire, Wales. In 1461, a large farmhouse was built on the site. In 1690, the house was built by Sir William Williams. Between the 1830s and 1850s, major changes happened during the time of Sir John Hay Williams, who transformed the house into a mock castle. In 1886, Sir William Grenville Williams modernized the house by introducing central heating and adding new features to the Entrance and Staircase Hall. In 1902, due to increasing debts, Sir William Grenville Williams moved to Pengwern. His family were the last Williams to live in the castle. From 1915 to 1918, the house and grounds were leased to the British Army for use as an Officers' Mess, recuperation hospital and training ground. In 1919, much of the land (1870 acres) and the contents of the house were sold.

From 1920, Bodelwyddan Castle was sold to the Lowther College and used as a boarding school for girls. In 1982, the house was purchased by Clwyd County Council and a process of refurbishment began. By 1988, the castle had been restored to its former Victorian country house glory and became a partner of the National Portrait Gallery. From 1994 until the present, part of the house was leased to Warner Breaks and became an adults only hotel complex. The Bodelwyddan Castle Trust was formed and given the responsibility of maintaining the remainder of the building and the collections within.

Bodelwyddan Castle is reputed to have many ghosts. An apparition of a Victorian lady has been seen at the far end of the Sculpture Gallery and has been likened to a faded photograph. In the cellar, which is the oldest part of the house, there is an alleged spirit of a man who likes to play tricks on investigators. In the Dining Room, a female spirit calling herself Emilia has reputedly made contact during vigils in this room. It is believed that it may be connected to her portrait which is hanging above the fireplace in the room. Members of staff and visitors to the castle have heard footsteps clearly in the Entrance Hall and the Watts Hall. Whining sounds and growling noises have also been heard. In the Gift Shop and in the First Floor Galleries a dark hooded figure has been seen. On the Jacobean Staircase, shadowy figures have been seen and staff and visitors have experienced the sensation of being followed and have felt their clothes being tugged.

In the Kitchen, a lady in a blue dress has been seen in the Kitchen Area of Caffi Castel. Poltergeist activity has also been witnessed. In the Library, footsteps have been heard and the scent of tobacco smoke is often smelt in this area. In the Changing Room exhibition area, World War One soldiers have been seen in uniform and have also been witnessed in the grounds of the castle. In the Victorian Toys and Games Room, which is allegedly the most active room in the house, people have reported feeling sick and also headaches. The ghosts of two children have been reported looking out of the window in this room, dripping wet and unhappy. Could these be the children who drowned in a nearby lake with their nanny whilst ice skating one winter?

On the night of 14 November 2009 we arrived at the castle where we were met by Janet, Lucy and Kay. After an initial talk we accompanied them on an informative tour of the castle, whilst I was taking notes on the castle's haunted hotspots. After a short drink we split into two teams to cover the castle. Team one consisted of me, Glynn, Matt Yarwood, Janet and two guests. Team two consisted of Sharon, Nicky, Richard, Lucy and Kay and another two guests.

My team took our first vigil in the cellar, whilst team two took the first floor rooms. We began by conducting a table tipping session in the cellar. We started asking out if there were any spirits present that could make themselves known to us. For a while nothing untoward occurred, but then the table started vibrating. As we continued asking out questions, we allegedly came into contact with a male spirit who murdered his wife or mistress and who was buried behind the wall in the bedroom upstairs. The table would shake, tilt and drag across the floor in response to questions. Whether this was due to a paranormal influence (RSPK) or the psychological phenomenon called the ideomotor effect is unclear. But the experiment was interesting nonetheless. We came off the table and separated into individuals in the large cellar and again, started asking out questions. During the vigils, various small knocks and bangs could be heard, but these were probably down to natural extraneous sound.

From here, we made our way to the upstairs floors where our next vigil was a bedroom which was the only one accessible as the other bedrooms were now made into private offices and were locked. We sat down on the floor and began asking out. During this vigil, nothing anomalous was reported. From here, we made our way up into the Toys and Games Room. This room was allegedly the most paranormally active building in the house. I started asking out, but nothing occurred at the beginning.

Glynn picked up the name Daniel, psychically, and we asked out if there was a Daniel present with us. As I asked out, rapping sounds were being heard, twice for yes and once for no. from the questioning we supposedly established that this was the boy that had drowned in the lake with his sister and nanny. I asked out how old was he? There were eight distinct knocks in succession. The raps for yes and no were recorded both on audio and video. It seemed as if the raps were coming from a partition board in the corner of the room near Glynn. We could see Glynn and knew it was him.

During the vigil, footfalls were heard coming from the floor as if somebody unseen was moving about. During this questioning period where we were hearing raps in response to questions, the alleged entity seemed to start rapping from the floor using the floorboards to communicate with us. One of the guests asked out if there was a Michael also present with us (the guest was supposedly a sensitive also) and we heard taps coming from the other side of the room in response. We thought that this might be his brother that drowned along with Daniel in the lake, but this information was wrong as he did not have a brother as far as we know, but just had a sister that drowned alongside him in the lake. Could the historical information have been wrong? Could it have been a brother and not a sister that had drowned? Whether this was some other alleged spirit trying to communicate with us is unclear.

From this vigil, we decided to meet up with the others and take a break. Sharon from team two reported hearing a man's laugh and also breathing sounds next to her ear. In the Library, Sharon reported seeing someone move in the shadows and took a photograph. When looking back at the photograph, there was a large misty-looking light anomaly where Sharon had seen the shadow move. The photo seems to back up her testimony and is not a dust particle, lint, or a bug which are usually causes of photographic light anomalies. Team two also reported hearing growling sounds coming from outside the Toys and Games Room.

Whilst we were having another break, Glynn had to nip out to the toilet. Glynn reported hearing a man's moan at the top of the cellar, and when I went to the toilet I heard what sounded like something had moved or had fallen to the floor, but this could have been one of the other investigators moving around in the café. When I mentioned the incident to them, they reported that nothing had fallen.

After the break we started conducting vigils downstairs. We started off in the Sculpture Gallery, then moved through to the Ladies room, the Dining room, the Library, the Changing Exhibition area and also the Billiard Room. In all of these vigils, nothing anomalous was observed. We next moved into the Gift Shop area near to the main entrance and asked out if any spirits could shake the large wooden doors. Nothing happened, but as we turned to leave, the double wooden doors shook as if somebody was shaking them from the outside. Janet immediately went to look out of the window to see if any security was checking the doors to see if they were locked, but nobody was there.

From here both teams got together to conduct a table tipping experiment at the bottom of the main staircase. Nothing happened at first, but then whilst asking out, the table started to vibrate, then started tilting towards me, for yes and no questions. The table also dragged along the floor when asked to do so. The alleged entity we were in communication with was an alleged murderer who caused suffering to people whether by rape or molestation. The spirit also said it was scared to move on because it was afraid of going to hell, so remained grounded instead. We conducted one more vigil in the Victorian Toys and Games room, but on this occasion nothing untoward occurred. This brought a fascinating investigation to an end.

CASE FILE: MICHELHAM PRIORY, SUSSEX

Set on a medieval moated island and dating back to 1229, Michelham Priory is beautiful and impressive. No one who approaches it through the fourteenth century gatehouse can fail to be moved by the sight that greets them. The priory was owned by the Augustinians until the Dissolution of the Monasteries (1536-1540), after which it passed through several different ownerships until being purchased by Thomas Sackville in 1599. The Sackvilles owned the freehold for the next 300 years and let it to a succession of tenant farmers who proceeded to surround the main house with barn and farm buildings.

In 1896 James Eglington Gwynne brought the priory and set about restoring the medieval buildings. His progress generated a great deal of animosity from the then tenants who, stung by their evictions, threatened to murder the new owners. However, the matter was soon smoothed over and life at the priory remained settled for the next fifty or so years. In 1959, it was given to the Sussex Archaeological Trust and it is they who run it as a lovely tourist attraction.

Over the years the priory has acquired the reputation of being one of the South East's most active haunted locations. The building is said to house a plethora of ghosts and spirits. Strange noises and sounds have been heard echoing throughout the house in the dead of night. Apparitions have been known to manifest in front of startled witnesses and just as quickly vanish. A ghostly white horse has been seen to pass through the doors of the gatehouse and a spectral grey lady has also been seen to pass through the gatehouse on occasions. A man in a black cloak has been seen to slowly descend the stairs from the ceiling and walk diagonally across the air to the floor. A second apparition, that of a woman dressed in a Tudor gown has also been seen to descend from the ceiling and follow the exact route as the ghost of the man in a black cloak.

Other ghosts that are said to haunt the old priory are a woman who is allegedly looking for her child who drowned in the moat and has been seen to wander the upper floor of the gatehouse and from which strange noises are heard when it is known to be empty. There is also the ghost of a little boy who has been seen in the Kitchen area. There are reports of strange smells such as burning hair and a feeling of uneasiness that tends to be felt in certain areas of the building, as well as phantom music which has also occasionally been heard.

On the 3 July 2010, The Office of Parapsychological Studies arranged for an investigation of Michelham Priory. The team for the night consisted of me, Sharon, Glynn, Charlotte and several guests. After a quick tour of the priory, the group split into two teams. Team one consisted of me, Sharon, Charlotte and two guests, and team two consisted of Glynn and four guests. My team decided to conduct the vigils in the upstairs rooms and the second team downstairs. Beforehand I had set up two trigger object experiments. One was in the Friar's Chamber Room and was a crucifix experiment and the other, downstairs in the Music Room, was a coin experiment. My team took with us EMF meters, a Natural Tri-Field meter, digital voice recorder, digital cameras and an Ultrasonic detector.

We started our investigation first in the Evacuees' Room. During the vigil, we all heard loud clear whistling as if someone was going around doing their daily work. Again, later on during the vigil, we heard the same whistling. We thought nothing of this at the time but Glynn later confirmed there was nobody in the owner's flat above us and nobody else was in the priory at the time of the whistling apart from the second team who said they did not hear the whistle at all during that time.

From here, we conducted our next vigils in the Nursery and the Music Room. Whilst asking out questions to the environment, loud spiking noises from the Natural Tri-Field meter began to register. Again these were loud, clear and at times seemed to respond to questions intelligently as if there was a disturbance in the electromagnetic field. Apart from this unusual occurrence, no other personal experiences were reported. We decided to take a break to see if team two had reported anything unusual. Team two said that they heard a number of audible phenomena such as a woman's whimper and a man's groan. After the break, we decided to conduct our next vigils downstairs whilst the second team took the upstairs rooms.

We started in the Kitchen area and started asking out. Loud spikes on the Natural Tri-Field meter again were heard which seemed to respond to questions. From here, we conducted our next vigil in the Music room which may have proved interesting because, as I was trying to goad alleged spirits into making themselves known, team two reported that they were table tipping at the time and the table was dragging itself along the floor, which we could hear clearly from downstairs. As I intentionally got angry with the atmosphere, so did the table become more intense in its movements. The Natural Tri-Field meter also began to spike more intently the angrier I was getting.

Whilst upstairs during our vigils, my group tried a table tipping session but without success. During this vigil, we kept hearing footfalls from the floor above us as if somebody was walking around. I used the walkie talkie to speak to Glynn who said that they all had been staying pretty much still apart from one of their team which decided to wander off on his own accord. So this footfall we heard is more than likely down to the team member that wandered off.

I and one of the guests decided to conduct a vigil at the bottom of the stairs area where the apparition of a lady has been seen to descend the stairs, but nothing abnormal occurred. From here my team decided to conduct a vigil in the Gate House, so we made our way upstairs. As we sat down and started asking out questions to any spirits present, we began to hear faint intelligent taps in response to questions and the sound of someone moving about near the corner of the room near the window. The shuffling sounds seemed to respond to questions regarding the woman whose child drowned in the moat outside. As we asked out 'my lady' the shuffling sounds became slightly louder as if someone was walking about, but we could not see anything that could account for the noise.

During the vigil, team two came into the Gatehouse while I headed back over to the priory to go to the toilet and sweep the place by myself whilst everyone was outside. As I tried to get back into the priory, I found that the main door had been bolted from the inside, so I could not get back inside. I went around to the other side of the priory and managed to get in. Later I found out that team two had not bolted the door either, and they had to find their way through the same door I had come through. So, who bolted the door? None of the team had and we are quite sure that Matt, who let us into the place had not bolted it as we still had our equipment inside. The owners also were not home at the time. A mystery indeed.

Whilst everyone was in the Gatehouse, I conducted a sweep of the priory with the digital voice recorder. It was quiet throughout apart from an incident in the Friar's Chamber, when I heard a man's voice speaking to me which sounded fairly loud, but could not work out what it said. A couple of seconds later, Sharon and the rest of the team had come back. After one more vigil we decided to call it a night on the investigation. We checked on the trigger objects and nothing seemed to have moved during the course of the night. Whilst tidying up, and whilst in the room near the main staircase, the biggest mystery of the night occurred. As I, Sharon, Glynn and two guests were tidying up after ourselves, the strong smell of lavender hit us. The smell had been prevalent in this room during the course of the night and we could not find the cause of it. Just as we were about to leave the room, we heard the creak of a door opening. One of our team had seen the door of a five hundred year-old dresser open of its own accord.

I looked in the dresser and found the cause of the smell, a basket of dry lavender was in the dresser. I put my hand in the basket and there it was, mystery solved! Or was it? Another mystery presented itself: who opened the cupboard door to reveal the basket of lavender? I checked the drawers and the cupboard and found that the left hand door which had opened was wedged together with a piece of tissue paper to stop it from opening and the right hand door was wedged together with a piece of blue tack.

So I closed the door to try and make it open by itself by applying force and vibration by walking past it and sure enough it opened, but the only problem with this hypothesis was I had to do some jumping around in front of it to make it open, so I and a guest tried to cause it to open by both walking in front of it (heavily), but it did not open on this occasion. Although we could find an explanation for the opening of the dresser, by vibrations over a given time period causing the door to open, it would have needed a good deal of vibrational force to open it and people were going past the dresser all night without it opening. The uncanny thing about this was that I was looking for a natural explanation for the lavender smell, and low and behold! The door opened revealing the lavender basket! If it was synchronicity or coincidence, it was one of the best I have seen! Very strange indeed. This brought an end to a most excellent investigation at Michelham Priory.

On the 14 July 2012, we conducted a second investigation at the priory. Not much in the way of paranormal occurrences was reported, apart from an incident that happened to me in the room downstairs next to the Dining Room. I was asking out for physical phenomena to occur, and as I was stretched out on the floor, I heard a shuffling sound on the carpet and realized my leg was being pulled by something invisible, which startled me. I later found out that my experience of my leg being pulled was also experienced by Jen Yarwood in the Dining Room. She reported that her trouser leg had also been pulled whilst she had sat on the window ledge.

Lisa Welch also reported that she had felt that her arm had been tapped in the room where I had my experience.

During the course of the night, in many rooms of the house, anomalous readings on the Natural Tri-Field meter were heard and, in the Gatehouse, footfalls were heard by everyone between the sound of heavy rain outside, as if somebody was moving about in the corner of the top floor. Again, anomalous readings were also recorded coming from the Natural Tri-Field meter in the Gatehouse. Sharon's team also reported moans and groaning sounds where some have been captured using digital voice recorders. Other odd noises like bangs and raps were also heard in the Gatehouse, but this could have been expansion and contraction of wood whilst the night cooled in conjunction with the rain outside. An interesting investigation though.

CASE FILE: CHILLINGHAM CASTLE, NORTHUMBRIA

Chillingham Castle is a dark and foreboding place of twisting stone stairways, echoing corridors, creepy dank and dark dungeons and creaking doors. Its inner courtyard is one of the most atmospheric in England. Its balustrades, pillars, balconies and romantic galleries could have come straight from the pages of Arthurian legend; and it would hardly come as a surprise if you encountered an apparition burnished in armour, clanking his way up the sweeping stone staircase that delivers the spellbound visitor into the castle's sprawling interior.

Chillingham Castle began life as a twelfth century stronghold. In 1246, the Grey family stormed the castle and evicted the then current owners. Their descendants have remained in possession of the castle ever since. Henry III stayed here in 1255, as did Edward I in 1298, en route to vanquish William Wallace who was making a nuisance of himself in Scotland. Later, Sir Thomas Grey was given permission to fortify the family stronghold and, in 1344, Chillingham became a castle. Embellished and adorned by successive generations, the last of the descendants, by then the Tankervilles, moved out in 1933 and the proud bastion was allowed to fall into ruin.

An aura of melancholic decay had soon descended on its once mighty walls, as damp and rot chewed their way through the building. Then, in 1983, Sir Humphrey Wakefield, whose wife is a member of the Grey family, was allowed to take over the decaying ruin and began a restoration that is still ongoing (unfortunately some so called paranormal investigation groups decide to try and stop that by stealing and vandalising medieval artifacts!) the castle was thus awakened from its long slumber.

Several ghosts are known to wander this magnificent house. The most famous is that of the so-called radiant boy. He is a childish wraith that is seen in the castles Pink Room and whose heart rending cries of either pain or fear echo through the old corridors upon the stroke of midnight. In the past, the cries always seemed to emanate from a spot near where the passage is cut through the ten feet thick wall into the adjoining tower. As they faded away, a bright halo of light would appear and a figure of a young boy, dressed in blue, would approach those sleeping in the room. Later the bones of a child, surrounded by decaying fragments of blue cloth were found behind the wall. They were given a Christian burial and thereafter the blue boy was seen no more. Until that is, Sir Humphrey began letting the room. Some guests complain of a blue flash that shoots out of the wall in the dead of night.

Another unquiet soul said to stalk the castle is the ghost of Lady Berkeley, wife of Lord Grey, whose husband ran off with her own sister, Lady Henrietta. Lady Berkeley was left abandoned at the castle with only her baby daughter for company. The rustle of her dress is sometimes heard as her invisible revenant sweeps across the rambling corridors of the medieval castle, searching for her cheating husband, whilst leaving a cold chill in her and her witnesses' wake. Other types of phenomena that have been reported from the castle are light anomalies, cold spots, objects moving about of their own accord as well as unexplained sounds and olfactory phenomena (smells).

On Saturday 23 April 2011 The Office of Parapsychological Studies finally managed to conduct an investigation at this most haunted of castles. The team for the night consisted of me, Sharon, Glynn, Charlotte, Chris Berry and four guests. We were met by Graham who ran us through the health and safety rules and then showed us the house areas we were allowed to explore. After the walk round we split into three groups of three each. Team one consisted of me, Chris and a guest, team two, of Sharon, Charlotte and Glynn and team three, the remaining guests.

After setting up trigger object experiments, my team decided to conduct our first vigils in the Chapel and the Great Hall. Although my team did not experience any anomalous phenomena in the Chapel, Sharon and Charlotte did report being tugged on their clothes and pamphlets moving whilst they were conducting their vigil. Whilst we were in the Great Hall and asking out if there were any intelligent spirits that could make themselves possibly known, we started hearing tapping sounds coming from the far end of the hall. So, we sat around an area where it seemed to emanate from. We could hear the tapping sound coming from a stool which sat empty in front of us. The tapping sounds were quite loud and then seemed to move to the fireplace, then to a corner of the hall, then back again to the stool. This cycle was repeated fairly regularly, and it seemed as if where we sat it would move to another place, then another place. We could not seem to find a rational explanation for this phenomenon and felt that it was having a game with us. We also strongly felt that we were being watched by something we could not see.

Whilst Sharon's team was in the Edward I Room, Sharon, Glynn and Charlotte all reported seeing light anomalies which seemed to move around the balcony in the room fairly rapidly. Light anomalies were also reported by my team and also the guests' team later on during the investigation, which they kept to themselves so they could be corroborated later with the rest of the teams. Whilst my team were in the Edward I Room, I, Chris and our guest also reported seeing the strange lights that seemed to move across the balcony and ceiling. The lights looked dull and hazy white when they materialized and moved. At one point a large patch of light materialized in a corner of the upper balcony with the inner wall with which it could be seen through. It almost looked like the shape of a person then disappeared.

Because the rest of the teams also reported the same light phenomenon, we decided to try and replicate what we had seen. So I and our guest went back up to the Edward I Room, whilst I sent Chris outside with a strong torch to see whether, if anybody outside of the room down below shone a torch about which reflected light through the upper windows, this created the same appearance as the lights we had seen. It did not. We tried all four windows from many different angles of the castle and could find no indication that this was the source of the said phenomenon. Car headlights were also ruled out.

It later transpired after talking to our host Graham what we had experienced. As it turned out, many other people had also reported the light anomalies. He said it would almost be impossible for it to be one of the team, as the side of the castle which the windows to the Edward I Room were facing were Sir Humphrey's personal land and were his personal gardens, so no access for us was possible. The only possible explanation were that it was either Sir Humphrey, or one of his family moving about in the garden with torches to check on security. This did seem improbable especially at the late times of the vigils in question.

Later on during the investigation, we decided to conduct another vigil in the Great Hall, but this time with Sharon and Charlotte also. Again, whilst we were asking out, we heard yet again, the strange tapping sounds coming from the fireplace, but this time they were fainter but proved interesting nonetheless. Glynn came up with some brilliant information psychically which was not documented publicly, but which was also corroborated later on. Other experiences that were reported from the vigils were banging sounds and what Sharon reported as 'walking through a vortex of a pleasant smell' which could not be accounted for.

CASE FILE: WOODCHESTER MANSION, GLOUCESTERSHIRE

Woodchester Mansion in Stroud, Gloucestershire was originally the estate of the Ducie family. Legend holds that when the second Earl of Ducie threw a lavish dinner to celebrate his succession to the earldom in 1840, he was somewhat taken aback when his father's ghost interrupted the festivities by occupying the seat that he was attending to sit in at the head of the table. Indeed, it gave him such a fright that he left the place never to return.

In 1845 the northern part of the estate was purchased by William Leigh, an immensely wealthy gentleman and recent convert to Catholicism. Leigh set about planning a house that would stand as a lasting testimony to his Catholic leanings and approached Augustus Welby Pugin, the master of gothic revival, whose designs included the Houses of Parliament. The two men however, did not see eye to eye, especially where money was concerned, and by the 1850s the project was given to a much younger local architect, Benjamin Bucknall.

Bucknall set about designing a truly grandiose house, and for sixteen years craftsman and builders laboured on its construction. Then suddenly in 1868, for reasons which have never been explained, the workers downed theirs tools and left the site. Rumours persist that the workers left because of a murder on the site. It has also been suggested that paranormal activity may have been responsible. The likeliest explanation however, is that the project proved too costly and the money ran out, even for William Leigh's deep pockets, and was simply abandoned.

Whatever the explanation, the result today is that on entering the mansion, you step back into a time warp and onto a mid-nineteenth century building site. Ladders remain propped up where they were left against exposed walls, fireplaces hang suspended in mid-air, doors lead to nowhere, and upstairs corridors end at precarious drops. The unfinished construction emphasizes the sheer magnitude of what this remarkable house would have looked like if completed.

Following William Leigh's death in 1873 his son, also William, asked Bucknall to supply him with two quotes, one for completion, and the other for demolition. When both proved expensive, the mansion was simply abandoned, although there was a sudden flurry of activity in 1894 when the drawing room was hurriedly completed for a visit by Cardinal Vaughan, Roman Catholic Archbishop of Westminster. This, however, was the only room ever to be finished and thereafter the house was neglected.

The ghosts of the mansion are somewhat varied. Without doubt one of the most curious parts of the house is the chapel. Some people claim to have smelt freshly extinguished candles there, although no candles have been burning prior to the manifestation of the mysterious olfactory phenomenon. Others have sighted the apparition of a short man standing in one of the chapel doorways. He does nothing except gaze up at the ornate windows and gives the impression that he is somewhat concerned about them. It has been suggested that he may be the ghost of a stonemason and that he is anxious about the damage to the stonework caused by water penetration. The sound of masonry falling has also been heard in the chapel area.

The spectral figures of American and Canadian soldiers, who were both stationed here during the Second World War, have also been seen. The figure of a Roman centurion has likewise been seen at various points around the grounds of the mansion as well as a strange dwarf-like figure that was spotted outside the mansion. Unexplained light anomalies, noises and other shadowy forms have also been seen inside the building. In March 2011 my organization conducted an investigation at Woodchester Mansion, but we found little evidence on this occasion to suggest the house was haunted. A few incidents occurred such as noises and some apparent breaths but these could have been down to natural environmental causes. I did hear a growling sound which Sharon had also heard earlier in the investigation.

One incident did stand out however and that was when people have been reported to have been scratched in the kitchen and scullery area. Whilst in the car, Sharon noticed that there was a two-inch scratch on my neck which faded away completely the next day. It could possibly have been done by me, but if I did it, I did not notice as I never felt a thing; the scratch was not even very painful.

THREE

CASE FILES OF CLASSIC GHOSTS, HAUNTINGS AND POLTERGEISTS

CASE FILE: BORLEY RECTORY, ESSEX AND SUFFOLK BORDER

Borley Rectory has become notorious for the title of 'Britain's most haunted house', if not the world's most haunted. The rectory itself was built in 1863 and scores of people, even to this day have said they have seen, heard and felt things from this active area. The famous Borley nun has been seen by dozens of people including three former rectors of the parish, doctors, visiting clergymen and occupants of the cottage (all that remains of the original rectory after it was destroyed by fire in 1939), past and present. The main investigator of this most famous case was none other than early psychical researcher, Harry Price. He wrote two books on this case: *The Most Haunted House in England* (1940), and *The End of Borley Rectory* (1946).

Borley Rectory was known as an ugly and gaunt red brick building in an isolated spot that could only be approached by a winding, lonely, country lane. Opposite the old rectory site is St Mary's Church which also has a history of haunted happenings which we will explore later on in this chapter. The Rev. H. D. E. Bull built the rectory and added to it over time for his ever increasing family. He died in 1892 in the haunted Blue Room. His son, the Rev. Harry Bull also died in the same room in 1927. The Rev. Guy Eric Smith occupied the rectory next from 1928 to 1930, and then the Rev. Lionel Foyster occupied it from 1930 to 1935. The next occupant, the Rev. Alfred C. Henning, never actually lived in the rectory but owned it from 1936 till his death in 1955.

Legend has it that a monastery once occupied the site and that a monk tried to elope with a nun from the local nunnery and who was hanged for his misdemeanour and the nun bricked up alive in the rectory. The phantom nun has been said to walk every 28 July but has been seen many times outside of that date. There was a window bricked up here that was said to have stopped the mournful, pale looking apparition of the nun looking in at the family as they were having dinner.

Ethel Bull, the last to survive of several children of Rev. H. D. E. Bull told legendary ghost hunter Peter Underwood of a remarkable experience she had whilst with three of her sisters on the afternoon of 28 July 1900. Ethel, Freda and Mabel were returning from a garden party in the late afternoon and as they reached the gate of the old rectory they all saw an apparition of a nun gliding along a path known as 'the Nun's walk'. They could not discern any facial features on the phantom, but the nun appeared solid and no sound was heard. Ethel thought that the nun was playing with its beads. Ethel and Mabel stood by the gate observing the apparition whilst Freda ran into the house to fetch their fourth sister, Elsie, who also saw the figure, and thought nothing strange about it. So, she began to approach the nun. As she approached closer the apparition vanished. Mr. P. Shaw Jeffrey, a former headmaster of Colchester Grammar School told Underwood that he saw the ghostly nun several times in either 1885 0r 1886. Harry Bull himself also reported that he had seen the nun.

The ghostly ringing of bells was heard by Rev, Harry Bull and P. Shaw Jeffrey and no explanation could be found that could account for the sounds. Harry Bull also reported seeing a phantom coach and horses that is said to draw up to the house, enter the house and disappear up the staircase and vanish. Before Harry Bull's death he said he would make mothballs fly about the old rectory to prove that the afterlife exists. When he did pass, mothballs did indeed fly around the rectory.

The next occupants of Borley were Eric Smith and his wife, and it was not long before they started to report strange and inexplicable phenomena. Mrs Smith saw what she described as a ghostly horse drawn coach in the drive with its lights blazing. Other strange phenomena occurred whilst they were in incumbency. Footfalls were heard, rooms in the rectory lit up mysteriously, bells rang when no human hands were present and Eric Smith reported hearing a voice say 'Don't Carlos. Don't!' whilst he was near an archway near the chapel. Smith went to the papers and they approached famous psychical researcher Harry Price, who spent twenty years of his life researching the haunting of Borley Rectory.

October 1930 brought the rectory's next tenants, the Rev. L. A. Foyster and his much younger wife, Marianne. Foyster was also a relative of the Bulls. During their incumbency, the paranormal activity reached its peak: written and scribbled messages appeared on walls and pieces of paper, asking for light, mass and prayers. Bottles apported and asported (materialized and de-materialized) and were also seen to fly about the building. Articles and objects also appeared and disappeared; moans, groans, bangings, rappings, ringing of bells and other phenomena were also reported. Apparitional figures were also seen. Rev. Foyster kept a diary of the events that occurred. Dom Richard approached Peter Underwood in 1956 and told him that he had personally witnessed moving objects without physical contact, penciled wall writing, spontaneous outbreaks of fire, doors unlocking and re-locking and bell ringing.

Captain V. M. Deane told Peter Underwood at a ghost club meeting in 1948 that he himself witnessed bottles and stones that fell amongst witnesses. They also handled the objects themselves afterwards. Mr. Guy L'Estrange said that he saw bottles being thrown and broken. He also stated that one almost hit his ear by an inch and that he also heard the violent bell ringing of the thirty bells in the hall.

Rev. Foyster died in 1945, and his younger wife emigrated to Canada. When the Foysters left Borley Rectory, Harry Price rented the property for a year for a proper scientific investigation of the haunting. He arranged to be joined by a host of investigators of high integrity on his haunted quest at the rectory. The principal investigator was Sidney Glanville who was a retired consulting engineer and became deeply interested in the case. He compiled a dossier of the haunting entitled; 'The Locked Book of Private Information'. Price acquired it and had it bound and fitted with a lock. Glanville became convinced that the haunting of Borley Rectory was a genuine affair based on his own experiences and other eye witnesses, all of which is collected in the dossier.

Many other people apart from the tenants and investigators experienced paranormal occurrences in and around Borley Rectory. The Rectory Cottage and its tenants, the Coopers (the cottage which is also the only building left standing after the fire, which is also reputedly haunted), had their own experiences to relate. They reported that they would hear a padding sound night after night and would tell of seeing a dark shape in their bedroom and a pungent smell that accompanied it. They also witnessed the phantom coach and horses as well as a hooded figure in the courtyard.

Other tenants such as the Arbons, the Turners, the Bacons, and the Williams who occupied the cottage since all reported strange phenomena occurring. In 1926, a carpenter saw the sad faced figure of the nun waiting at the gate of the rectory on four successive occasions in the morning whilst on his way to work. On the last occasion, it occurred to him that she might want help, but as he approached her, she vanished and he never saw the ghost again. A local doctor also had a similar experience when he saw the phantom nun.

The rectory was sold to Captain Gregson in December 1938, and in 1939 an oil lamp was accidently knocked over and the place was gutted by fire. During the fire witnesses reported seeing mysterious figures walking through the flames. Months after the fire the Cambridge Commission conducted extensive investigations at the ruined site until 1944. They reported unusual temperature variations, a luminous patch, footfalls, bangs and knocks (eighteen were heard in a row on one occasion); stone throwing, olfactory phenomena and anomalous lights were also witnessed.

During the Christmas holiday season of 1939, the Rev. Canon W. J. Phythian Adams, D.D, and Canon of Carlisle read Harry Price's classic book *The Most Haunted House in England* and came up with the theory that a young female French Roman Catholic was brought over to this country in the seventeenth or eighteenth century, in which she was betrayed and murdered and her remains buried in the cellar of the old rectory. Phythian Adams suggested that Price start digging, which he did, and they came across a jaw bone which they and medical experts believed to be that of a young woman. The examination of the jaw bone showed a deep seated abscess which would have caused much pain to the owner of the jaw bone. If this is indeed the jaw bone of the legendary nun, then it is no wonder that people who witnessed her said that she looked pale, sad and forlorn! The remains were buried in Liston Churchyard.

Since the rectory burnt down, the ghostly nun has been seen many times on or near the rectory site and across the road in St Mary's churchyard. Terence Bacon, who occupied the cottage, said that he saw the phantom nun on no less than three times and a Mr Williams once. As stated St Mary's church and churchyard across from the rectory cottage is haunted. There are many reports of footfalls from an invisible presence in and around the church. One Ghost Club investigator, one September night with the full moon ablaze, heard heavy footsteps hurrying towards the church. He said they sounded like a woman's tread, and when he got up to meet whoever was approaching, was astonished that they ceased immediately and no one appeared. Ghostly organ music has been heard on occasion coming from the locked and empty church. The music was heard in 1970 by a group of scientists conducting investigations at the church.

In 1949 the Rev. Stanley Kipling visited Borley to read an obituary for a funeral for a friend, and as he stood at the west door of the church, he saw the unmistakable figure of a veiled girl in the churchyard, presumably the nun. As he watched she walked behind some bushes and then vanished. He disclosed that she appeared to be frail, aged between eighteen and twenty three, and he distinctly saw a nun's hood on her head from which some thick veiling hung down. Some months later two investigators reported seeing a ghostly form in black walk silently towards the priest's door at the church and then disappear.

A Mr Cole once saw the ghostly nun in Borley churchyard in 1951. The nun seemed rather sad and was sheltering under a tree. He said she looked quite normal and she wore a black hood, a white collar, a golden coloured bodice and a black skirt which stood open about eight inches down the front showing a blue underdress. Mr. Cole started to approach her and as he did she disappeared.

In 1956, Peter Rowe, a retired Bank of England official and member of The Ghost Club and The Society for Psychical Research, went to Borley with a friend whom he was telling stories of the phantom nun. Peter stopped the car by the gate to the rectory garden and his friend turned towards Rowe as he listened to the story of the nun. His friend suddenly saw a nun-like apparition run past the gate with short quick steps towards the end of the old rectory garden. He got out of the car quickly to investigate, but found nobody there.

Unusual olfactory odours have been experienced at the now long gone rectory and also when it was standing. The pleasant smells of violets and incense have been experienced as well as the putrid smells of rotting corpses. They seem to be localized and stationary even when the weather is bad. Other anomalous phenomena reported are raps and knocks, the panting of a dog, the sound of heavy furniture being moved, smashing crockery, voices of a jovial nature and strange lights. This case is probably the most famous case in the world which continues to fascinate, astonish and fire the imagination of what a true haunted house should be.

CASE FILE: THE ENFIELD POLTERGEIST

At about 9.30pm on 31 August 1977, a poltergeist made itself known to the Hodgeson family who lived in a semidetached council house in the suburb of Enfield in North London. As Mrs Hodgeson (a divorced woman in her 40s) was putting her four children to bed in one of three upstairs bedrooms, Janet (then aged eleven) and one of her brothers (ten) said they could hear a shuffling sound. As Mrs Hodgeson entered the bedroom, they were all astonished to see a large chest of drawers move around 18 inches across the floor. She moved it back into place, only for it to move again and then refused to be budged when tried to be moved back into its normal place. They then heard four loud knocks that came from wall.

Mrs Hodgeson was terrified. She called on her neighbours, Vic and Peggy Nottingham. As they began a search of their friends' house, knocking sounds began to come from a wall beside them as they were making their way down the Hodgeson's staircase. They searched inside the house and out, but nobody was in sight. The Hodgesons decided to call the police at around 11.00pm. Two officers arrived and they themselves witnessed a chair slide across the living room floor. WPC Carolyn Heeps signed a written statement of what she witnessed.

The next day, marbles and toy bricks began to fly around the house at great speed. When the objects were picked up, they were found to be unusually warm and the bombardment of flying objects went on for around three days. On 4 September they were at their wits end and decided they wanted expert help. They called The Daily Mirror newspaper in the hope that they might put them in touch with someone who could come to their aid.

Reporters Douglas Bence and newspaper photographer Graham Morris spent the evening with the Hodgeson's. Nothing occurred, but just after they left at around 2.30pm on the Monday morning, as they were driving off, Peggy Nottingham's father called them back to say that toy bricks began to be thrown about again. As Morris stood in the living room doorway, with everyone visible in his wide angle lens on his camera, a toy brick flew at him and hit him hard on the forehead as he pressed the shutter. It left a large bruise on his forehead.

Senior reporter George Fallows, who was impressed, suggested to the Hodgesons calling in the Society for Psychical Research. Enter Maurice Grosse, an inventor and businessman who had lost his daughter a year before in a motorcycle accident, who coincidentally was named Janet. On his first visit, Grosse did not witness anything paranormal, but on 8 September between 10.00 and 11.00pm, he witnessed a marble that flew through the air towards him. Chimes on the living room wall began to sway to and fro and he witnessed a door open and close on three or four occasions. He witnessed a shirt fly off a pile of clothing on the kitchen table and fall to the floor (this was also witnessed by Guy Lyon Playfair on another occasion) and finally a sudden cold breeze that moved up from his feet to his head.

On 10 September, the Enfield poltergeist made front-page headlines in The Daily Mirror: 'The House of Strange happenings'. Author Guy Lyon Playfair telephoned Maurice Grosse and asked if he needed help on the case, which was readily accepted. On 11 September, on Playfair's first visit, he was standing with Graham Morris outside Janet's bedroom. As they were looking through an open door, a marble hit the linoleum floor right in front of Playfair's feet. The strange thing was that the marble did not roll or bounce but came to a sudden halt.

The knocking and rapping on walls became a nightly occurrence and seemed intelligent in nature. It would rap two knocks for yes and once for no to simple questions. One evening as they were having a lengthy conversation with the alleged entity, Grosse asked how many years had the entity lived in the house. Immediately there were fifty three raps and were recorded on audio. The poltergeist began to beat out nonsensical rhythms and Grosse asked; 'Are you having a game with me?' Two seconds later, a cardboard box full of soft toys and cushions lifted off the corner of the bedroom and flew over the bed and hit Maurice on the forehead. It had travelled around eight feet.

On another occasion, Guy Playfair watched Janet get up from an armchair and began to walk towards him, when he saw the armchair slide along the floor and crash over backwards. Other strange occurrences in the house began to make themselves apparent, especially to equipment. Photographer Graham Morris found on three separate occasions that his camera flash, although should be fully charged, was drained of battery power. A Newvicon infrared sensitive television camera was brought in by investigators only to find that lights on the machine would all come on at once and the tape inside became so jammed that the entire machine had to be dismantled to free it. Cassette tapes were found broken or mysteriously wiped, a metal part in one of the recorders was found to have bent by itself and on one occasion the tape recorder itself disappeared completely only to appear about an hour later underneath a dressing table which had fallen forwards onto Janet's bed, nearly crushing her.

Janet spent six weeks in Maudsey Hospital in South London, where she underwent extensive tests for signs of physical and mental abnormalities; none were found. Physicist David Robertson from Birkbeck College at the University of London was sent to assist. A few days after his arrival, a strange series of events took place. A bizarre male voice which sounded like a gruff old man seemed to start manifesting from Janet. The voice was named Bill became the prominent identity of the poltergeist. During one questioning period the voice said that he went blind and died of a brain haemorrhage in a chair downstairs. This and other voices were captured on audio.

David Robertson wasted no time in conducting some practical experimentation. He was hoping to observe Janet levitating. He asked Janet if she could bounce up and down on her bed and attempt to take off; as he did so, he was ordered to get out of the room by the voice. Janet called out to Robertson that she was being levitated, but he found that the door would not open as a bed had been pushed against it. Janet's sister, Rose became scared and went to fetch her neighbour, Peggy Nottingham. Janet tried another levitation, with the door closed and claimed that she not only had just risen into the air, but had passed through her wall and through into Peggy Nottingham's room next to it.

When Peggy went into her house she found a book of Janet's entitled *Fun and Games for Children*, which had not been there on her bedroom floor before. David Robertson asked if she could make a large and heavy plastic covered sofa cushion disappear to obtain evidence of teleportation of matter through matter. A tradesman walking past the Hodgeson house at the time suddenly witnessed a red cushion appear on the roof of their house. He also witnessed Janet through the window 'floating horizontally across the room' with books, dolls and cushions flying about as if they were all attached to an elastic cord. Another witness, Mrs Hazel Short also witnessed Janet floating horizontally in the air and calculated she must have been around twenty-eight inches above her bed.

Graham Morris also succeeded in capturing alleged poltergeist phenomena on camera, some in a sequence of photos. One shows two pillows, one of which is allegedly floating in mid air and the other of which is on the floor, but apparently in motion. Another, shows Jane's bedclothes seemingly being pulled off her whilst the curtain next to her bed is twisting in a tight spiral and seems to be blowing into the room by a breeze, although the window behind it is closed. The curtain twisting was observed several times by Janet who also claimed that it had wrapped around her neck, trying to strangle her.

Whilst trying to gather evidence for the scientific community, Grosse managed to record the entity voice on a laryngograph, an instrument that registered patterns made by radio frequency waves as they pass through the larynx. The results confirmed that the voice was not produced by Janet's normal vocal cords, but by the false vocal cords which trained actors can learn to use but for most people is a painful process which cannot be carried on for long. Janet and the voice could go for at least three hours or more without her normal voice being affected at all. Under normal circumstances this could destroy the vocal cords altogether.

It was alleged that apparitions were also seen throughout the fourteen months of the Enfield haunting. Whilst Janet was recuperating from her six weeks in hospital, the Hodgesons decided to go away on a holiday to Clacton to just get away from it all. John Burcombe had let himself in to the Hodgesons to collect the mail and to make sure everything was alright in the house. As he entered the front room, he was astonished to see the apparition of a man sitting in one of the dining room chairs. He was facing away from Burcombe with his back to him. He described a middle aged, grey haired old man, dressed in a blue and white striped shirt. Burcombe went to challenge the old man thinking he was an intruder, but he vanished before his eyes. The ghostly old man was seen from time to time as well as the apparition of a young child, dark shadowy forms crossing rooms and on the stairs and the legs of a man wearing blue trousers walking up the stairs, faces appearing through windows and the doppelganger of none other than Maurice Grosse.

The closest thing to a properly controlled scientific experiment came when David Robertson attached a piece of metal to a strain gauge in the hope of capturing psychokinetic phenomena. Any strain on the metal would be recorded scientifically on paper. During a two hour session with Janet, she was under constant observation and whilst not touching the metal, several strong deflections appeared on the chart. The metal bent through 15 degrees before it snapped in half.

In 1982, four years after when the poltergeist phenomena ceased at the Hodgesons, Janet took part in a strictly controlled experiment at Birbeck College, in London. It was supervised by Professor J. B. Hasted, Head of the Physics Department as well as by David Robertson and Maurice Grosse. The purpose of the experiment, one of a series of experiments, also using different subjects, was to examine the phenomenon of people losing weight during paranormal incidents, specifically the poltergeist phenomenon, in relation to levitation.

Janet was a natural candidate for the experiment as she had already claimed to others that she did indeed levitate. For the experiment, she was placed in a chair on a special platform that also functioned as a weighing scale. This was connected to a computer and chart recorder, which monitored any changes in weight deviation. Is someone were to jump on the platform, the chart would show a peak above the stable bassline trace and would be followed by a downward deviation on the chart when the body re-lands.

Whilst Janet had sat on the platform, the scientific apparatus began to behave in an abnormal way. The observers found that although Janet had sat perfectly still on the chair the pen on the chart recorder moved steadily upwards for about thirty seconds and also registered large peaks. Two of the peaks were so strong that the pen had literally ran off the top of the paper! According to the chart Janet had lost two pounds in weight for at least thirty seconds. Hasted could not explain the deviations in weight in normal terms.

Although some sceptics suggest fraudulent activity in the Enfield case (it is true that Janet was caught out on several occasions trying to fool investigators, this is usually due to attention seeking when genuine phenomena becomes slack so try to keep investigators interested), but there were around 2000 incidents involving around thirty different witnesses over a fourteen month period before the phenomena ceased. This I still believe is a truly remarkable case in parapsychology.

CASE FILE: THE WALSINGHAM HAUNTING.

One of my favorite stories of a haunted house comes from America and concerns the Walsingham family. The farmer owned a house by the Savannah River and was not a superstitious fellow. At the start the farmer thought that the beginnings of the haunting were just mischievous pranks by neighbours; then things took a decidedly horrifying turn. Banging doors were heard, bells started ringing for no apparent reason and chairs were thrown about after the family retired to bed. The house dog, which was a mastiff called Don Caesar, was found one day in the hall barking furiously with anger and staring at the wall in front of him, although nobody was there. At last he pounced; with a terrifying yelp the dog was flung back down by a powerful force and had its neck broken. The cat, on the other hand, enjoyed the favour of the entity. She would come through the door purring as if she was escorting some person who had been stroking her back. The cat would then climb on a chair, rubbing herself against it with pleasure.

The ghost started to disturb the family throughout most nights and sleep became next to impossible to come by. The strange audible sounds consisted of shouts, groans and hideous laughter and a horrifying wail which either came from the ceiling where the family would be sitting or from under the house. One night the youngest daughter, Amelia, was using the toilet when she suddenly felt a hand lay softly on her shoulder. She thought it was her mother or her sister, and as she looked up at the glass she was shocked to find no reflection in the mirror but her own, but she could plainly see a man's large hand resting on her arm. She screamed until she could scream no more. The rest of the family came running in, but there was no sign of the phantom hand.

Not long afterwards, farmer Walsingham was walking through the garden after a light rain, when he saw footsteps forming beside his own and they seemed to be barefooted. As he walked, the footsteps also followed beside his as if someone invisible was walking with him. The Walsinghams started thinking about leaving the property and any doubts they had were settled one night when they were sat for dinner. Whilst the family were around a dining room table a loud groan was heard in the upstairs room above. They did not take too much notice of this sound as they were becoming more or less used to the unnerving sounds, until someone pointed to a stain forming on the white tablecloth. There was a liquid dripping on the table from the ceiling above. The liquid seemed to be freshly shed blood and they watched it drip slowly down. Mr Walsingham and some of his guests ran upstairs to find the source of the mysterious blood. They pulled back the carpet and ripped up the floorboards, only to find them dry and bare. They were even covered by a thin layer of dust. The blood continued to drip down onto the dining table below. By the time it had stopped, there was a bloody stain the size of a dinner plate and when chemists were brought in to examine the stain the next day they confirmed that it was indeed human blood.

The Walsinghams left the house and never returned. The house became a tourist attraction and no one wanted to move in. The first person who dared to stay there overnight was a man called Horace Gunn who accepted a bet that he would not stay in the house for twenty four hours. Soon after dark he tried to light a fire in one of the rooms and light a lamp, but found it impossible to do so. An icy breath kept blowing out each of the matches as he tried to light them. At this point he wanted to leave, but he persevered.

For a while, nothing else occurred, but whilst he was lying asleep in bed, he was suddenly woken by a horrifying yell from underneath the house. He said it sounded like a cry of rage or deep pain. Footfalls were heard running up and down the staircase and from room to room as if someone was being pursued. This happened for around an hour and then suddenly stopped. There was absolute quiet and Horace began to breathe more easily. Suddenly, he noticed a light on the wall opposite which brightened in intensity until it resembled a disc of fire, and to his terror he realized that the light came from a human head, with no body, moving slowly along the wall at the height of a man. The terrifying head appeared to be that of someone old, with hair that was long and grey, matted with dark clots of blood which oozed from a deep wound in the temple. The cheeks were sunken and the whole face seemed to be in suffering and in misery. The head's eyes were wide open and gleaming whilst the glassy eyeballs seemed to follow the wretched Horace Gunn who was terrified by what he was witnessing and could not cry out. Gunn said that he could not tell if the old face was that of a man or woman. At last the apparition disappeared but the terrible sounds continued as if they were made by several people.

The house also shook with the horrifying audible phenomena and Gunn stated, 'The groaning and wailing that broke forth from every direction was something terrific, and an unearthly rattle and banging as of china and tin pans being flung to the ground from the upper storey added to the deafening noise'. Finally Horace tried to escape. Feeling nervously in the dark along the wall trying to avoid the horrors, he had almost reached the door when he suddenly felt himself seized by the ankle by an unseen force and was thrown violently to the floor. He was grasped around the throat by ice cold, unseen hands and was choked incessantly. He fought for his life but was overpowered.

Gunn's friends found him the next day unconscious and his throat was black with bruises with the marks of long fingers with curved nails. He was brought out of his unconscious state with much difficulty and he never recovered from his experience. He said there was not enough money in the world that could persuade him to stay in that house again.

CASE FILE: GHOSTS IN THE TOWER.

The Tower of London has been called the most haunted building in the world. It could well be true, considering how many ghosts and apparitions have been witnessed here over the years. Originally the tower was built by William the Conqueror in 1078, and it has a tragic place in English history. It has been a fortress, palace, prison, arsenal, a mint and a menagerie and is remembered because of its long list of famous state prisoners held here. Many of them were also executed within its walls.

One Saturday night in October 1817 Edward Swifte, keeper of the crown jewels, who resided in the tower until his retirement in 1852, was having supper with his wife, her sister and their young son in the sitting room of the Jewel House (then called the Martin Tower and thought to have been the prison of Anne Boleyn). The doors and windows to the room were closed. Swifte's wife was just about to take a drink when she shouted out: 'Good God! What's that?' They both saw a cylindrical apparition which looked more like a glass tube about the size of someone's arm hovering between the ceiling and the table. Its contents appeared to be a dense fluid, white and blue, mixing within the cylinder. The shape remained in the same place for around two minutes and slowly moved towards Swifte's sister-in-law, following the shape of the table.

The form passed in front of Swifte and his son and then moved behind his wife. Mrs Swifte broke down and collapsed onto the table. She screamed out, 'Oh Christ! It has seized me!' Mr. Swifte picked up a chair and threw it at the apparition which then disappeared. After questioning, it was revealed that although Edward Swifte and his wife saw the strange form, his son and sister-in-law never saw anything.

Several days after this encounter, a sentry guard at the Jewel House saw the apparition of a grizzly bear manifest from under the door to the Jewel Room. The guard rushed at the apparition promptly with a bayonet which stuck in the door. The guard then fainted. Several days later the sentry died allegedly from fright. Another guard, Sir George Younghusband, a later keeper at the Jewel House, stated that on several occasions he often saw the apparition of one of the Earls of Northumberland pass up and down the narrow walk of the ramparts of Martin's Tower which today is called Northumberland Walk. Several other sentries also saw the ghost, and sentry duty ended up being doubled.

The Bloody Tower, built by Henry III, is where the Princes in the Tower were supposedly murdered by Richard III. Edward V was acclaimed King of England before he was thirteen years old, but he never lived to be crowned and was kept in the Tower with his brother Richard, Duke of York. Both were smothered to death. They were buried quickly in the basement of Wakefield Tower and then moved again to be buried at the foot of the staircase leading from the White Tower to the chapel St John. It has been reported that their sad ghosts have been seen from time to time walking hand in hand in the Tower. Thomas Overbury was also murdered here in the Bloody Tower. Other famous guests here that were incarcerated were Sir Walter Raleigh, Guy Fawkes and the infamous Judge Jefferies, who died in the Tower. It has been reported that unearthly moans, groans and agonized screams have also been heard in the Bloody Tower on occasion. The phantom of Sir Walter Raleigh has been seen from time to time at a spot near to the Bloody Tower, called Raleigh's Walk.

As reported earlier in the book, the apparition of Anne Boleyn has been seen at the Tower of London. Her restless form has been seen in the area of the White Tower and on Tower Green. It has been reported that when she has been sighted the audible sound of footfall also has been heard. The most striking ghostly manifestation to take place at the Tower is that of the execution of the Countess of Salisbury, daughter of the Duke of Clarence. She was beheaded on orders from King Henry VIII. The frightening scene of her execution is said to be re-enacted on the anniversary of her death. The ghostly spectacle encompasses the ghost of the Countess, seen and heard screaming with terror as she is being chased around by the phantom executioner with axe in hand. When he finally reaches the countess, he is seen to hack off her head with repeated blows; the scene then vanishes.

The ghost of Henry VI has been seen in the Wakefield Tower, where he is said to have been knifed to death as he knelt in prayer. His mournful spectre is said to manifest on the anniversary of his murder as the clock approaches midnight. He is seen to walk with around until the clock strikes 12.00am and he then disappears into a wall. His ghost has not been reported for a long time now.

In the White Tower, a ghostly white lady has been seen from time to time. On one occasion she was seen by a group of children waving to them from a building opposite. Sentry guards have also smelt her pungent perfume, which makes them retch, around the entrance to St John's Chapel. Also from the White Tower comes a more amusing tale. On one occasion a guard who was on patrol, Arthur Crick, decided to rest on his duties. Sitting on a ledge he decided to take off his right shoe and whilst massaging his foot, heard a voice, 'There's only you and I here' which elicited a response from Crick, 'Just let me get this bloody shoe on and there'll only be you!'

In the Gallery where Henry VIII's impressive armour is displayed, several guards have reported a crushing sensation that suddenly descends upon them as they enter the Gallery. One night a sentry guard was patrolling the chamber and got the sudden and unnerving sensation that someone had thrown a heavy cloak over him. As he struggled to free himself the garment was seized from behind and was pulled tight around his throat by the invisible ghostly attacker. He managed to break free and ran back to the guardroom where marks on his throat were clearly invisible.

CASE FILE: GHOSTS IN A ROYAL PALACE

Another of my favourite haunted royal buildings is Hampton Court in Middlesex, South West London. It was constructed in 1529 by Cardinal Wolsey on the banks of the River Thames. The Cardinal lived in luxury in this magnificent palace and his hospitality became the talk of Europe. Later, Cardinal Wolsey presented the palace to King Henry VIII and was then accused of treason by the king as he failed to obtain an annulment of Henry's marriage to Catherine of Aragon. Henry VIII introduced his second wife Anne Boleyn to the luxurious palace, but she was later beheaded in 1536. Her apparition has been seen wandering the long corridors and passageways and wears a blue dress. She was seen by a servant who recognized the ghost from a portrait. At the time Henry was married to Anne, he was also courting Jane Seymour (1509–1537). She was to be his third wife.

Jane bore Henry a son, Edward, who was born on 12 October 1537, but Jane died of natural causes and has been seen on the anniversary of her son's birth. She has been seen all in white, carrying a lighted candle, gliding through the long corridors with her head bent in sadness. Her ghost emerges from a doorway in the Queen's Old Apartments and glides noiselessly around the stairway and through to the Silver Stick Gallery. Some servants witnessed the apparition and handed in their notice because they reported 'a tall lady, with a long train and a shining face' walking through closed doors holding a taper and then gliding down the stairs.

The most famous ghost of Hampton Court is that of Catherine Howard. Catherine became Henry's fifth wife. She was still a young teenager when she married Henry but found the king repulsive. She began a liaison with Thomas Culpeper and the talk between the servants found its way to King Henry who was furious at her betrayal. Culpeper was thrown in the Tower of London and then executed. Howard herself was imprisoned in her own chambers in Hampton Court. Whilst Catherine lay brooding in her chamber on her inevitable fate, she decided to try and plead with Henry to spare her life.

On 4 November, 1541, knowing that King Henry would be at prayer in the chapel, she broke free from her guards and ran through what is now known as the Haunted Gallery. She threw herself at the door, screaming at the king to grant her an audience. Henry VIII listened in silence and the guards came racing back through the gallery to recapture the hysterical queen and took her back to her chambers, but to no avail: her fate was sealed. On 13 February 1542, aged just twenty, she bravely went to the block. As the axe fell she kept on smiling. Many people have reported seeing her ghost and she is reported as being dressed in a white gown, with long flowing hair, racing towards the chapel. Her face is contorted with terror and the apparition is accompanied with an unearthly scream.

Many visitors have reported hearing a woman's ear-piercing shriek come from the gallery area which then fades away. There are also people who have reported an unusual, icy coldness which seems to emanate from around the doors of the chapel. The feeling of sadness also is purveyed along with the cold spot. After the gallery was opened to the public, an artist was sketching some tapestry when he witnessed a disembodied ringed hand appear in front of it. He sketched the hand and ring and later found that the ring was actually worn by Catherine Howard. Other folk have been reported to have fainted, and when regaining consciousness, they report a sudden chill followed by the feeling of being punched.

Before the outbreak of World War II, a man called Norman Lamplugh lived in the palace for many years. On one occasion, he was holding a garden party in the palace when he saw a little boy (along with his brother Earnest) aged around eight years old walking through the group of guests on the lawn. Both Norman and Earnest were confused for two reasons: they both knew that no children were present in the party and secondly, they were stumped by the child's appearance. The boy had abnormally long fair hair and was dressed in a black and white period costume of the time of King Charles II. His breeches and doublet appeared to be black velvet and he also wore shiny black shoes with big silver buckles and white hose.

As the two men were discussing the strange appearance of the boy, he approached the stairs and mounted them in confidence and walked right past Norman and Earnest. The two men made room for the boy as he passed and at no time did the boy look at the two men, but just made his way up the stairs to the top of the house and then entered a room that had no exit except the door at the top of the stairwell. He then vanished. Footsteps have also been reported in the vicinity of the stairs, especially on the night of 26 February, the anniversary of the death of Sir Christopher Wren.

Henry VIII's apparition has also been seen from time to time in and around the palace. He lived here with five of his six wives. His apparition is also seen in Windsor Castle dressed all in his garb wandering the castle. In Fountain Court, two figures used to be seen and were witnessed by Lady Hildyard, who had luxury apartments overlooking the court. She also reported hearing rappings and other strange noises during the night time hours. Later, when workmen were laying new drains in Fountain Court, they discovered two feet below the surface the perfectly preserved remains of two young cavaliers in the dress of the Civil War period.

A ghostly white lady has also been seen in and around Hampton Court. She is reputed to haunt the Landing Stage and a number of fisherman reported seeing her some years ago. There is also the ghost of Archbishop Laud which has been seen by residents of the house, strolling along slowly without a sound in the vicinity of the rooms he once knew so well. His apparition has also been seen in the library of St John's College in Oxford, rolling his head along the floor.

Another ghost seen in the palace is that of Sybil Penn, also known as 'The Lady in Grey'. She was the foster mother of Edward VI. She was the nurse of Henry VIII's only legitimate son, Edward. She watched over the sickly child anxiously and conscientiously. Edward never forgot Mrs Penn; neither did Mary Tudor or Elizabeth I who granted her a pension and apartments at Hampton Court. In 1562 Penn and Elizabeth suffered an attack of smallpox. Queen Elizabeth survived but was scarred for the rest of her life but Sybil Penn died on 6 November. The Ponsonby family occupied the rooms in the palace where Sybil Penn had lived and worked. They used to complain about hearing the sound of a spinning wheel and a woman's voice which they could not account for. The sounds originated from one of the walls in the south west wing and the noises became so regular that the Board of Works was called in. They discovered a chamber which contained a much used spinning wheel and other women's artifacts.

Around this time in 1881, a sentry on duty one day outside Sybil Penn's apartments saw a female apparition dressed in a long grey robe and hood manifest through Sybil Penn's former rooms and vanish in front of his eyes. Another sentry deserted his post when he saw a phantom of an old woman in a grey dress pass through a wall. Both said that the figure they saw looked like Sybil Penn herself. The discovery of the spinning wheel seems to have triggered the strange happenings associated with Sybil Penn and many people reported phenomena in the vicinity of Penn's apartments. Servants reported that they were awakened at night by the feeling of cold hands on their faces and also the sound of footfalls walking around them. Muttering sounds were heard as well as loud crashing and banging noises during the night. Some also reported finding the whole apartment bathed in a unearthly light.

Princess Frederica of Hanover, who stayed at Hampton Court, reported that she came face to face with the apparition of Sybil Penn. She stated it was a 'tall gaunt figure, dressed in a long grey robe, with a hood on her head, and her lanky hands outstretched before her'. She stated that the apparition resembled that of the stone effigy of Sybil Penn.

In February 2015 a remarkable photograph was taken by a twelve year-old girl, Holly Hampsheir. She was taking a photograph of her cousin, Brook McGee, also twelve, on an iPhone in the King's Apartments. On one of the frames there seems to be a woman dressed all in grey, with long tattered hair standing next to the fireplace. The strange thing is she seems to be around eight feet tall! Sceptics have stated that it could well be a glitch in the digital processing of the picture known as an iPhone panorama glitch, but there does seem to be something genuinely disturbing and creepy with this picture. It is quite possible that the girls may have genuinely caught a photo of the 'Lady in Grey'.

A police constable with over twenty years' experience in the force said that he witnessed a group of ghosts in the palace grounds. As he was standing by the main gates, he noticed a party of people coming towards him along Ditton Walk. They consisted of some eight to nine ladies and two men in evening dress. He stated that the only sound he had heard coming from them was the sound of the rustling of dresses as they approached him. He opened the gates for them to pass, whereupon they changed their direction and headed north towards the Flower Post Gates.

The ghostly party formed themselves into a procession with the men leading them, then vanished before the constable's eyes.

Another ghostly account to come from the palace is that of two devoted friends of whom one, after the death of her first husband, married a German count and went to live in Germany with her little girl Maud. The other was granted residence at the palace. One night when going to bed, the lady saw the apparition of a woman dressed entirely in black climbing the wide staircase opposite the door to her chamber. There was no sound accompanying the manifestation. She did notice that she also wore white gloves. As the form made its way towards her, she was horrified that it was in fact the ghost of her friend. She then screamed with terror, and passed out. Several days later she received a letter from Maud informing her that the Baroness (her friend) had died. The lady travelled to Germany where it was revealed that on the Baroness's deathbed she requested that she be buried in black with white gloves. When the lady saw her apparition at Hampton Court, it was revealed that in fact it was on the very day the Baroness had died.

After a costume performance of *Twelfth Night* at Hampton Court, actor and producer Leslie Finch told Peter Underwood, the late great psychical researcher, that he was walking towards one of the gateways with Lady Grant who had apartments at the palace, when he saw a grey, misty figure in Tudor dress approach them and felt a sudden coldness. At the time, he thought it must have been one of the actresses of the costume performance and he moved to let her pass. Lady Grant looked at him strangely as she did not witness the ghost at all but did feel the same sudden coldness that he felt.

During the 1966 season of Son et Lumiere at Hampton Court, a member of the audience said he witnessed the figure of Cardinal Wolsey under one of the archways and thought that an actor was taking part in the performance. On 7 October 2003 security staff heard alarms activated by fire doors which should always have been closed. They checked the CCTV footage to find out what happened. They were astonished to see a skeletal figure, dressed in a long cloak emerge from behind the doors. Staff stated that it could not be anyone in period costume as there was no one there in costume on the day in question. Staff also stated that these doors in this part of the palace are also off limits to members of the public.

CASE FILE: WHALEY HOUSE

Whaley House in San Diego is considered to be one of America's most haunted houses, which opened its doors as a museum in 1960; many paranormal occurrences have been reported since. The house occupied what was once the site of a public gallows which saw many executions. The house was designed and built by Thomas Whaley in 1857 and was considered a mansion in San Diego at the time. The house was used for more than just a family residence. It contained a granary, was the County Court House and later became a theatre, a general store, a billiard room, ballroom, school and a polling station.

Thomas and his wife Anna Eloise moved into Whaley House on 22 August 1857. They had three children, and left as they needed more space in the house, then moved back to Whaley in 1868. Tragedy struck Whaley on 19 August 1885. Violet, one of Whaley's daughters, took her life in the house by shooting herself in the heart as her marriage had broken down. Six family members died in Whaley house, Thomas Junior, Violet, Anna Eloise, Francis, George and Corrine.

The first occurrence of a ghost in Whaley House was of 'Yankee Jim' whose real name was James Robinson. He was convicted of Grand Larceny and was hanged on the gallows in 1852. When the family moved in they could hear heavy footsteps walking around the house. They also reported windows being thrown open although no one had released the window latches. Several visitors to the house have reported the tightening around the throat around the archway that leads to the music room. It is the spot where James Robinson was hanged.

The apparition of Thomas Whaley himself has been seen standing at the top of the stairs or in his bedroom wearing his long coat and a top hat. The smell of Cuban cigars (his favourite) has been picked up by visitors to the house. They report that it is overpowering and have had to leave the room. People have also reported hearing his loud laughter all around the house from time to time. Anna Eloise was a keen piano player and had a beautiful voice. Her ghost has been seen all over Whaley House and there is the olfactory phenomenon of perfume as her apparition floats past. She has also been spotted in the garden picking flowers. It is recorded that Anna always had a vase of flowers in the house at all times. The sound of music has been heard coming from the music room and the keys on the piano have been seen to move when nobody is playing.

One of the more playful ghosts that supposedly haunts Whaley is that of Marion, who was Thomas and Anna Whaley's red-haired granddaughter who died aged eleven after she accidentally consumed a large amount of ant poison. The apparition is usually witnessed by children and appears so solid and lifelike that children do not realize they have witnessed a ghost until she vanishes. She reportedly prefers the attention of girls as the ghost playfully pulls young girls' hair and tugs their arms. She also tickles them and makes them laugh.

Another tragedy that took place at Whaley House is that of a girl who was running down the hill situated outside the house's grounds who accidentally ran into a clothes line which wrapped around her neck and strangled her. She was taken into the house and she died on the kitchen table. It has been reported that her apparition has been seen running around in the garden and has been seen in the kitchen. Pots and pans have also been known to move around of their own volition.

Another ghost that is regularly seen by children is that of a terrier dog called Dolly Varden. People have witnessed seeing a small spotted dog running down the hallway and into the dining room with its ears flapping and tail wagging. The spectral dog is also known to lick the toes of anyone wearing open toed shoes. Little Thomas Junior was the youngest and first of the immediate family members to die in the house and his cries can be heard coming from his upstairs bedroom. Dolly the dog has been seen running upstairs into Thomas's bedroom and out again as if to get someone's attention.

Another phenomenon reported from Whaley House is poltergeist activity such as the rocking chair moving forward and back on its own, bedroom window curtains have been seen blowing around although the windows are sealed shut and strange human-like pillow indentations as if someone invisible is laying there.

CASE FILE: LONDON'S HAUNTED BOOK SHOP.

The story of Number 50, Berkeley Square is one of Britain's most famous ghost stories and reputedly concerns one of London's most haunted buildings. The location is now occupied by the Maggs Brothers antiquarian bookshop, but before this there were many horrifying ghost stories attached to this house and surrounding area. A Colonel Kearsey was visiting a relative in the square one day and was shown a room. As he entered the room and by the light of the burning fire in the fireplace he saw a woman in a long dress and a broad brimmed hat sitting in an armchair by the fire. She was crying bitterly and when he approached her asking if she was all right, she arose from the chair and without looking at him passed through the heavy curtains and disappeared through the shuttered windows.

Lord Lyttleton spent a night in Number 50, specifically the 'haunted room', and armed with two blunderbusses loaded with buckshot and silver sixpences, the latter said to ward off evil spirits. He reported that during the night, he fired at a formless entity that leapt at him from the shadows which fell to the floor and then disappeared. A woman also went out of her mind after spending the night in the haunted room.

There is an account of a Scottish child who was tortured or frightened to death in the nursery and whose apparition has been witnessed from time to time wearing a plaid frock, sobbing and wringing its hands in the upper part of the house. A young woman once lived at Number 50 with her lecherous uncle and committed suicide by throwing herself out of the top window; her ghost has been seen clinging to the ledge and screaming before falling to her death.

The most famous story coming from house concerns two sailors who wandered into Number 50 many, many years ago when the house was up for let. Believing they had found a resting place for the night, they broke inside. One of the sailors produced a candle which was conveniently kept in his pocket. He lit it, then the sailors made their way upstairs where they made a fire in the grate. They settled themselves in the four poster bed and fell asleep. An hour later they were awoken by the sound of footfalls which did not sound human. The footsteps came upstairs and through the door.

They rushed for the stairs but as they tried to flee a dark formless entity barred the way. They stated that it 'crept, panted and shuffled across the room making scratching sounds on the bare boards which might have been the scraping of horny claws'. The entity then leapt on one of the sailors who staggered back against the window, crying out for help as the glass and framework of the window shattered. Pursued by the screams of his friend, the other sailor managed to escape from the house and collapsed in the street where he was found by a policeman. When he recovered, they went back inside the room in Number 50 to find it empty. On looking outside the smashed window they saw the body of the other sailor impaled on the spiked railings of the courtyard with his neck broken. They assumed that he was either pushed or he had tried to escape his paranormal assailant. The matter was then closed.

During the 1870s the occupants of neighbouring houses told of loud cries and strange noises emanating from the locked and empty building at night. The sounds of heavy furniture was heard being dragged across bare boards, along with the sounds of bells ringing, windows being thrown up, as well as stones, books and other objects being thrown down into the street below. At one time it was reported that the notorious haunted room had been kept locked and there were stories of a lunatic who died there. Others spoke of a housemaid who was found lying on the floor of the haunted bedroom and convulsing. She refused to give a statement of what she had witnessed, but just said that it was 'just too horrible'. She died the next day in St George's Hospital. In another account, another visitor volunteered to spend a night in the haunted bedroom but only on condition that help would be forthcoming if needed. He did and was found dead with his eyes fixed upon the same spot with terror on his face.

One morning in 2001, Julian Wilson, who was one of the booksellers with Maggs Brothers was alone in the accounts department (the haunted room), when he suddenly encountered a column of brown mist move quickly across the room and vanish. Not long after this encounter a cleaner experienced the feeling of someone or something standing behind her. On looking round she found that the room was empty. On another occasion a man was shocked when his glasses were snatched from his hand and flung to the floor as he was walking up the stairs. Number 50 Berkeley Square truly seems to be a house of horrors.

CASE FILE: THE MACKENZIE POLTERGEIST

Greyfriars Kirkyard in Edinburgh, Scotland houses the infamous Black Mausoleum, the tomb of George 'Bloody' Mackenzie. Twelve hundred survivors of the Covenanter movement were imprisoned in what is known as the Covenanter's Prison on the orders of Charles II after their defeat at the Battle of Bothwell Brig. Many of them died from starvation or disease and the other thousands (the remainder of them) were executed by the King's advocate, 'Bloody' George Mackenzie. Mackenzie was interred in Greyfriars in 1691 within sight of the Covenanter's Prison.

During recent years a malevolent haunting seems to have been triggered here in the Covenanter's Prison. It all seems to have started around 1999. People have reportedly been scratched and bruised after being punched by an invisible assailant, people have passed out, peoples hair has been pulled or torn out, strange pins and needle like sensations have been felt along with the feeling of sudden coldness, knocking and rapping sounds coming from tombs, people reporting being shoved or pushed, nausea and dizziness, the sensation of an invisible man's arm grabbing an arm or a leg, breathing sounds in a person's ear, the feeling of sadness and despair, the feeling of being watched and that a person is not alone, obnoxious smells are reported, dead animals have been found in front of the Black Mausoleum, people being burned and bitten, electrical equipment faltering or failing and other strange anomalies.

Apparitional sightings have been of a dark shape that is seen in the shadows, a man with blue eyes and a cloak has been reported, a hooded figure with a featureless face has been seen, a young girl aged around eight or nine years old wearing a white lace dress has been reported. There have been over 350 reported incidents here and it is now closed because of the 'attacks' until there is a guided tour. I was taken on a personal tour of the Covenanter's Prison and I must say that there is something very oppressive in this part of the Kirkyard.

CASE FILE: THE GHOSTS OF CHINGLE HALL

Chingle Hall in Goosnargh, near Preston in Lancashire is another one of Britain's most haunted buildings. The house is over seven hundred years old and is tucked away at the end of its own lane. The house is believed to have been the birthplace of John Wall, a Franciscan priest who was one of the last English Catholic Martyrs. The hall belonged to the Wall family in 1585 and John was born in 1620. He was executed at Worcester in 1679 and his head is said to have been conducted on a grand tour of the Continent before being smuggled back to Chingle.

Here it was either buried in the grounds or hidden somewhere in the house, where several hidden places have been discovered over the years. The apparition of John Wall himself has been seen here on many occasions. There is many phenomena reported at Chingle; footfalls are heard walking about the passages and rooms as well as on the bridge that crosses the moat. Door latches have been heard to move, doors opening and closing, objects are moved, water formations appear from nowhere, dogs sense something that is not seen, people feel icy cold and chilled to the bone, and the feeling of being watched when no one is there, raps and knocking sounds being heard, and a ghostly monk has been seen on many occasions in and around the hall. The monk has been sighted peering through a window, a cowled head and pale face which appears briefly then vanishes.

One visitor stated that they had seen two monk-like figures in the act of praying in a room in the hall. When the visitor approached them they disappeared through a wall. In the haunted priest's room upstairs, the apparition of a man with shoulder length hair has been seen to walk past the outside window. The window is twelve feet higher than ground level, so he would have been seen to float past, not walk. Another visitor to Chingle saw a greenish type figure in the porch. As the visitor stopped the ghost turned and walked back into the dining room and disappeared.

A Mrs Walmeley was pushed in the back whilst she was alone in the lounge, a Mrs McKay felt a wave of cold air come over her and then was astonished to witness flowers lift up out of a vase whilst a table lamp and picture was shaking. A Mrs Rigby was having a cup of tea with Mrs Howarth in the lounge when they both witnessed a wooden plaque fly off the wall over the fireplace and land in the centre of the room. Another visitor to Chingle and her young son looked back on leaving Chingle Hall and observed a human looking apparition looking out of the window from the hall, specifically the priest's room. They both described the figure as dressed in white or light grey robes. They turned their headlights on from the car and directed them at the window; the form was still there and they described it as black or dense.

Michael Bingham was a young New Zealander who visited Chingle Hall. Whilst he was in the priest's room, he heard sounds as if bricks were being moved. The sounds seemed to originate in the area of the open priest's hole and he was startled to see a ghostly hand moving the bricks. As he watched, the hand froze and then vanished. Michael also heard footfalls on many occasions and also saw a cowled figure like a monk from time to time. Many people believe the ghost at Chingle Hall is that of John Wall, a man of God, and that he would do no one any harm.

In 1979, two members of the Ghost Club came to Chingle for an investigation at the ancient hall. Whilst they were in the priest's room loud bangs and thuds came from the direction of the priest's hole and seemed to then move across the floor towards one of the investigators. The sounds then seemed to come from underneath the floor under the investigator's feet, in which the investigator felt the floor vibrate. He then moved to the other side of the room towards the other investigator, but the bangs and knocks continued moving until they reached the chimney and then ceased.

A bit later on during the investigation, the sounds started again in a different part of the room. The sounds moved inside a cabinet, moved out and were so powerful that they managed to shake a chair on which an investigator was sitting. The banging then moved towards the fireplace, moved outside of the room and moved into the doorway. The sounds ceased then started yet again. This time they moved from the floor up to the ceiling, across then stopped. A bit later, Mr Knowles came in and knocked three times in the name of Jesus Christ. All of a sudden three loud knocks came back as a response.

Several more investigations were carried out at Chingle by the Ghost Club members in which other phenomena were reported. Andrew Usher reported that at around 6.45pm one night, he was looking out of a window in Chingle Hall when he saw an apparition of a monk in a brown habit walk towards the drive. He stated that he ran outside to greet the individual but nobody was there. This location is a place I have always wanted to investigate, but unfortunately they do not now allow investigations to be held here, due to the hall being privately owned.

CASE FILE: THE DUNSTABLE HITCHHIKER

One of the most disturbing ghostly I can personally imagine is with an apparitional hitchhiker. One Friday evening in October 1979 Roy Fulton, a twenty-six year-old carpet fitter was coming home from a darts match near the small Bedfordshire village of Stanbridge when he saw a man standing by the roadside with his thumb raised for an obvious lift. Roy Fulton stopped his van and saw that the hitchhiker was a young man with a white shirt and dark trousers. He got into Fulton's van but was uncommunicative. When Fulton asked where the man wanted to go he just pointed his finger towards Dunstable.

Fulton thought nothing of this and just thought that some hitchhikers do not like to talk much or he might be deaf and mute. They had been travelling at around a steady forty miles per hour when Fulton decided to 'break the ice' and talk to the stranger. He stated: 'I turned around to offer him a cigarette and the bloke had disappeared. I braked, had a quick look in the back seat to see if he was there. He wasn't, and I just gripped the wheel and drove like hell!'

He drove to a local police station to tell them his strange tale and was visibly shaken by his experience. The police found that Fulton was reliable and stated that: 'He was an ordinary sort of chap, and not the worse for alcohol. He had only drunk a couple of lagers during the darts match'. The case was never explained. A strange tale indeed.

CASE FILE: GLAMIS CASTLE

Glamis Castle near Forfar in Angus, Scotland is set amongst the beautiful Grampian mountains. It is the seat of the Earl of Strathmore and Kinghorne and was first built in the fifteenth century. What is left of the castle today was built at a later date. Much of the castle as we see it today with its large soaring towers, was rebuilt in the seventeenth century, when it acquired its French chateau look. It was also the home of Lady Elizabeth Bowes Lyon, the Queen Mother.

There are many ghosts and apparitions known to wander the castle's rooms and corridors. It is the castle in which Duncan was supposedly murdered by Macbeth and where an indelible bloodstain remained forever where King Malcolm II is said to have been killed. The whole floor was then boarded over. One of the apparitions is that of a little grey lady and was seen by Lord Strathmore; he walked into the chapel one afternoon and saw the figure kneeling in one of the pews. He also saw her once walking into the chapel. The Dowager Countess Granville also saw her kneeling in one of the pews in the chapel. It was a sunny afternoon and she saw the sun coming through the windows which shone through the figure.

In one of the secret rooms at the castle, one of Glamis Castle's legends was born. It is here that 'Earl Beardie' one of the lords of Glamis, was playing cards one night. In spite of the coming Sabbath he was reluctant to give up the game of cards they were playing. As soon as the clock struck midnight, it was said the devil manifested and asked if he might join in the game. Earl Beardie sold his soul to the devil and died soon after. Many people heard the ghostly sounds of swearing and cursing coming from the secret chamber at night, and in an attempt to subdue the disturbances, the room was bricked up. Unfortunately this did not stop the activity and it is still reported today that the bearded ghost of the earl is roams the rooms and corridors of Glamis. There are also reports of guests waking up to find the ghostly earl leaning over their beds with an evil intent.

There is another famous legend that comes from Glamis: the legend of the monster said to have been born around 1800 which should have become the heir. The monster is said to have been a man that was deformed and misshapen to a horrible degree. It was supposed to have no neck, small arms and legs, was immensely strong and looked like a flabby egg. It is said that a secret room was built for the creature, which was kept from the prying eyes of everyone. Its existence was only known to four men at a time: the Earl of Strathmore and his son, the family lawyer and a factor of the estate.

Each eldest son was told the secret when they reached the age of twenty one, and records show that there was indeed a secret chamber built in 1684. It is said that the creature lived to an incredibly old age and may have died in 1921. It is also said that the story may have accounted for why the succeeding Lords of Strathmore were unhappy men. One lady of Strathmore asked one of the factors outright if the story was true. They said that 'It is fortunate that you do not know the truth, for if you did, you would never be happy'.

Lord Halifax was adamant that Glamis Castle was haunted. He recounted that he saw the ghost of 'Earl Beardie', and was told that two visiting children often saw shadowy forms wandering about the corridors and passageways of the castle in the vicinity of the Blue Room. The children would not sleep in the room. A small dressing room off the Queen Mother's main bedroom was said to have been haunted at one time. People who slept there often found the bedclothes being pulled off them in the middle of the night, but after the room became a bathroom no more disturbances came from it.

There is another room at the castle where the door is said to open by itself every night, even though it will be bolted or wedged by some heavy object. There is also an apparition of a tongueless woman who runs across the park, pointing in anguish to her bloody mouth. There is another apparition known as 'Jack the Runner' who is a strange ghost, as the figure is said to be thin and runs up the long drive of the castle. Another ghost, that of a madman, has been seen to walk on stormy nights on a portion of the roof.

On a spot known as 'The Mad Earl's Walk', an apparition of a small black boy has been seen sitting in front of the door to the Queen Mother's sitting room, and is said to have been a page boy who was mistreated. There are accounts of people hearing loud knocking and hammering coming from the oldest part of the castle, and a figure of a woman has been seen floating above the castle's clock tower surrounded by a red glow. The apparition is thought to be that of a Lady of Glamis who was burned at the stake on Castle Hill in Edinburgh. She was said to have been charged with witchcraft and with intent to poison King James V.

Even more ghosts are said to haunt Glamis Castle. Once, when a Provost of Perth was occupying a room at Glamis, a tall figure of a man walked into the room. He was said to have been dressed in a long, dark cloak that was fastened at the throat with a clasp. A ghostly woman with mournful eyes and a pale face has been seen staring out of a lattice window on an upper floor, with hands clutching the glass panes.

There is also the story of some visiting youngsters who decided to try and find the secret chamber, so they decided to visit every room and hang towels and sheets from outside the window to mark them (the total known number of rooms at the castle is one hundred), and when they gathered outside they saw that there were seven more rooms that had no towels or sheets to mark them. They were sure they had visited all of the rooms. There must be more secrets at Glamis Castle than we are aware of.

CASE FILE: THE SALLIE HOUSE

Another of America's most haunted houses is the Sallie house in Atchison, Kansas. The house was built at the turn of the century and was originally the home of an Atchison doctor who practised from his home. The doctor and his family lived on the upper floors whilst downstairs was used as the surgery and examination rooms. Sallie was a young girl, aged six, who was brought to the doctors one day suffering from a serious illness.

There are allegedly two different stories that tell what happened next. In one of the story it is alleged that Sallie had been up all night with major stomach ache. The doctor realized that she might have appendicitis and decided to operate on her. The little girl supposedly panicked when she saw the surgery tools and the doctor was forced to hold her down. The girl fought with him and was not under any gas when he made his first incision. She screamed but the doctor would not stop the procedure as he feared the appendix might burst causing peritonitis. She died on the operating table and according to some it is her last memories of him, seeing him torture her before she died, that brought about the haunting. In the second story it is said that Sallie was suffering from severe respiratory problems due to pneumonia, but was wrongly diagnosed with a less severe illness and she died. With regret, the doctor moved away from the house never to return.

In 1993, paranormal activity began to be reported from the house when a young couple moved in. The dog began to growl and bark at something invisible, especially around the second floor near the nursery. Lights would dim and brighten on their own, appliances would turn themselves on and off, pictures hanging on the walls would be found upside down and on one occasion, when the family had returned from a night out they found that the toys in the nursery had been arranged in a circle on the floor.

The poltergeist activity then took a more violent turn. Spontaneous fires began to break out around the house and the husband began to suffer from tactile physical attacks from an entity. The first attack happened when he walked into the room that was once the doctor's surgery. He felt suddenly cold and chilled to the bone and then long bloody scratches appeared on his arm. Attacks continued which left him terrified, with scratches and welts all over his body. He stated that there was always a sudden and severe drop in temperature before he felt invisible nails scratching him. The wife and baby were never attacked by the entity but it was suggested that it was the ghost of Sallie making her presence known.

The husband said he saw the apparition of Sallie on two separate occasions and other strange phenomena included strangely melted candles with burnt finger marks. The husband on one occasion heard a woman's voice say 'Here's your remote' as the TV remote was placed on his chest by unseen hands. One night, when the husband was asleep, he dreamed of being pulled out of his bed by a little girl, by his wrists. On waking he found burn marks on his wrist that looked like the fingerprints of a small girl. On another occasion when he was asleep on the couch he suddenly sat up and said in a strange voice 'He's mine!' then laid back down. On awakening twenty minutes later he said he did not even remember the incident.

On the family's photographs appeared strange phenomena such as streaks and lights and on film was caught scratches and marks appearing on the husband's body by the investigative team for the television show, 'Sightings'. The last straw occurred when the husband was shoved by an invisible force from behind, nearly pushing him over the upstairs banisters. The family moved away never to return but the husband still reported psychic attacks, though less severe, and eventually they stopped altogether. Later investigations from different paranormal teams have produced several EVPs and other anomalous phenomena.

FOUR

CASE FILES: THE REAL STORIES BEHIND GHOST MOVIES

CASE FILE: THE AMITYVILLE HORROR

In 1979, the movie *The Amityville Horror* was released, followed by many other sequels and spin-offs. In 2005 a remake was made, and the real story first came to light in the book *The Amityville Horror* by Jay Anson. But what was the real reason for the supposed haunting? On 13 November 1974 a young man from New York, 24 year-old, Ronald DeFeo, ran into a local bar screaming that someone had broken into his home at 112 Ocean Avenue, Long Island and murdered six members of his family. His mother, father, two brothers and two sisters were found shot dead in their beds. The police did not believe him and he was arrested on multiple counts of murder and sentenced to serve six life sentences.

The house was put up for sale and was empty for a year before the next occupants to move into the house were the Lutzes. They thought that the house was a bargain when they purchased it for $80,000. The couple were impressed by the three-storey Dutch Colonial residence, with its boathouse, swimming pool and garage. The house was built in 1928. George Lutz was a 28 year-old ex-marine and his wife Kathy was a housewife, looking after their two small sons, Daniel and Christopher and their daughter, Melissa. They moved into the empty house on 18 December 1975, but a month later they fled the house because of the alleged terrors that befell them.

It all started with overpowering olfactory phenomena pervading the house, which they described as 'rotting meat', and a strange black slime-like substance that began appearing over the bathroom fittings. They tried to remove the muck, but to no avail. Next came a swarm of flies around a second floor bedroom and the front door was ripped from its hinges with just one remaining attached. George reported that he constantly felt cold and could not get warm despite a huge fire being lit in the living room. Not long afterwards the Lutzes discovered cloven hoof tracks in the snow which stopped short of the front door, which was ripped almost from its frame. The Lutzes believed that no human could have been strong enough to rip the door from its frame. It began to occur to the Lutzes that their new home was haunted by unseen forces and that it was a nightmare rather than a dream house.

Kathy said she was the first person to be victimized by the entities. She stated that invisible arms tried to embrace her and that a force was trying to take possession of her body. She thought that escape was impossible and that it was inevitable that she was going to die. It was not just the Lutzes that supposedly felt the effects of a presence in the house. A priest that had befriended them, Father Pecoraro was called in to bless the house. As he was sprinkling holy water around whilst saying prayers he heard a male voice say, 'Get Out'! Later he was struck down by an unknown infection and the priest stated that the rectory where he lived was also filled by putrid smells that drove any visitor away to get some air outside. The priest did not tell the Lutzes about his experience in the house but telephoned them to warn them not to use the room. While he was speaking he stated that the line cut out and that he had developed blisters on his hands that resembled the crucifixion wounds of Jesus Christ.

George Lutz recounted that he had also experienced the sound of a marching band that paraded through the house. He stated that he could hear the sounds of stomping boots and horns blaring out. George said that to make that much sound from the ghostly band that there would have to have been at least fifty members! He also stated that the furniture had moved to make room for the invisible band.

Other anomalous phenomena occurred around the house; the manifestation of black slime occurred as well as red weals that appeared over Kathy's body as if she had been slashed and struck with a red hot poker. The levitation of Kathy happened whilst she was in bed and a demonic pig-like entity with bright red eyes was seen staring through one of the windows and was also the alleged invisible playmate of Melissa, called Jodie. George reported hearing the sound of the door slamming on multiple occasions, and when he went to investigate nobody was there. Scratching and thumping sounds were also prevalent in the house at night and George stated that his personality was changing as if he was being manipulated by an unseen force.

George recalled that allegedly on the 10 January 1976 he awoke with a compulsion to flee the house. He shouted at his wife but could not rouse her. Then, as he watched, his wife began to transform into a ninety year-old hag; her hair became dirty, old and disheveled, she dribbled and creases and wrinkles appeared on her face. George stated that it took several hours before she became normal again. This is where one of three supposed levitations took place. Other apparitional forms were allegedly seen in the house. One was a gigantic hooded entity in white and the other was a demon with horns with half its face shot away. On 14 January 1976, the Lutzes left the house, never to return.

There are many contradictions in the stories told and has become a muddled and complicated case, but is now generally regarded by parapsychologists and psychical researchers as a hoax. Dr Steven Kaplan, Director of the Parapsychology Institute of America, said that after many months of study and many interviews with people associated with the Amityville case: 'We found no evidence to support any claim of a haunted house. What we did find is a couple who had purchased a house they economically could not afford. It is our professional opinion that the story of its haunting is mostly fiction'. Recent owners at 112 Ocean Avenue have reported that they have experienced no unusual phenomena occurring in the house.

CASE FILE: THE EXORCIST

In 1973, my favorite horror movie of all time was released, *The Exorcist*. The book and screenplay were written by William Peter Blatty and tell the story of a young girl named Reagan McNeil who becomes possessed by a demon called Pazuzu. The film shocked audiences all over the world. People were reported fleeing the cinemas in terror, and also fainting in the aisles in the cinema. The film was later deemed too shocking to show and was later banned. Since then, however, the ban was lifted and the film remains a fan favourite. The real story however, is not based around a young girl but a young boy called Robbie Mannheim.

Robbie Mannheim was born in Cottage City, Maryland and was an only child. He spent a great deal of time with his Aunt Harriet, who was also a spiritualist medium. His aunt disregarded the supposed rules of involving children in the summoning of the dead and introduced Robbie to the infamous Ouija board. Later, his Aunt Harriet died and he tried contacting her spirit through the use of the Ouija board. Some people believed that the use of the board caused him to become possessed by an alleged evil spirit. A poltergeist began to make itself known to Robbie. Furniture was moved around, vases and other household objects flew around the house, and the sound of marching feet was heard (this sounds similar to what George Lutz had heard in the Amityville Horror case).

The poltergeist then began to victimize Robbie. The word 'hell' manifested on Robbie's chest as well as the word 'spite' and when a vial of holy water was placed next to Robbie, it smashed into pieces. This was enough for Robbie's parents who contacted Fr Raymond Bishop for help. Fr Bishop asked for Robbie to sleep at his house in order to observe the phenomena surrounding the boy. During the night the priest heard scratching sounds and witnessed an armchair tilting up.

Fr Bishop decided to have the fourteen year-old boy exorcized at a local Jesuit hospital, where his behaviour became even more disturbing. While Robbie writhed in his hospital bed the priest began to read the Roman Ritual of exorcism. He was taunting the priest in Latin and then lashed out at the priest with a loose bed spring, causing a deep cut down the priest's right arm that required more than a hundred stitches. Robbie was then sent home and ended up defecating over the walls in the house and began again speaking in a strange guttural voice.

Another two priests, Fr Walter H. Halloran and Fr William Bowdern, tried exorcizing the boy thirty times and witnessed some startling phenomena including the word 'evil' appearing on his skin. Eventually, during the final exorcism, the priests reported a tremendous thunderclap and Robbie said: 'It's over'!

What are we to make of such stories regarding possession? There are many psychological theories that could explain some of the phenomena experienced. Automatism causes involuntary physical actions, obsessive compulsive disorder can cause irrational fears, paranoia might lead someone to believe they are possessed by demonic forces and Gilles de la Tourette's syndrome causes involuntary tics and abusive and foul language. A religious belief along with suggestion can all play their part in an alleged possession. They may not explain all the facts relating to possession, but could go a long way to explain the phenomenon if looking at it objectively.

CASE FILE: THE ENTITY

The film *The Entity* was released in 1983 and tells the story of a woman called Carlotta Moran who was subjected to rape and abuse by an negative entity. The name Carlotta Moran, however, was not her real name; this was a fictional name made for the book and movie. Her real name was Doris Bither and the case was investigated by my friend and colleague Dr Barry Taff and his associate at the time, Kerry Gaynor. The case came about when Doris overheard Kerry Gaynor and a friend of his in conversation regarding haunted houses. She approached them cautiously and made herself known to them. The two parapsychologists made their first visit to Doris's house on August 22, 1974. The family consisted of Doris, aged thirty, a daughter aged six and three sons aged between ten thirteen and sixteen.

One of the phenomena experienced by the family was a semi-solid apparition around six feet tall which the family called Mr Whose-it. Doris recounted that she and her eldest son encountered two dark Asian figures that manifested within their mother's bedroom and which seemed to be fighting with each other. This was experienced several times and Doris claimed to have physically bumped into an apparition in the hallway.

The most extraordinary of incidents that was related to Barry Taff and Kerry Gaynor was that Doris reported that she had been physically sexually assaulted by three semi-invisible entities. She told the parapsychologists that two small apparitions held her down by the wrists and ankles whilst the third one raped her. After the terrifying ordeal Doris stated that it had left behind large black and blue bruises, especially around the groin area, ankles and wrists, inner thigh and the breasts. This ordeal happened on several other occasions also. In another extraordinary account, Doris reported that during one of the attacks her eldest son heard the attack from another room and as he entered the bedroom he witnessed his mother being thrown around the room by the entities. When he tried to help her he said an invisible force picked him up and threw him back into the wall.

On the second investigation at the house, Barry Taff and Kerry Gaynor reported that the temperature in Doris's bedroom was unusually low compared to other parts of the house and that the cold was penetrating. The parapsychologists also reported the smell of decomposing flesh that could be found in a morgue and also that there was a feeling of overpressure in the inner ear. Poltergeist phenomena were also reported by the parapsychologists. In one instance, whilst Gaynor was in the kitchen talking to the eldest son, a kitchen cabinet door swung open and out flew a frying pan whilst he was standing one foot away from the cabinet. During the investigation several photographs were taken by the scientists to try and catch images of the phenomena that were being reported. They stated that the Polaroid photographs each came out as if they were bleached white and blurred.

In the third investigation, a female photographer also accompanied the parapsychologists. On entering the bedroom the woman reported that there was a horrible stench that pervaded the bedroom and was making her feel nauseous. On more than twenty occasions they all collectively witnessed small, pulsing flashes of light and when the female photographer got home she became very ill and vomited before retiring to bed.

On the fourth investigation, the parapsychologists decided to conduct a séance in the hope of manifesting the phenomenon that was plaguing Doris. During the course of the séance, Taff and Gaynor reported extremely intense, three-dimensional lights that would change shape and vary in luminosity which approached various individuals within the circle. The lights also returned during their next investigation with thirty individuals from the UCLA Parapsychology Laboratory. The lights were bright green in colour and would intensify in brightness when Doris swore and cursed at the lights. The parapsychologists attempted to communicate with the light anomalies and to their astonishment, the lights communicated back by sharp, fast flashing lights. Doris reported that while she was in the bathroom she heard the black poster boards which were hung up in her bedroom by duct tape for experimental purposes being forcibly torn down, taking some of the paint and plaster with them.

On their sixth visit, Barry Taff, Kerry Gaynor and twenty other individuals witnessed the anomalous lights take the apparitional form of the top torso of a muscular man, lime green in colour and three-dimensional in shape but with no discernable features. Two investigators passed out after witnessing the manifestation and never went back to the house again. On another investigation, Doris reported that she and her son witnessed two candelabras fly off the kitchen sink, fly across the room and strike Doris on the arm. Gaynor and Taff both witnessed the red bruise on Doris's arm. They also reported that a large wooden board tore itself from its secure position beneath a bedroom wall window, fly fifteen feet through the air, narrowly missing her son's head, which Doris also managed to avoid. During many of the investigations some genuine light anomalies were caught on film; one shows a three-dimensional arc of light which seems free floating in nature and others which defy explanation.

The case is a fascinating case in which two renowned parapsychologists witnessed a host of parapsychological occurrences. There are not many parapsychologists who witness such a spectacle (I have witnessed many phenomena like these at The Ancient Ram Inn in Gloucestershire, as stated earlier in the book) and who are fortunate (or unfortunate – depending on how you look at such things). I believe, as Dr Barry Taff and Kerry Gaynor do, that the phenomena may have been caused not by discarnate malignant forces, but by extreme RSPK. Dr Taff said in his book, *Aliens Above, Ghosts Below* that 'Doris was a deeply troubled woman, whose claims of spectral rape were due in large part to extreme emotional distress coupled with an overactive imagination and libidinous fantasies', and that the phenomena reported were 'the direct product of her tortured unconscious mind and not of her environment'.

I personally wish to thank my friend and colleague Dr Barry Taff for letting me use some notes from his book, *Aliens Above, Ghosts Below*.

CASE FILE: AN AMERICAN HAUNTING

An American Haunting is a 2005 movie based on the true account of the Bell Witch poltergeist case which began in the early months of 1817, in Robertson County, Tennessee. The family at the centre of the disturbances was John Bell, his wife Lucy and their nine children. There were four children on whom the disturbances seemed to concentrate on: Elizabeth Bell, also known as Betsy; John, who was the eldest; Richard who was ten; and Joel who was nine.

The manifestations began one night when the family was disturbed by sounds which sounded like rats running about. On other occasions the family reported that the noises sounded more like a dog pawing at the door trying to get in. These sounds escalated over the coming weeks. The noises the family heard ceased when the family investigated the strange sounds, and no rats or other animals were ever found.

In the spring of 1818 loud knocking, thumping and bangs were heard which echoed through the farmhouse. On other occasions an unusual noise which sounded like a person smacking his lips in anticipation over food soon began, as well as choking and gurgling sounds which sounded like someone was being throttled or choked to death. Next came the physical phenomena. Whilst the children slept in their beds at night, the bedclothes were thrown off the bed which frightened and terrified them. Richard awoke one time to find an invisible force pulling at his hair; his screams awoke the household.

The poltergeist soon began to centre itself on Betsy Bell; her hair was pulled night after night and stones were thrown at her, even inside the house. Some violent poltergeist phenomena began to manifest by way of slapping Betsy's face. Her brother was talking to her at the time when an invisible hand slapped her and her brother witnessed her cheek redden where she was struck. Enough was enough for John Bell. He called on his neighbour John Johnson, who was an avid Bible reader to see if he could help. When Johnson called at the Bell house, all was quiet for a while, when he heard the sound of the smacking lips manifest. He shouted out 'Stop it! In the name of the Lord!' the sound ceased immediately. Some people believed it was the children playing tricks around the house, after all there were nine children in house, so proof was needed from other witnesses outside of the family circle.

There were indeed other witnesses. On one occasion a visitor expressed his opinion that the disturbances were the result of the children playing pranks. He was immediately slapped by an unseen presence. The phenomena began to manifest outside of the house also, especially on the track that led to a local church and school. Next to the track were some bushes, and as the children passed the thicket they would be pelted by sticks, although like the stones, they were never actually hit by the objects but just narrowly missed. The boy Joel picked up the sticks to throw back and as he did, the sticks were thrown back with much more force. The children searched the bushes to see if someone was there, but to no avail.

The neighbours of the Bell House became accustomed to the strange goings on, so they started to play games with the poltergeist. They would rap on the kitchen table and the poltergeist would rap back in response. The playing of games with the poltergeist only heightened the activity that was taking place. Other unusual sounds began to make themselves apparent, humanlike grunts and groans occurred along with whistling and whispering noises. The sounds were faint and indistinct at first but as the days went on, words and phrases began to be heard. One of the poltergeist's first utterances was, 'I was a spirit that was once happy, but I have been disturbed, and am now unhappy!'

Some of the poltergeist's other vocal words were of an abusive nature, such as swearing and cursing and also some of a sexual nature. The poltergeist seemed to despise John Bell and called him 'Old Jack Bell' and would torment him. The poltergeist turned its intentions away from Betsy, and instead turned to John Bell. It would slap him and throw stones at John and he seemed to have mysteriously contracted lock jaw and a swollen tongue and he could not talk and eat for days on end.

The Bell family also had a slave called Anky who lived with them to help with household chores. The voice followed Anky through the house making derogatory racial remarks. On one occasion, the slave girl was covered with what looked like saliva, as if she had been repeatedly spat on. When asked who the voice was, the poltergeist said that it was the spirit of a Native American who had been buried on the site of the farmhouse and the haunting was the result of a protest against the building of a white person's home on top of the spirit's bones that lay under it. It then discarded this explanation and stated that it was 'Old Kate Batts' Witch'.

Kate Batts was a local black woman who earned a living as a nurse and social worker to the black community. She was called in for questioning but denied having anything to do with the haunting. Batts also denied having anything to do with witchcraft, but the name 'Old Kate Batts' Witch stuck and the poltergeist became known as the Bell Witch. Other voices joined the Bell Witch, a gruff male voice stated that its name was Black Dog, a young boy's voice manifested and said its name was Jerusalem and a woman came through calling herself Mathematics.

All the voices started singing songs and also telling rude jokes. The disturbances sounded as if the Bell family were having a drunken party in the house. The voices also started talking about the local people and their embarrassing medical problems. It also talked about couples' sexual behaviours. The voices also made accusations regarding drunkenness, theft and violence which could not be proved or denied. The voices also took to reading passages from the local minister's sermon whilst joking and mocking them.

The poltergeist whispered in Betsy's ear that it knew the location of a pile of gold. The children took spades and shovels and spent hours digging at the specified spot without finding a thing, but when they got home the Bell Witch just laughed at them for days on end about the ghostly prank. The poltergeist enjoyed playing other pranks on people, such as placing pins in beds and on chairs, the poltergeist seemed to have a fascination with shoes, as the shoes would be moved from place to place and were pulled off peoples feet when they sat down.

John Bell ended up being targeted with most of the later incidents. In one incident, he had stepped out of the front door of the house to go to work when a force grabbed his feet so he could not walk. He then felt the invisible hands let go and then was punched hard in the face. He staggered from the blow and sat down on a log to recover. The poltergeist then threw him off the log and cackled with laughter as it threw John Bell's arms and legs about. When it finally let him go the entity began to sing rude and abusive songs. Richard helped John back to the house where he had to rest for a couple of days.

The poltergeist phenomena were not always as aggressive. Sometimes it would be pleasant to the rest of the household. When Mrs Bell became ill, the Bell Witch would stay about in her vicinity, weeping and moaning, 'Lucy, Oh poor Lucy!' and then apported some hazelnuts beside her bedside table. Betsy said, 'Oh, but we have no nutcrackers!' Instantly, two pounds' worth of shelled hazelnuts materialized by the bed. Also a bunch of grapes then materialized from nowhere on Mrs Bell's bed. The poltergeist then said, 'These will be good for her health'.

On Betsy Bell's birthday, the poltergeist presented her with a large basket of fruit, including bananas, oranges and grapes which, again, apported from nowhere. The voice commented, 'Those came from the West Indies, I brought them myself!' By this time, the poltergeist outbreak had been going on at least two years (an unusually long time for a poltergeist case infestation, as they normally end within eighteen months or less). In 1819, Betsy fell in love with a local boy named Joshua Gardner, the Bell Witch became aware of the relationship between the two and the poltergeist took a violent dislike to it. The voice would follow Betsy around the house saying, 'Please Betsy Bell, don't have Joshua Gardner, Don't marry Joshua Gardner'.

Its next step was to start insulting the boy, but this did not work so it began a new tactic, it would tell the rest of the Bell household that they were kissing and where Joshua was placing his hands on Betsy and how she reacted. It would taunt and make fun of Betsy and in the end the pressure got so great that the couple broke up. One of Joshua's friends, in a fury, went to the Bell household and pushed his way into the house and shouted out, 'Take any shape you desire, so that I may get my hands on you!' After a few seconds an invisible force punched the friend hard in the face and then in the stomach, causing him to double up in pain; he was gasping for breath as the force had winded him. He then left the house to recover from the entity's beating.

The Bell Witch poltergeist infestation was coming to an end. On 18 December 1820, John Bell began to feel unwell and said he was going to bed earlier than usual. The next day, the family tried to rouse him but found him unconscious. The poltergeist voiced, 'It's useless for you to try and relieve old Jack, I've got him this time! He will never get up from that bed again'. They called the local doctor, and when he arrived, he noticed a small bottle that neither he nor anyone else recognized. The Bell Witch voiced again, 'I put it there, and I gave old Jack a dose last night while he was asleep, which fixed him'.

John Bell died the next day without ever gaining consciousness. On the day of the funeral, the poltergeist moved objects around the house and sang songs, one of which was a popular bar song in the day, 'Row me up some brandy oh'. The apparent murder of John Bell by an alleged poltergeist made the case famous today. There are not many recorded incidents of a poltergeist causing the death of a human person.

After the funeral the poltergeist phenomena became quieter than normal. John Bell Junior asked the Bell Witch if he could speak to his dead father to which the poltergeist replied 'He is no longer of this world'. The poltergeist then stated that all survival after death was fraudulent, and told John Bell Junior to look out of the window. As he did he saw invisible footprints being made in the snow, as if someone invisible was walking towards the house. The Bell With told John that the prints were identical to those of Old Jack Bell.

Several weeks later, whilst the Bell family were sitting for supper, they all heard a loud crashing and rumbling sound coming from the chimney. A strange dark spherical apparition rolled out of the chimney and exploded in a cloud of smoke. The poltergeist then shouted out, 'I am going and will be gone for seven years'. The smoke cleared it vanished.

Seven years had passed and by this time Mrs Lucy Bell and two of her youngest children were the only ones left present in the farmhouse. The phenomena once again began with the sound of scratching and bedclothes being pulled off. The remaining family ignored the strange goings on and several days later the phenomena ceased altogether. John Junior claimed that he heard the Bell Witch say that it was now leaving again and would be back again in one hundred and seven years, which would have made it back in 1935. It did not appear ever again.

What are we to make of this case? It seems entirely plausible to me that the poltergeist disturbances were due to RSPK by its first human epicentre, Elizabeth (Betsy) Bell. It seems that her unconscious thought processes, her anger, frustration and inner turmoil were directed at her father John Bell for one reason or another. It has been speculated that Betsy was abused by her father, sexually or otherwise, and because of her keeping the dreaded secret locked up inside, she vented her anger at her father psychically. Again, there is no real proof of this, but it could explain why the poltergeist disturbances moved on from Betsy to her father and possibly killing him in the end. The alleged murder could well have been down to suicide, by knowing what he did to his daughter, and because of his guilt, he poisoned himself. Or, perhaps as he was tormented by the poltergeist, he could no longer take the manifestations that were occurring and again took his own life. Another intriguing possibility is that could Betsy have murdered her father in his sleep physically – that is, in an altered state of consciousness and because of the abuse that may have been going on, she may have given him the poison as he slept. The poltergeist did say that it was 'it' that gave Old Jack Bell the poison and he would never awake from his slumber, so it is entirely possible that if it was RSPK directed at her father and poltergeists are of the unconscious/subconscious mind and not some intelligent discarnate entity, then it was indeed Betsy Bell that murdered her father, psychically or otherwise. A fascinating case indeed.

CASE FILE: THE HAUNTED

In 1991 a television movie based on the Smurl family's haunting, and I believe one of the best ghost movies around, found its way onto television instead of the cinema. The film *The Haunted* tells the story of 'one family's nightmare', involving a malevolent force that plagued their family home. The Smurls lived in West Pittson, Pennsylvania, and their home became a scene of a horrific and diabolical haunting which lasted until 1987, and gained worldwide publicity. It was one of the cases that famous demonologists Ed and Lorraine Warren investigated.

The Smurl family consisted of twin daughters Carin and Shannon, daughters Dawn and Heather the youngest, together with the father and mother, Jack and Janet Smurl. The family lived in a duplex house which was built in 1896. The Smurls were devout Catholics and they attended regular church meetings; the family were well known and liked in the neighborhood. In 1974 things started to happen. A strange looking stain appeared on one of their new carpets without explanation and disappeared just as mysteriously as it had appeared. On another occasion, Jack's television set suddenly spontaneously combusted. In the bathroom, the bath suite such as the sink would be found with scratch marks on them and the toilet would flush of its own accord. Several pipes in the house began to be found with mysterious leaks even though they would be repaired several times. The family also found scratch marks on the walls and woodwork throughout the house, with no explanation.

In 1975 Dawn, the eldest daughter, would often wake during the night to see apparitional people floating around the bedroom, and footsteps were heard regularly coming from upstairs when no one was there. Poltergeist activity began to make itself apparent. Dressing table draws would open and shut, things would go missing and turn up in odd places, radios would turn themselves on even though they were not plugged in and the rocking chairs would rock back and forth as if someone was sitting there. On some occasions a vile smell like a rotting corpse could be smelt coming throughout parts of the house. Almost everyone in the family claimed that they were being touched on occasion by an unseen hand.

In 1985 the activity started to get worse. The temperature in the house was always icy cold and the Smurls found it increasingly difficult to keep the house heated. John and Mary next door would hear loud, abusive and foul language coming from the Smurls' house although they were not home at the time. On several occasions a black amorphous shape was seen floating around the house. On one occasion, the Smurls went camping for the weekend to escape the barrage of paranormal activity that was constant, and on sitting around the fire, looked up to see the dark apparitional shape standing there. There was no escape! So they went back home.

Once the Smurls arrived home, they were greeted by neighbours who said that while the Smurl family were away camping, screaming and shouting was heard coming from the empty house as if someone was being murdered or beaten. The local police were called to the scene, only to find nothing out of the ordinary. In one incident whilst Janet was sleeping she awoke to find herself being pulled out of her bed by an unknown force and flung about the bedroom screaming. Jack was purportedly raped by a horrific looking female entity which he described as 'an old woman with a young body, her eyes were red and her gums green'. Jack also said he witnessed an entity which he described as 'a pig standing on two legs'.

The family's German Shepherd dog, Simon, was repeatedly picked up and thrown. Finally, after a light fitting was torn from the ceiling in the kitchen, they sought help from demonologists Ed and Lorraine Warren. The Warren said that there were three spirits and demonic entities, hell bent on destroying the Smurl family. They said that whilst they were investigating and saying prayers the demonic spirit shook a mirror and a chest of drawers and spelling out, 'You filthy bastard, get out of this house!' later, Janet was attacked again and pig-like noises could be heard coming from the walls. The Smurls tried to gain support from the church, but the Roman Catholic Diocese of Scranton said that their involvement would be unlikely. The Warrens brought in Fr McKenna who conducted the ancient rite of exorcism which did nothing but antagonize the alleged demon.

Over the next few weeks after Fr McKenna left the house, Carin became seriously ill from a strange fever and almost died. Janet awoke to find marks and strange bites on her arms and Janet again pleaded with the church to intervene. After many refusals, she decided to go to the media and unfortunately, as normally happens in these cases, the Smurl home became a tourist attraction for the sceptics, press and amateur ghost hunters. The media coverage shamed the Scranton diocese into assisting the Smurls in their paranormal predicament. Ed and Lorraine Warren also conducted a mass exorcism with several priests and the disturbances ceased for around four months.

In 1986, just before Christmas, the paranormal phenomena started again. Frustrated, terrified and hopeless, the Smurls decided to move out. However, weeks later, after having moved into their new home, they realized the activity had followed them. In 1988, the church performed a fourth exorcism and the manifestations stopped for good. Again this case has many detractors saying that the entire episode was a hoax, but it is up to the reader to decide what is real and what is not.

CASE FILE: WHEN THE LIGHTS WENT OUT

In 2012 the film *When the Lights Went Out* was released. The story was based on the Black Monk of Pontefract case which happened in the old market town, in East Riding, Yorkshire from 1966 to 1969. It was the Pritchard family which owned the three bedroom, semi-detached house at Number 30, East Drive. Joe Pritchard was an owner of a pet shop in Leeds city centre and had a wife, Jean Pritchard and their two children; Phillip was aged fifteen and their daughter Diane was twelve.

The poltergeist first made its presence felt on 1 September 1966. John, Jean and their daughter Diane were away on holiday for a week in the West Country and Sarah Scholes, Jean Pritchard's mother, was at number 30, East Drive looking after her grandson, Phillip. Just after midday, a strange freezing gust of wind came from nowhere and slammed the back door, which was open, shut. Outside it was a warm and sunny day.

Later, Phillip was bringing his grandmother a cup of tea when he saw in the small living room falling ash drifting down from between the floor and ceiling and covering the carpet and furniture. They said it was a grayish chalk, white like powder. While this was continuing in the living room, formations of water began to appear on the kitchen floor. They fetched a neighbour and her married daughter, Marie Kelly, to help clean up the mess. No sooner had they cleaned up the mess in the kitchen than more puddles of water began to appear from nowhere. Marie lifted up the kitchen lino to find no leakage or moisture of any kind.

Out of desperation they called the local water board and they arrived that afternoon. The engineer said that the water was probably due to condensation. Things returned to normal for a few hours, but later on in the evening, the poltergeist phenomena returned. As Sarah and her grandson were watching television, in the kitchen a tea dispenser started to work on its own accord. The hall light began turning on and off and as Sarah went to find out what was going on, she found a plant pot with soil strewn all over and half way up the stairs. Then she listened as crockery, plates and cups started rattling away in the kitchen cupboards and thundering knocks started emanating from upstairs which shook the house. Mrs Scholes went round to her neighbours, the Mountains, to see if they were conducting some building work. It was not them as they also heard the hammering sounds coming from the Pritchards. Later the sounds ceased.

Marie Kelly went home whilst Phillip Pritchard was getting ready for bed. As Sarah went to check on Phillip, they were both astonished to see the wardrobe in Phillip's room start shaking side to side and making its way out. Now terrified, she decided to stay at her daughter's house whilst Phillip stayed at Vic and Marie Kelly's. Mrs Scholes's son-in-law decided to make a call to the police. They arrived to find all was calm and normal. After the police had left they began talking about ghosts and the paranormal. Marie said she knew somebody who was interested in the paranormal and told him his name was Mr O'Donald, who lived a couple of streets away. Sarah decided to see if he was still awake and to call on him. Fortunately for the Pritchards he was still awake and he accompanied them back to Number 30 to see what was happening.

After half an hour's talking and no sign of anything abnormal, Mr O'Donald went back home. As the Kellys were walking through the hallway, they heard a crash and found a framed photograph and some small paintings had been thrown to the floor. The photograph of the Pritchards' wedding day had been torn from top to bottom as if vandalized. Later, on Saturday afternoon, the Pritchards returned from their weekend away and were told of the bizarre occurrences which had been happening in the house whilst they were away. As they sat talking the strange cold gust of wind again announced itself and in conjunction with that came the sound of several loud knocks which came from upstairs. The atmosphere in the room again became normal and nothing unusual occurred for another two years.

On 26 August 1968, the poltergeist returned with a vengeance. Whilst Jean Pritchard was drinking tea with her daughter they both heard a noise out in the hallway. They investigated and found a quilt from Diane's bedroom lying at the bottom of the stairs. They went back to wallpapering her daughter's bedroom and were again disturbed by a clattering sound. This time they found the counterpane from Phillip Pritchard's bedroom lying in the hall downstairs with several knocked over plant pots.

Sarah Scholes began to cry fearing that the disturbances from two years previously were beginning again. That night, unable to sleep due to the warm weather, Jean Pritchard decided to make herself some tea. On the first floor landing the temperature had dropped cold and the painting equipment started to come to life. A pasting brush and bucket jumped up and were thrown against the wall where she was standing and a roll of wallpaper began rocking from side to side on its end in the middle of the floor. She grabbed the wall paper and found the carpet sweeper suddenly swung towards her. She dropped to the floor in terror and screamed. She crawled into the bedroom where her screams awoke her husband and two children.

They all watched as different items and objects were thrown about and, incredibly, watched as a wooden pelmet that was covering the curtain rail in the bedroom was suddenly torn away and hurled out through the open window into the back garden. Joe Pritchard slammed the bedroom door shut and they went back into the main bedroom. From Diane's room they could hear objects being thrown against the inside of the bedroom door, then the psychic episode ended.

Over the next days and weeks more strange phenomena began to happen. Lights would turn themselves on and off, clothes and other household objects were found scattered over the stairs, such as books, ornaments and even food. Incessant knocking and rapping was heard coming from the rooms which was so loud that it could be heard up and down the street. It seemed the poltergeist was centred on Diane Pritchard who was then aged fourteen. Stories were run in the papers on the Pontefract haunting and it became a local media sensation. People would linger outside the house to hear the bangings and knockings, and amateur ghosthunters would camp outside the house hoping to experience some of the phenomena.

In September 1968, the Pritchards invited Christian minister, the Rev. Davy to visit them at number 30 East Drive, in the hope that he would perform an exorcism of the property. The minister suggested that the events in the house were probably down to subsidence and the heightened atmosphere in the house attributed to the suggestion that the house was haunted by ghosts and spirits. As the Rev. Davy continued to talk, loud knocking noises were heard and a brass candlestick flew off the mantelpiece and landed at Davy's feet. A second candlestick then lifted up off the mantelpiece, travelled horizontally through the air, then landed on the carpet. Seconds later, a tremendous crashing noise was hard coming from the kitchen which sent the Rev Davy and the Pritchards running in to see what happened. Amazingly, they found all the crockery, plates, saucers and cups lying scattered on the kitchen floor unbroken. Rev. Davy decided there was an evil presence in the house and suggested that the Pritchards should move house, which they refused to do.

Later that evening, Diane Pritchard decided to go to bed; the temperature in the house started to yet again drop, a sign she said that another host of paranormal activity was about to start. Suddenly, all the lights in the house went out, and the family was plunged into darkness. On previous occasions, Joe Pritchard had found that the poltergeist had switched off the main switch under the stairs, so decided to investigate. He then saw a shadowy movement in the hallway, and an oak hall stand with a number of items resting on top, a sewing machine and other ornaments, slid along the floor and trapped Diane in the corner at the bottom of the stairs. Diane then tried to push the stand away but she tripped and fell backwards, and found her hair caught between the sewing machine and the stand which the machine was resting upon. The lights in the house then came back on. Joe and Philip found the oak stand almost immovable, as if a force was holding it against the girl. The force dissipated and they managed to move the furniture off Diane. Terrified and shaken, Diane decided to go upstairs to her bedroom, but the poltergeist was not done yet. As she lay in bed she was disturbed to find her bedclothes being pulled away from her by an invisible presence. Suddenly, the mattress was overturned throwing Diane onto the bedroom floor. The Pritchards reported this on no less than four occasions that one night.

One Saturday evening in the winter months of 1968, after being on an evening out, Jean Pritchard was in the kitchen making a coffee when the light in the kitchen started flickering on and off. All of a sudden whilst Rene Holden was sitting in the living room a cushion struck her in the face, the lights all went out and objects and items were thrown around the living room. Rene said perhaps that they should try a séance, so they all stood around in a circle whilst holding hands. Suddenly, they were pelted by stones which seemed to emanate from upstairs, then followed a mattress, sheets and clothes. So they decided to abandon the séance in their own best interests.

Vic Kelly tried to perform his own exorcism at number 30 with holy water blessed by the local Catholic priest, but this seemed to antagonize the entity, which responded by making loud knockings and streams of water apporting through the living room ceiling. Other fantastic feats of a psychic nature allegedly occurred: a full jug of milk supposedly made its way from the refrigerator, floated across the kitchen and tipped its contents over Joe Pritchard's sister, Maude Preece. Maude's fur gloves apparently floated in the air, with invisible hands that beat in time to Maude's Christian song 'Onward Christian Soldiers'. A grandmother clock lifted off the wall and was thrown down the stairs, large footprints appeared in the hall carpet overnight, a brass crucifix allegedly took off from the mantelpiece and stuck on Diane Pritchard's back like a magnet, a set of house keys materialized and came down the chimney and eggs de-materialized out of their box and then re-appeared in mid-air before exploding their contents all over the room.

In the spring of 1969 the entity began to appear in visible form. One night after Jean and Joe retired to bed and with the light off, the bedroom door suddenly swung open revealing, in the light coming through the landing window, a tall hooded apparition. Joe turned the bedside light on, but the figure had disappeared. Several days later, May Mountain the Pritchards' neighbour was standing by the kitchen sink in her own house, when she got the feeling that someone was stood behind her. She turned around and was astounded to see a tall monk-like figure dressed in black robes with a cowl which covered its face. It was standing an arm's length away. She stood on the spotterrified and seconds later the apparition vanished.

The apparition soon became known as 'The Black Monk' and was seen on a further two occasions. One evening, Jean Pritchard and Rene Holden came back from a spiritualist church. Also accompanying them was a driver who brought them back. As they were sitting in the living room drinking tea and coffee, the lights suddenly went out. Mrs Holden then felt a hand touch the back of her head and in the light that was coming in from the streetlights outside, she saw the apparition of a figure dressed all in long dark robes standing right behind her. The apparition vanished within a few seconds and the light came back on. On another occasion, Philip and Diane Pritchard were in the living room watching television when they saw a dark figure through the glass door leading to the dining room. Phillip thought it was one of the neighbours that had come in, so got up to investigate. He managed to see the apparition of the 'black monk' sinking through the kitchen floor and vanishing.

The haunting reached its peak in May 1969 when one final act of paranormal violence was directed at Diane Pritchard. One evening she was walking through the hallway into the kitchen when suddenly, the lights again went out. Jean and Phillip heard a terrifying scream and rushed out into the hall, only to witness Diane being dragged upstairs by an invisible presence by her cardigan. She was struggling and fighting to get free, whilst her mother and brother were trying to pull her away from the poltergeist. Suddenly the force dissipated, and they all ended up a heap together at the bottom of the stairs. Diane's throat was covered with red claw marks, but on that night the disturbances ended for good. I would like to say a big thank you to Paul Adams for allowing me to use some of his notes for this account.

CASE FILE: THE HAUNTING IN CONNECTICUT

The Haunting in Connecticut was released in 2009 and tells the story of a family that moves into an abandoned old funeral home with their seriously ill son who suddenly find themselves drawn into a house of nightmares. The real story surrounds the Snedeker family who moved into their house on 30 June 1986. The house was big and spacious and was cheap to rent. The reason they moved was because their son, who had cancer of the immune system, was closer to hospital. When the Snedekers moved in, they found that their house used to be a mortuary called Hallahan Funeral Home. It was a funeral home and mortuary for many years and the family found abandoned mortuary equipment hidden behind the basement wall. The family also found a graveyard at the back and also drawers full of photographs of corpses.

Soon after, the Snedekers started reporting unusual phenomena. Strange sounds would be heard, extreme cold temperatures could be felt along with apparitions of dead people being seen; bed covers were also pulled away from family members during the night. On the first night in the house, Phillip was awakened by hearing someone call his name and on another occasion whilst Phillip was sharing his room with his brother Brad, they both saw four apparitions standing in the corner in the room. A toy robot which was standing next to the four figures activated and started moving around erratically. The four apparitions all turned as one to look at the boys and they ran upstairs to Carmen, who went downstairs to investigate. No one was there.

One of the apparitions was said to be seen regularly and was powerful in nature. Carmen Snedeker describes: 'They were incredibly powerful, one of them was very thin with high cheek bones and long black hair and pitch black eyes, and another had white hair and eyes and was wearing a pin stripe tuxedo and his feet were constantly in motion'. Carmen reported that she was not aware that the house was a former funeral home but one of the neighbours said that they were fully aware what the house was once used for. In one incident Carmen was mopping the basement floor when suddenly the water turned blood red. In another she said that the dishes and pots would suddenly find themselves back in the cupboards. The Snedekers also said that lights would flicker on and off even when there were no light bulbs in their sockets. The sounds of voices were heard, items began disappearing and they even heard the sound of hundreds of birds taking flight. Phillip, who was undergoing radiation treatment at the time for his cancer, began to exhibit personality traits such as withdrawal into himself and anger (whether this was due to his therapy or his life threatening disease is unclear).

Phillip began writing poetry with necrophilia themes. In one episode he attacked his cousin and intended to rape her. He was taken away from the house and diagnosed as a schizophrenic. He was not allowed to return home until he was better. Carmen and her niece reported that they were raped repeatedly and beaten by invisible entities as well as her husband. The stench of rotting flesh was also smelt throughout the house. In one alleged terrifying incident, Carmen was taking a shower when all of a sudden the shower curtain enveloped and tightened around her face; unable to breathe she screamed for Tammy, who managed to rip a hole in the curtain allowing Carmen to breathe.

The Snedekers brought in demonologists Ed and Lorraine Warren who moved into the property for several weeks. They claimed they also witnessed family members being punched, slapped, beaten and pushed by demonic entities. The Warrens allegedly performed a full scale exorcism of the property and declared it clear.

CASE FILE: THE CONJURING

In 2013 the movie *The Conjuring* hit the cinemas and became a worldwide success. The movie tells the story of a family plagued by a demonic spirit who later possesses its victim. The true story behind the film is known as the Harrisville haunting and concerns the Perron family. The family consisted of Roger Perron and his wife Carolyn and their five children, Andrea (Annie), Nancy, Christine, Cindy, and April.

The parents decided that they wanted to move their children for a quieter life in the countryside in Harrisville, Rhode Island, and moved in the winter of 1970. The house was built in 1736 and belonged to the Arnolds. Eight generations of the Arnolds lived and died on the estate. Mrs John Arnold, at the ripe old age of 93, hanged herself from the rafters in the barn. Other losses of life included suicides, hangings and poisonings, a murder and rape of eleven year-old Prudence Arnold which was never solved, two sudden drownings in the creek located near to the house, and four men who mysteriously froze to death on the land. When the Perrons moved into their 'dream' house the estate agent told them to 'Leave the lights on at night'.

Unusual things started to happen to the Perrons from the first day of moving in. on some nights the daughters slept in Andrea's bed as she stated that the sisters 'Came crawling into bed with her, trembling and crying in terror'. At first the Perrons thought that the ghosts inhabiting their house were harmless and they described the apparitions as opaque and somewhat solid in appearance. One of the ghosts smelt of flowers whilst another would gently kiss the girls goodnight in their beds every night. Another ghost they witnessed was that of a young boy that would push toy cars around. One apparition which the Perrons assumed was female seemed to be a welcome presence in the house. They would often hear the sound of sweeping coming from the kitchen. When they entered the room, they would find the broom in a different spot in the kitchen with a pile of neatly swept dirt sitting on the floor waiting to be picked up and put in the dustbin. Another spirit said to inhabit the house was that of Johnny Arnold (Manny), who had committed suicide by hanging himself in the attic in the 1700s. The children loved Manny and he would appear to the children, with a crooked smile on his face, standing nearby and quietly watching the children go about their business. If eye contact was made with Manny, he would withdraw from sight just as quickly as he appeared.

As well as the apparitions, the Perrons witnessed other remarkable phenomena: toilets flushing by themselves, washers turning on, taps running. Beds would levitate several inches off the floor, telephone handsets would float in the air and slam down on their phone base when someone entered the room and various household items would glide about on their own accord. Often, chairs would be pulled from beneath an unsuspecting guest and pictures would fall from walls. The Perrons also described seeing an orange coloured substance like blood ooze from a wall then vanish. Some of the alleged ghost phenomena were nasty in nature. Some would yank the girls' legs and hair during the middle of the night, and others would bang on the front door with such force that the entire house would shake.

Some doors would slam shut on their own accord as well as being frozen to the spot without being able to shut no matter how much force was applied to them. One entity in the house on some occasions kept the Perrons awake at night by crying out, 'Mama! Maaaama!' Another ghost would torture eight year-old Cindy by telling her over and over, 'There are seven dead soldiers buried in the wall'. One of the Perrons recalled a small apparition of a four year-old walking about the house and crying and calling for his mother. One of the spirits has been alleged to have molested some of the children, but this has never been disclosed by the Perrons.

The most terrifying entity said to have haunted the Perrons targeted Mrs Perron herself. The spirit called Bathsheba was said to be the ghost of Bathsheba Sherman who lived in the house in the early nineteenth century. She was apparently a Satanist and witch and died there after hanging herself from a tree behind the barn. Bathsheba Thayer was born in 1812 in Rhode Island and married fellow islander Judson Sherman on 10 March 1844. When alive, Bathsheba lived a life of seclusion and she became an outcast in the community because she was accused of killing her young baby in a sacrifice to Satan. The baby's body had been impaled in the head with a sharp instrument. Lacking evidence the case was dropped. Bathsheba is said to have had three other children who did not live beyond the age of four. These children could have been her other victims, and it was not just her children who suffered. She is known to have tortured her staff, often starving them and beating them for minor errors. When Bathsheba died on 25 May 1885, the coroner in his report stated that he had never seen anything like it, her emaciated body had eerily solidified and seemingly turned to stone.

Bathsheba's ghost was said to be a vile hideous creature described as having a face similar to a desiccated beehive. Her face was covered in cobwebs with no real human features other than vermin and insects crawling from crevices etched into the wrinkled skin of her face. Her head was round and grey and sat leaning off to one side as if her neck had been broken, whilst a putrid stench permeated the room when the apparition was present. The entity tortured Carolyn Perron whilst it also lusted after Mr Perron. Machinery and other electrical items kept breaking down in the house and whilst working on them to repair them down in the cellar, Mr Perron often felt The entity touching him, gently caressing his neck and running its hands down his back. It became apparent that Bethsheba wanted Carolyn out of the house. In one horrifying account, 'Mrs Perron said she awoke before dawn one morning to find an apparition by her bed, the head of an old woman hanging off to one side over an old grey dress. There was a voice reverberating, "Get out. Get Out. I'll drive you out with death and gloom"'.

Bathsheba's ghost would pinch and slap Carolyn and also throw household items at her. Carolyn had a fear of fire and this was used by the entity to strike fear and terror into Carolyn as the ghost would bang torches against her bed and demand that she leave the house permanently. Although the attacks on Carolyn Perron were at first cruel, they began to get harsher. In one incident, she was lying on the couch when she felt a sharp pain in the calf of her leg. She looked and found a puncture wound that looked as if a large sewing needle had been stabbed in her leg. The psychic attacks did not prevent Carolyn staying in the house so the entity decided to use a different tactic.

Enter demonologists Ed and Lorraine Warren. The Perrons approached the Warrens at one of their lectures on the paranormal and pleaded with them for help. It was believed that Carolyn Perron was possessed by the spirit of Bathsheba and wanted the Warrens to help save their mother. On the night of the exorcism by the Warrens, daughter Andrea Perron remembered, 'The night I thought I saw my mother die was the most terrifying night of all. She spoke in a voice we had never heard before and a power not of this world threw her twenty feet into another room'.

In the movie *The Conjuring*, the Warrens rid the woman of the evil spirit, but in reality they were not successful. In fact things got worse around the family. As the situation got out of hand, the Perrons asked the Warrens to leave the premises immediately. The Perrons decided to flee their haunted house but had to wait ten long years with the malevolent forces still terrorizing them before they managed to find the financial resources and leave. The family soon learned that every occupant previously (apart from a local minister and his family) of the estate had reported paranormal activity. Before the Perrons moved in the owner had been renovating the home when he suddenly stopped work and fled the house screaming, leaving behind his tools and car. It is known that renovations, alterations and modifications on a house may stir up paranormal activity. Perhaps the spirits inhabiting their former homes do not like 'their' houses being touched?

The owner after the Perrons, Norma Sutcliffe, who purchased the property in 1983, states that she and her husband Gerry and various visitors to the home have also reported paranormal phenomena coming from the old Arnold estate. They experienced the door banging in the front hall, sounds of people talking in other rooms, the sounds of footsteps scurrying around the house and an incident where Gerry's chair began vibrating in the study. They claimed also to see a glowing blue light shooting across a room, fog-like apparitions floating throughout rooms of the house and strange vibrations that were so intense that they felt the house was falling apart.

Several visitors to the house have also reported seeing an apparition of an elderly woman, with her hair in a bun, moving silently through the house.

CASE FILE: ANNABELLE

In 2014 the prequel to *The Conjuring*, *Annabelle* was released. It tells the story of an ornamental doll that becomes possessed by the spirit of a cult member. The doll itself was sinister in appearance to start with but that was not what the doll really looked like. In fact the doll was a plush-looking and soft Raggedy Ann doll. In 1970 a mother purchased the antique doll from a hobby store and it was a present for her daughter Donna for her birthday. Donna at the time was a student in college who was preparing to graduate with her nursing degree and resided in a tiny apartment with her roommate Angie.

As Donna was pleased with her gift, she placed the doll on her bed as a decoration and did not give it a second thought until a few days later. In that time, both Donna and Angie noticed that there was something very strange and sinister about the doll. The doll allegedly moved around on its own accord. Donna and Angie would often come home to find the doll in a completely different room from where they had originally left it. Sometimes the doll would be found cross-legged on the couch with its arms folded, on other times it was found upright, standing on its feet, leaning against a chair in the dining room. On several occasions, Donna placed the doll on the couch before leaving for work and would return home to find the doll back in her room on the bed with the door closed.

Annabelle the doll could not only move around but could write, it seemed. About a month into their experiences Donna and Angie began to find penciled messages on parchment paper that read, 'Help us' and 'Help Lou'. The hand writing belonged looked like it belonged to a small child. The strange part about the messages was not the wording, but the way they were written. At the time Donna never kept any parchment paper in the house. One night Donna came home to find the doll had once again moved. This time it was on her bed. She inspected the doll and fear began to take hold. On the back of the doll's hands she found what looked like drops of blood and also on its chest. Scared, she began to seek help from somewhere. Donna contacted a medium and a séance was held. The alleged spirit inhabiting the doll was that of Annabelle Higgins. Annabelle was a young girl that resided on the property before Donna's apartments were built. She was only seven when her lifeless body was found in a field upon which the apartment block now stood.

The spirit said through the medium that she felt comfortable with Donna and Angie and wanted to stay with them to be loved. They gave the spirit permission to stay with them, but things began to take a more malevolent turn. Lou never liked the doll and he awoke one night in a panic. He was paralyzed and couldn't move. He moved his eyes down towards his feet and he saw Annabelle the doll. The doll began to move slowly up his leg, moved towards his chest and the doll began to strangle Lou. Lou passed out from asphyxiation and awoke the next morning. He was determined to get rid of the possessed doll.

On the next day, Lou and Angie were preparing a trip out and were reading maps in her apartment. Suddenly, rustling sounds could be heard coming from Donna's room. Thinking they had an intruder, Lou made his way over to the room and turned on the light. The noises stopped and he found Annabelle tossed on the floor in the corner. He walked towards the doll and had the distinct feeling that there was a presence behind him. He turned around but nobody was there, within seconds he grabbed his chest and doubled over. He was cut and bleeding and he opened his blood stained shirt revealing seven claw marks, three vertically and four horizontally which felt like hot burns. The scratches healed almost immediately and by the second day they had completely disappeared.

Donna came to believe that the spirit that was inhabiting the doll was not that of a little girl but something inhuman. She contacted a priest, Fr Cooke who in turn contacted Ed and Lorraine Warren. The Warrens believed that it was a demonic inhuman spirit that possessed the doll and asked Fr Cooke to perform the rite of exorcism. After the exorcism, the Warrens took the doll with them and placed it on the back seat of the car. It is alleged that as they were travelling back to their home the car mysteriously swerved and stalled and they were nearly on the verge of crashing the car, but Ed reached into his black bag and pulled out a vial of holy water dousing the doll and making the sign of the cross over it. The disturbances stopped immediately.

The Warrens finally reached home and Ed placed the doll in a chair next to his desk. He stated that on several occasions the doll would levitate and also move from room to room over the ensuing weeks. In one account Fr Jason Bradford, a Catholic exorcist came to the house. He saw the doll sitting in the chair and picked it up. He said to it, 'You're just a rag doll Annabelle, you can't hurt anyone'. And he put the doll back in the chair. He left the Warrens an hour later and as he was driving home he approached a busy intersection. His brakes failed and he was nearly killed in a fatal car accident which destroyed the car.

The Warrens placed the doll in a special case and put it in their Occult Museum where today it can still be seen. In one account a young man came to the museum on his motorcycle with his girlfriend. After hearing Ed's account on the doll, he defiantly made his way to the case, banged on it and said if the doll can put scratches on people, he also wanted to be scratched. Ed remarked 'Son, you need to leave' and made him leave the museum. On his way home the young motorcyclist and his girlfriend were laughing and making fun of the doll when he mysteriously lost control of the bike and rode into a tree. The motorcyclist was killed instantly and his girlfriend was hospitalized for over a year. Make up your own minds on this story!

END

BIBLIOGRAPHY

Adams, Paul & Brazil, Eddie
>   Extreme Hauntings: Britain's Most Terrifying Ghosts. The History Press, 2013.

Berger, Arthur; Berger, Joyce
>   The Encyclopedia of Parapsychology and Psychical Research. Paragon House Publishers, 1991.

Broughton, Richard
>   Parapsychology: The Controversial Science. Rider & Co Publishers, 1992.

Brookesmith, Peter
>   Ghosts, Orbis Publishing Limited. Black Cat Imprint, 1992.

Currie, Ian
>   You Cannot Die: The Incredible Findings of a Century of Research on Death. Element Books Ltd, 1995.

French, Chris
>   "Anomalistic Psychology", 2000, British Investigators Training Course Advanced Level (AITC): The Scientific Investigation & Research of Anomalous Phenomena, MAPIT, 2000.

Farson, Daniel
>   The Hamlyn Book of Ghosts in Fact and fiction. The Hamlyn Publishing Group Limited, Fourth Impression, 1982.

Graves, Zachary
>   Ghosts: The Complete Guide to the Supernatural. Canary Press, 2011.

Henry, Jane
>   Parapsychology: Research on Exceptional Experiences. Routledge Publishing, 2004.

Innes, Brian
>   The Catalogue of Ghost Sightings. Blitz Editions, 1998.

Irwin J, Harvey; Watt, Caroline

An Introduction to Parapsychology. 5th Edition. McFarland & Company, Inc. Publishers, 2007.

Jones, Richard,
    Haunted Castles Of Britain And Ireland. New Holland, 2003.

Kelley, Douglas.
    MHs.M2: Advanced Metaphysical Concepts, Institute of Metaphysical Humanistic Science.

Kelley, Douglas.
    MHs.M16: Paranormal Science, Institute of Metaphysical Humanistic Science.

Kelley, Douglas, Irwin, Ingrid.
    MHs.29: Electronic Voice Phenomena, Institute of Metaphysical Humanistic Science.

Matthews, Rupert
    Poltergeists and Other Hauntings. Arcturus Publishing Ltd, 2009.

Mera, Steve
    The British Investigators Training Course (BITC): The Scientific Investigation & Research of Anomalous Phenomena, MAPIT, 2006.

Mera, Steve
    The British Investigator's Training Course Advanced Level (AITC): The Scientific Investigation & Research of Anomalous Phenomena, MAPIT, 2010.

Phenomena Magazine
    Issue 39, July, 2012. Issue 33, January, 2012.

Radin, Dean
    What is Parapsychology? Parapsychology FAQ. American Institute of Parapsychology, 1995.

Roberts, Ron; Groome, David
    Parapsychology: The Science of Unusual Experience. Hodder Arnold Publications, 2001.

Roland, Paul
    Hauntings: True Stories of Unquiet Spirits. Arcturus Publishing Ltd, 2008.

Schoch M. Robert; Yonavjak, Logan
    The Parapsychology Revolution: A Concise Anthology of Paranormal and Psychical Research. Tarcher/Penguin, 2008.

Taff, Barry E,
    Aliens Above, Ghosts Below. Cosmic Pantheon Press, 2011.

Underwood, Peter
    The A-Z Of British Ghosts. Chancellor Press, 1992.

Underwood, Peter
    This Haunted Isle. Brockhampton Press, 1998.

Young, Francis
    English Catholics and the Supernatural, 1553–1829, Ashgate Publishing, 2013.

WEB AND INTERNET SOURCES

The New England Society for Psychical Research (www.warrens.net)

Paranormal Witness (www.paranormal-witness.wikia.com)

www.zoey24.hubpages.com

www.altereddimensions.net

ABOUT THE AUTHOR

Dr Robert Young is a parapsychologist, metaphysicist and founder of The Office of Parapsychological Studies in Nottinghamshire, England. He holds the BITC and AITC certificates in anomalous phenomena and parapsychology from The Scientific Establishment of Parapsychology in Manchester. He holds diplomas in Psychology and Quantum Theory and obtained his Ph.D. in Metaphysics, specializing in Parapsychology, from the Institute of Metaphysical Humanistic Science along with his Bachelor's and Master's degrees. He also holds a Certificate in Parapsychological Studies from The American Institute of Parapsychology and is England's representative to the organisation. He also is a member of The Rhine Research Centre and The American Institute of Parapsychology.

For investigations and research, please contact Dr Rob Young at parapsy.co.uk or email him at: itstherob@hotmail.com.

Made in the USA
San Bernardino, CA
17 July 2016